Staffordshire Library and Information Services
Please return or renew by the last date shown

If not required by other readers, this item may be renewed in person, by post or telephone, online or by email.
To renew, either the book or ticket are required.

24 Hour Renewal Line
0845 33 00 740

Staffordshire
County Council

Philip Mansel is a historian of France and the Middle East. He has lived in Paris, Beirut and Istanbul, and often visited Aleppo. In 2012 he won the London Library Life in Literature Award, and in 2013 became a Chevalier des Arts et des Lettres. His most recent publication is *The Eagle in Splendour: Inside the Court of Napoleon* (2015). *Aleppo: The Rise and Fall of Syria's Great Merchant City* is his third book on cosmopolitan cities of the Middle East, after *Constantinople: City of the World's Desire* (1995), on Istanbul, and *Levant: Splendour and Catastrophe on the Mediterranean* (2010), on Smyrna, Alexandria and Beirut.

ALEPPO

THE RISE AND FALL OF SYRIA'S
GREAT MERCHANT CITY

PHILIP MANSEL

I.B. TAURIS

LONDON · NEW YORK

Published in 2016 by
I.B.Tauris & Co. Ltd
London • New York
www.ibtauris.com

Copyright © 2016 Philip Mansel

ISBN: 978 1 78453 461 5
eISBN: 978 0 85772 924 8

A full CIP record for this book is available from the British Library
A full CIP record is available from the Library of Congress

Library of Congress Catalog Card Number: available

Typeset by Out of House Publishing
Printed and bound in Sweden by ScandBook AB

To May Gazalé Sikias and Mark Gazaleh

For the inhabitants of it, and the
concourse of people, it is an epitome of
the whole world.

Charles Robson, *Newes from Aleppo*,
18 May 1628

Contents

List of Illustrations   xi

Acknowledgements   xiii

Introduction   1

PART I A HISTORY

 1 The Ottoman City   7

 2 Emporium of the Orient World   11

 3 Consuls and Travellers   15

 4 Entertainments   23

 5 Muslims, Christians, Jews   26

 6 Catholics against Orthodox   32

 7 Janissaries against Ashraf   34

 8 Ottoman Renaissance   39

 9 The French Mandate   47

10 Independence   52

11 Years of the Assads 58

12 Death of a City 61

PART II THROUGH TRAVELLERS' EYES

13 *A Collection of Curious Travels and Voyages containing
Dr. Leonhart Rauwolff's Itinerary into the Eastern Countries*
(1693), Leonhard Rauwolff 69

14 *The Six Voyages of Jean-Baptiste Tavernier ... through Turkey
into Persia and the East Indies* (1678), Jean-Baptiste Tavernier 85

15 *The Natural History of Aleppo* (1756), Alexander Russell 92

16 *A Journal from Calcutta in Bengal, by Sea, to Busserah:
from thence across the Great Desart to Aleppo: and from thence
to Marseilles, and through France to England. In the Year 1750*
(1757), Bartholomew Plaisted 121

17 *Voyages and Travels of a Sea Officer* (1792), Francis Vernon 124

18 *Travels in Africa, Egypt and Syria from the Year 1792 to 1798*
(1799), William George Browne 127

19 *Travels in Syria and the Holy Land* (1822), John Lewis
Burckhardt 133

20 *Travels among the Arab Tribes inhabiting the Countries East of
Syria and Palestine* (1825), James Silk Buckingham 143

21 *Narrative of a Tour through Some Parts of the Turkish Empire*
(1829), John Fuller 154

22 *The Ansaryii (or Assassins), with Travels in the Further East
in 1850–51* (1851), Lt. the Hon. Frederick Walpole R.N. 158

23 *The Lands of the Saracen; or, Pictures of Palestine, Asia Minor,
Sicily and Spain* (1854), Bayard Taylor 169

24 *Personal Narrative in Letters; Principally from Turkey, in the Years
1830–33* (1856), Francis William Newman 176

25 *Through Turkish Arabia: A Journey from the Mediterranean to
Bombay by the Euphrates and Tigris Valleys and the Persian
Gulf* (1894), Henry Swainson Cowper 186

26 *Syria: The Desert and the Sown* (1907) and *Amurath to Amurath* (1911), Gertrude Bell   199

27 *Dead Towns and Living Men* (1920), Leonard Woolley   215

Notes   219

Bibliography   233

Index   241

Illustrations

Maps

1 Aleppo and its region   xiv
2 Baedeker's map of Aleppo, 1912 (private collection)   xv

Plates

1 Panorama of Aleppo with the citadel in the background, *c.*1940 (Collection of May Gazalé Sikias)
2 Andrea Soldi, *Portrait of Henry Lannoy Hunter in Oriental Dress, Resting from Hunting, with a Manservant Holding Game,* *c.*1733–6 (Tate Images)
3 A souk in Aleppo (from Jean Sauvaget, *Alep. Essai sur le développement d'une grand ville syrienne, des origines au milieu du XIXe siècle,* Paris, 1941)
4 Khan al-Wazir (from Sauvaget, *Alep*)
5 The *iwan* of the Beit Jumblatt (from Sauvaget, *Alep*)
6 *Iwan* and courtyard of the Beit Ghazaleh (from Sauvaget, *Alep*)
7 Salon Marcopoli, *c.*1900 (Collection of May Gazalé Sikias)
8 A horse and its owner, outside Aleppo, *c.*1940 (Collection of May Gazalé Sikias)
9 A camel caravan outside Aleppo, *c.*1940 (Collection of May Gazalé Sikias)

10 Greek Catholic priests with members of the Ghazeleh family, *c.*1934 (Collection of May Gazalé Sikias)

11 Rue Baron, British troops, *c.*1942 (Collection of May Gazalé Sikias)

12 Amina al-Harriri with her son Ghassan in the family house near the Great Mosque, *c.*1939 (Collection of Zahed Tajeddin)

13 A costume ball at the Club d'Alep, 1952, formerly a Ghazeleh house (Collection of May Gazalé Sikias)

14 Fête-Dieu procession, 28 May 1964 (Collection of May Gazalé Sikas)

Acknowledgements

I am deeply grateful for information and comments to Sonia Anderson, Georges and Myriam Antaki, Edward Chaney, Peter Clark, Hussein el-Mudarris, Caroline Finkel, Julia Gonnella, Cecil Hourani, Basil Tallal Kudsi, Faisal Kudsi, Erol Makzume, Simon Mills, Nabih Moukayed, Aouni Abdul Rahim, Alan Rush, Olivier Salmon and Zahed Tajeddin. I owe a particular debt of gratitude to May Gazalé Sikias and Mark Gazaleh. They not only found many illustrations for this book, and provided invaluable information and comments, they also commissioned an early version of the text in 2011 as they were researching the history of the family house Beit Ghazaleh in Aleppo, in preparation for its planned opening as a Museum of Aleppo Memory.

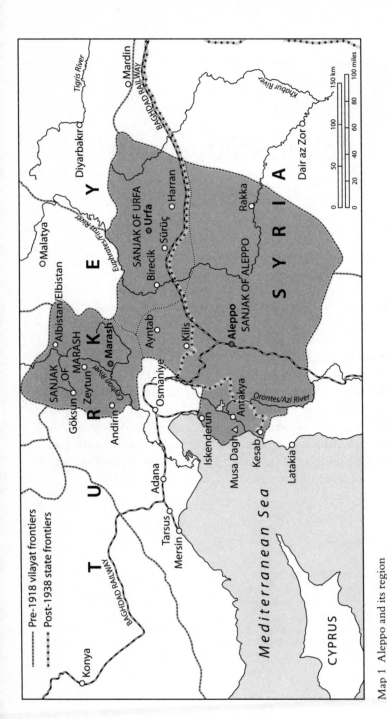

Map 1 Aleppo and its region

The new state frontiers ignored the old provincial boundaries, and left many Arabic-speakers in the new state of Turkey. The area around Iskenderun, including Antakya, of mixed Turkish and Arabic population, was ceded by France, acting as the mandatory power for Syria, to Turkey in 1938. After independence the government of Syria never officially recognised the cession.

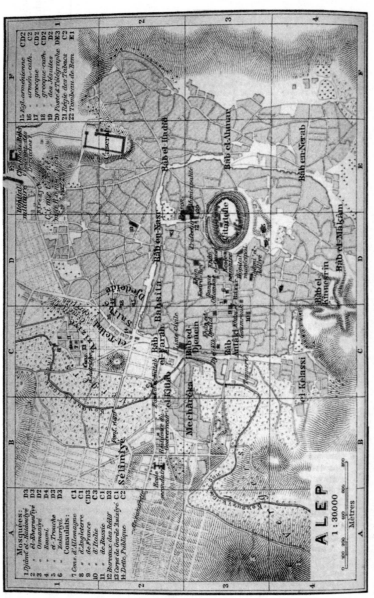

Map 2 Baedeker's map of Aleppo, 1912 (private collection)

This map shows the old city in the centre, with the new quarters being developed to the west. Mosques, khans, churches and consulates are shown as the most important buildings in the city.

Introduction

Cities have their own dynamism. Geography, economics and culture help them challenge the force of nationality and religion. The connections of everyday life can have more power than the commands of sects and states. Inhabitants need each other, or they would not be living in the same city. For many the city is their primary identity.

Aleppo, in particular, was a city with a rhythm of its own, challenging categories and generalisations. Lying between the desert and the sea, the mountains of Anatolia and the banks of the Euphrates, it was Arab and Turkish; Kurdish and Armenian; Christian, Muslim and Jewish. An Arabic-speaking city with a Muslim majority, under the Ottoman Empire Aleppo also became a centre of French culture and Catholic missions. Like many other cities in the region, it mixed East and West, Islam and Christianity. Until 2012 Aleppo was distinguished by its peaceful character. For 500 years, whatever their origin, its inhabitants had lived together relatively harmoniously. The reasons for this harmony, and for the current cataclysm, are the subject of this book.

Like Damascus 200 miles to the south, Aleppo is one of the oldest continuously inhabited cities in the world. Humans have lived in or near Aleppo since at least the fifth millennium BC. Thirty-four miles south-west of Aleppo are the remains of the ancient and wealthy kingdom of Ebla and its spectacular archive. One clay tablet of 2250 BC mentions a king of Aleppo.[1] According to legend, Abraham milked his flocks there and dispensed the milk as alms – hence, by some accounts, its name Halab, Arabic for milk.[2] Because of its geographical position, it was always changing masters. Successively Hittite, Assyrian, Babylonian, Persian, Seleucid and Armenian, Beroea – as Aleppo was then known – became Roman with the rest of Syria in 64 BC. Henceforth it looked west rather than east. A ring of classical ruins in the surrounding countryside, known as the 'dead cities', demonstrates its prosperity under the Roman Empire: Sigilla, Chalcis, Saint Simeon, and many others date from the fifth and sixth centuries. In some of them, modern Syrians are still living in Roman houses.[3]

After the Arab conquest in 637, Aleppo was ruled from Damascus by the Umayyad caliphs, masters of the Muslim world, and after 750 from Baghdad by the Abbasid caliphs. The Byzantine frontier was close. Wars and skirmishes were frequent. In 962 the Emperor Nicephorus Phocas briefly recaptured the city.

Subordinate to Damascus and Baghdad, Aleppo was always a second city, never a capital, except during the years 944–1003, when it flourished under the cultivated Shi'a dynasty of the Hamdanids. The poet al-Mutanabbi lived there for nine years, writing panegyrics to the Hamdanid ruler Saif al-Daula ('sword of the state'), 'the orient and the occident of the sun'. They show his love of the city of Aleppo and pride in Islam and the Arabs.

All the nations make claim to love Saif al-Daula …
The Arabs in the world are unique in being of his race, and the
    non-Arabs share with the Arabs in enjoying his beneficence.
    Allah has reserved his succour exclusively for Islam, even though
    all nations partake of his blessings.
Every time gardens welcomed us, we said to them,
Aleppo is our aim and you are merely the route.[4]

Despite its frontier position, Aleppo was already a great trading city. In 1184, when it was ruled by emirs of the Zengid dynasty, Ibn Jubayr, a traveller from Andalucia, praised the 'large markets arranged in long adjacent rows so that you pass from a row of shops of one craft into that of another until you have gone through all the urban industries', and the height and impregnability of the citadel.[5] Ibn Battuta from Tangier, who visited it two centuries later, also praised the beauty and grandeur of its markets.[6]

Aleppo's more recent history, during and after the Ottoman Empire, is the focus of this book. Since 1260 most of Syria had been ruled from Cairo by the Mamluk sultans. The citadel which towers over the city was rebuilt in the Mamluk period. The Mamluk sultans were increasingly opposed, over territory and leadership of Sunni Muslims, to the Ottoman sultans, who since 1453 had ruled their expanding empire from Constantinople. On 23 August 1516 Yavuz Selim ('Selim the Stern'), grandson of Mehmed the conqueror of Constantinople, defeated the Mamluk army at Marj Dabiq, thirty miles north of Aleppo: the Ottomans had better cannon and the Mamluk commander had been bribed in advance to desert. After eighteen days in Aleppo, Yavuz Selim moved on to Damascus and Cairo, where he completed the conquest of the Mamluk sultanate and received the allegiance of the Sherif of Mecca, a descendant of the Prophet Mohammed, who governed Mecca and Medina. Thenceforth, as the most powerful Muslim ruler, and 'guardian of the Two Holy Places' of Mecca and Medina, the Ottoman sultan also claimed to be caliph of the Muslims.[7]

According to local chroniclers, the people of Aleppo, exasperated by Mamluk over-taxation and lawlessness, had welcomed the Ottoman conquest. In 1520 a rebellion against Ottoman rule broke out in Damascus. Aleppo, however, remained loyal. That loyalty would last 400 years.[8]

PART I

A History

Chapter One

❁

The Ottoman City

Situated at the crossroads of Europe, Asia and Africa, ruling an area stretching from Bosnia to Yemen, the Ottoman Empire needed foreign allies. It favoured Constantinople's re-emergence as an international capital, after its decline in the last centuries of the Byzantine Empire. Mehmed the Conqueror and his successors encouraged or forced Turks, Greeks, Armenians and Jews to settle there, and welcomed European embassies. Similarly they favoured Aleppo's development as an international trading city. Part of the Ottoman Empire's enduring success, compared to previous Turkic states like the Seljuk sultanate in Anatolia, came from its ability to keep foreign allies and to incorporate different peoples and religions in its administrative and financial structures. Local Christian and Jewish hierarchies were made responsible for paying taxes and enforcing laws in their respective communities.

Aleppo shows that the Empire was not only an imperial autocracy, and a Muslim Turkish state, but also a complex of communities. Each group could follow its own faith and traditions. Self-interest and realism discouraged them from temptation to rebel. As long as the sultan's suzerainty was acknowledged, and taxes were paid, the Empire could rule with a light hand. Aleppo had found a state which suited it, both geographically and economically. It was no longer a frontier city, but an entrepôt at the centre of an empire.

Yavuz Selim's first acts in Aleppo announced the character of the Ottoman administration. They included the appointment of Turks, rather than Arabs, as governor and *kadi* (Muslim religious judge); the diminution of customs rates from 20 per cent to 5 per cent; and the lowering of the tax on Christian pilgrims going to Jerusalem.[1]

The governor of the province of Aleppo ruled a large area between the Mediterranean and the Euphrates. His authority was balanced by that of other officials appointed directly from Constantinople, the *aga* of the elite corps of 700 janissaries who controlled the city walls and the two military commanders of the city and the citadel. By the eighteenth century, according to Alexander Russell, a Scottish doctor residing in the city from 1740 to 1753, the governor was assisted by a *divan* or council, meeting every Friday. It included the principal government and religious officials, and

> the principal effendis [gentlemen] and Agas, together with the Shahbinder or head of the merchants [...] Business relating to the city and all parts of the Province is transacted in the divan, the Bashaw always affecting to be desirous of exact information. He inquires with much formality concerning the city markets, the disposition of the people, the state of trade and the condition of the villages.

In theory the governor could not inflict capital punishment without a formal trial and had to listen to opinions in the *divan*:

> The different interests operating in the Divan, in some measure counterbalance one another and not withstanding the frequent violation of the people's rights, the ordinary course of affairs proceeds more equitably than might be expected in a government where the people are commonly supposed to be the mere slaves of despotic power.[2]

Syrian *ulama* or religious authorities called the Ottoman sultan 'Sultan al-Rum' (Rum – an Arab and Turkish word for Anatolia, the area once ruled by Roman or Byzantine emperors). They regarded him as foreign, but in later periods often went to study in Constantinople, just as the different *kadis* (judges) and *sheikhs al-islam* (leading Muslim authorities) were generally sent from Constantinople to Aleppo.[3] As in other Ottoman provinces, the rivalry between Turks and Arabs, dating back to the ninth century when Turkish commanders had begun to dominate the Abbasid caliphate, was reflected in the military and political dominance of Turks. A seventeenth-century Ottoman historian born in Aleppo, Mustafa Naima, describes the fear of Aleppo and Ottoman officials felt by 'the Arabs of the sort acustomed to the desert and the open lands'.[4] The first governor of Aleppo of local origin, Ibrahim Pasha Katiraghasi, was not appointed until 1799, and lasted only five years.[5]

Aleppo functioned as an Ottoman base during the Empire's frequent wars with Iran under the Safavid shahs. They were caused by territorial disputes over control of Iraq, as well as by religious hatred between Sunni Ottomans and Shi'a Iranians – dating from quarrels over the succession to the Prophet Muhammad, between Sunni supporters of his Umayyad cousins and Shi'a followers of his son-in-law Ali. Ali had been murdered in 661 and his son Hussein in 680 – murders still dividing Shi'a and Sunni Muslims today. The geographical ambitions of the two empires envenomed the religious hatred of the two groups. After campaigning against Iran, Suleyman 'the Magnificent' himself spent part of the winters of 1534–5, 1548–9 and 1553–4 resting in Aleppo. It was the only Arabic-speaking city to receive regular visits from an Ottoman sultan.[6]

Since 1535 one of the Sultan's main allies had been the King of France: they were united by a shared fear of Spain and the House of Austria, as well as shared desire for trade. A sign of the Ottoman–French alliance, which would influence Aleppo for the subsequent 400 years, was the presence there in 1548–9 of the French ambassador Monsieur d'Aramon, at the same time as the Sultan, whom he was advising on tactics against Iran.[7]

Aleppo began to acquire an Ottoman layer of khans, mosques and fountains, in addition to its Umayyad, Ayyubid and Mamluk buildings. Inscriptions in honour of Ottoman sultans appeared on the walls of the Great Mosque, where the sultan's firmans or decrees were read out. The first Ottoman mosque was built by the governor Husrev Pasha in 1537–46.[8]

Ottoman rule favoured diversity. A German doctor called Leonhard Rauwolff, who visited the city in 1573 in search of medicinal herbs, heard a story that, when Suleyman the Magnificent was staying in Aleppo, there was debate in his council over whether, for their 'unsufferable

usury', to expel Jews from the province. The Sultan asked his advisers
to consider a flowerpot

> that held a quantity of fine flowers of divers colours, that was then in
> the room and bid them consider whether each of them in their col-
> our did not set out the other the better [...] The more sorts of nations
> I have in my dominions under me, as Turks, Moors, Grecians etc.,
> the greater authority they bring to my kingdoms and make them
> more famous. And that nothing may fall off from my greatness,
> I think it convenient that all that have been together long hitherto,
> may be kept and tolerated so still for the future.

The council agreed 'unanimously'.[9] Such Ottoman belief in the advan-
tages of diversity, also reflected in Mehmed II's policy of repeopling
Constantinople, in the recruitment of janissaries from non-Turks and
in numerous Ottoman texts praising the virtues of different races, is
another reason for the Empire's survival.[10]

The only serious threat to Ottoman authority came in the
early seventeenth century, from a family of Kurdish chiefs called
Canbulatoglu, ancestors of the Jumblatts, Druze leaders in Lebanon
today. In 1603–7 Ali Pasha, leader of the clan, led moves for auton-
omy or independence in Aleppo, encouraged by the Grand Duke of
Tuscany and his Order of Saint Stephen, who wanted to recreate the
crusader Kingdom of Jerusalem.[11] Far from being averse to foreign
intervention, local leaders often initiated it. Shah Abbas of Iran, who
was in communication with the Grand Duke of Tuscany, also had
plans to seize the city, and a Mediterranean port, in order to export
silk direct from Iran to Europe, without paying Ottoman customs
dues.[12]

Chapter Two

Emporium of the Orient World

Conquest had made Aleppo Ottoman; trade made it a world city. At the junction of Anatolia, the Fertile Crescent and the Syrian Desert, where the Silk Road approached the Mediterranean, Aleppo was a natural destination for merchants. Caravans of camels arrived every year from India, Iran, the Gulf, Erzerum, Damascus and the Arabian Peninsula. They halted in Aleppo before proceeding to the ports of Iskenderun on the Mediterranean, Smyrna on the Aegean, or Constantinople. In 1550 Jacques Gassot, a French diplomat, wrote of Aleppo: 'Elle est fort marchande et plus que Constantinople ou autre ville de Levant.'[1]

For the English traveller Thomas Coryate, Aleppo was 'the principall emporium of all Syria or rather of the Orient world'.[2] Leonhard Rauwolff observed

> great caravans of pack horses and asses, but more camels arrive there daily, from all foreign countries, viz. from Natalia, Armenia, Aegypt

and India etc. with convoys, so that the streets are so crouded that it is hard to pass by one another. Each of these Nations have their peculiar champ [khan] to themselves.[3]

In 1574 the most global of grand viziers, Sokollu Mehmed Pasha, who commissioned buildings from the Balkans to the Black Sea, also paid for the construction of the Khan al-Gumruk or customs inn, near the entrance to the main souk. A symbol of Aleppo's role as an international trading city, for centuries it would be the residence of the French, Dutch and English consuls. At one time there were 344 shops in the khan and its endowment made it one of the largest landowners in the city.[4]

Aleppo received a further boost after 1590, when Iskenderun on the Mediterranean, seventy-five miles away by road, was officially opened by the Ottoman government for international trade, replacing the previous port Payas, twenty miles to the north. Merchants in Aleppo were informed by messages tucked under pigeons' wings of the arrival of ships in Iskenderun. The journey took three or four days for people on horseback, but only six hours for well-trained pigeons.[5]

By 1600 there were fifty-three khans and fifty-six souks in Aleppo. The dark, narrow, vaulted souks were the largest in the Middle East. They stretched for twelve kilometres; through the souks of the rope-makers, the saddlers, the tanners or the spice-merchants, it was said that a blind man could make his way by following the smell of the merchandise.[6] There were also at least eight weekly markets outside the city walls, every Friday, where people from the surrounding countryside came to sell their produce.[7] Ten gates in the city walls later gave their names to districts of the city: among them Bab Antaki, the gate of the road to Antakya; Bab el-Nasr, the gate of victory; and Bab el-Farraj, the gate with a fine view of gardens outside the walls.[8] After Constantinople and Cairo, Aleppo was the third largest city in the Empire.

One of the first Englishmen to trade in Aleppo was John Eldred, later treasurer of the Levant Company, founded in 1581 to encourage England's trade with the Ottoman Empire. Arriving from Baghdad in 1586 in a caravan of 4,000 camels, he wrote: 'it is the great place of traffique for a dry towne [i.e. not a port] that is in all those parts; for hither resort Jewes, Tartarians, Persians, Armenians, Egyptians, Indians and many sorts of Christians and enjoy freedom of their consciences and bring thither many kinds of rich merchandises'.[9] Freedom of conscience, at that time, was unknown in most cities in Europe.

In 1596 Fynes Morison praised the courteous entertainment and 'plentifull diet, good lodging and most friendly conversation' of the English merchants, and their 'excellent wines': the white was local, the red came from Mount Lebanon. The presence of English traders inspired Shakespeare's line in *Macbeth* (1603–6), 'Her husband's to Aleppo gone, master o'er the Tiger'.[10]

Silk, soap, spices and goat-hair were among the main exports, textiles the main import: every year in the early seventeenth century England sold in Aleppo 12,000 pieces of cloth, known as 'londra'.[11] Until the nineteenth century many people in the Ottoman Empire dressed in cloth woven in Aleppo; turbans and belts were a speciality.[12]

From the mid sixteenth century, Armenians in Aleppo helped run the silk trade with Iran, where they had many co-religionists. In 1621 it was said that Iran exported 6,000 bales of silk to Europe via Aleppo, and similar figures were probably correct for most years when the Ottoman Empire and Iran were not fighting each other: hence the Shah's interest in acquiring Aleppo.[13] Reflecting Armenians' growing prominence, in 1616 the Armenian Church of the Forty Martyrs (Surp Karsunk) had been built as seat of the Armenian patriarch. For greater security, he had moved to Aleppo from Sis in Cilicia.[14] In 1617 an Armenian traveller called Simeon of Poland was struck by Armenians' prosperity and excellent schools, in 'the famed and glorious capital city of Aleppo'. In the 'very beautiful and delightful' domed Armenian church, 'the Franks have three altars where every Saturday and Sunday they serve mass'. One Armenian called Petik, chief of the customs of Aleppo, travelled 'like a pasha', escorted by cavalry and infantry. He and his brother donated funds for a second Armenian church. At this stage the city had 300 Armenian households, 'decent people, great merchants who travel to India, Baghdad and Isfahan. They eat superb food.'[15]

Venetian merchants also prospered in Aleppo, as they had since the Middle Ages. The Venetian consul had reported in 1615, '[T]he trade in Aleppo is as flourishing as ever, because there still come caravans from different places with valuable goods, especially silk.' At the end of the same year, however, his successor complained of 'the evident destruction of this market and especially of this our poor trade [...] all the Venetian merchants here are so downhearted and have to that degree lost courage that some think of returning home to Venice whereas others will travel to India or Persia.' Ottoman wars with Iran interrupted the supply of silk. After 1650, Smyrna, on the

Aegean, began to replace Aleppo as the city where Asia came shopping for Europe, and vice versa.[16]

Horses were another export. Again, location favoured Aleppo. Horses from the Arabian Desert were especially prized in Europe, as they were faster than its slow and heavy breeds. Aleppo was the natural place to buy them, since only Aleppo had easy access both to Europe and the Arabian Desert. By the mid seventeenth century it had become the main marketplace for 'Arabian' stallions. One Aleppo proverb stated: 'There are three fine things in life: an obedient wife, a large house, and a fast horse.'[17] Arab traders were said to know some horses' pedigrees, on both father's and mother's sides, for the last 500 years: 'proofs of nobility', wrote the French consul d'Arvieux, 'that many Nobles in France could not produce'.[18]

The best horses were in theory reserved for the sultan, but market forces could be more powerful than Ottoman decrees. In 1704 the English consul Thomas Darley sent the 'Darley Arabian', a horse over fifteen hands high, from Aleppo to his brother in England, via Iskenderun. Long remembered in Aleppo, it is one of the three ancestral 'foundation sires' of thoroughbred horses racing today.[19] As Donna Landry has shown, 'Lord Harley's Dun', another foundation sire, regarded as 'the finest horse that ever came over', was sent to his brother in England by Nathaniel Harley in 1715. Another famous stallion 'the Bloody-shouldered Arabian' – so called because of dark patches on its shoulders – considered 'worth his weight in gold', was shipped from Iskenderun in 1720 after a wait of three years in Aleppo owing to war in the Mediterranean.[20]

Aleppo proverbs reflected its spirit as a trading city, where deals were more important than ideals. One, tragically forgotten today, was: 'Excess is obnoxious, even in religious worship.'[21] Others were: 'He who has wealth will win the hand of the Sultan's daughter'; 'The piastre equips its owner with seven languages.' A man from Aleppo, it was said, could sell you a dried donkey-skin. What was sold in Cairo in a month was sold in Aleppo in a day.[22]

Chapter Three

Consuls and Travellers

Under the Ottoman Empire, while remaining an Arabic-speaking city with a Muslim majority, Aleppo also became a Levantine city. It resembled distant ports such as Smyrna or Alexandria, as well as neighbouring cities like Homs and Damascus. Levantine cities' characteristics included: location on or near the Eastern Mediterranean; the prominence of international trade and foreign consuls; the use of international languages, such as lingua franca or broken Italian, and later French; and relative tolerance, and numerical balance, between different communities. No single group was exclusively dominant.[1]

Aleppo became a city of consuls. Venice, France and England had ambassadors in Constantinople who obtained 'capitulations' which gave them the right to appoint consuls in the Empire and their nationals the right to trade and, in most legal disputes, to follow their own laws, administered by their consuls. In 1548 Venice transferred its consul from Tripoli on the coast to Aleppo, as Aleppo was 'where the merchants live and business is done'.[2] Subsequently France (1560), England (1583) and the Netherlands (1607) – five years before it sent its first ambassador to

Constantinople – also appointed consuls in Aleppo. The Aleppo consulates are – or, it is now necessary to write, were – among the oldest in
the world.[3]

A consul's duties were to execute the orders of his government and,
in the English case, of the Levant Company, which paid his salary; to
negotiate with local officials; to protect the rights and privileges, and
ensure the good behaviour, of his nation's merchants; to preside over
their assemblies; and to hire interpreters.[4] The state entry of a consul
into Aleppo, like that of an ambassador into Constantinople, celebrated
the bonds of respect and interest connecting the Ottoman Empire and
the powers of Europe. To the sound of gun salutes fired from the citadel,
a new consul would be escorted by janissaries and Ottoman officials (to
show watching crowds that he enjoyed the sultan's protection) in ceremonial uniform, as well as by his own grooms, ushers and interpreters,
and by his fellow consuls and European merchants, also wearing their
best clothes. Local bands played music. 'The whole city' cheered.

Subsequently consuls visited, and exchanged presents with, the governor and the *kadi*. Presents conveyed mutual need and respect across
religious and cultural boundaries, and were vital to ensure good relations with Ottoman authorities. Monsieur Gedoyen, on his arrival in
Aleppo as French consul in August 1624, for example, described at
length the presents he gave. Although France and the Ottoman Empire
were allies, he describes these presents as a form of tribute. No audience
was given by the governor to a consul unless the consul's presents had
first been weighed, measured and tested for quality. A consul also had to
give gratuities to the governor's servants.[5] Foreign powers still needed
the Ottoman Empire more than the other way round.

Through its consulate, and its priests, the influence of France was
felt in Aleppo long before French troops arrived in 1920. The 'salle
consulaire' in the French consulate in the Khan al-Gumruk contained
portraits, heraldic shields, tapestries and a red leather chair for the consul
'quand on tient assemblée'. 'You would not believe', claimed the consul
in 1693, 'how many people in this city come to see the furniture and
admire the portraits of our kings.'[6] Next to it was the consul's chapel,
served by French Jesuits, and a room furnished 'à la turque', with sofa
and divans, to receive people from Aleppo.[7]

Consuls in Aleppo became sources of information, innovations and
hospitality, as well as of protection and mediation. A consul was often
the first European to hear news of Arabia, the Gulf, Iran and India.

Through his despatches, ambassadors in Constantinople – and ministers in Westminster or Versailles – could 'feel the pulse of Asia'.[8] Consuls also supplied their governments with rare animals, plants and manuscripts. In 1668, for example, the French consul sent gazelles, canes and pistachios to Louis XIV's minister Colbert.[9] Greek and Arabic manuscripts were also purchased, on the death of local scholars, for the King and his ministers. As with Arabian horses, Europeans got the best, since they paid the most.[10]

Simultaneously consul of France and the Netherlands in 1679–86, the Chevalier d'Arvieux's memoirs and despatches give a vivid account of Aleppo in those years. He spoke Turkish, Arabic, Armenian, Greek and Hebrew, as well as knowing Spanish, Italian and Latin. He had been a merchant in Smyrna and Sidon, as well as French consul in Algiers and Tripoli, but also kept a job at the French court, as equerry to the governess of the *enfants de France*. Combining Versailles and Aleppo, he entertained his friends at the former with stories of the latter, and no doubt vice versa. His memoirs, published in six volumes in 1735, suggest that Aleppo worked like an elaborate machine, each piece of which helped make the others function. The frequent exchange of gifts kept the machinery well oiled. After d'Arvieux had made his state entry in 1679 on a richly harnessed white horse, wearing an embroidered red coat decorated with lace, he made visits to churches, merchants and officials. The heads of local guilds also came to visit him. He did not live in seclusion, and often wore local dress and a beard. Manners and ceremonies, as well as gifts, helped ensure the visits' success. The *kadi* received him with the Ottoman rituals of a pipe to smoke, coffee to drink and a perfume-sprinkler for his clothes, and expressed his desire for 'perfect correspondance'. Tobacco, grown near Aleppo, had revolutionised Ottoman life since its introduction from Europe earlier in the century: a pipe could be a status symbol as well as a pleasure.

The *mutsellim* or deputy of the governor served, and enjoyed, wine and liqueurs 'without a break' like other Ottoman officials, embraced him with tenderness and asked him to be his friend. D'Arvieux liked the local wine and the 'delicacy' of the local food and admired the marble walls and Venetian mirrors he found in Aleppo houses. He also praised the city's gardens and fruit, especially the peaches and grapes.[11] On 17 April 1681 a dinner d'Arvieux gave for Dutch visitors reflected Aleppo's spirit of diversity. There was 'service à la turque' (local food with many small dishes); wines and liqueurs 'à la grecque';

acrobats, Jewish dancers and an European orchestra; 'the company was very gay'.[12]

On the other hand d'Arvieux also faced disputes over customs rates, pilgrims, slaves and other issues, requiring lengthy correspondence with the French ambassador in Constantinople or the French government. The English consul and merchants were unfriendly. French merchants' assemblies were unruly. Marauding bedouin or drunken soldiers assaulted French subjects.[13] 'The 'zèle mal réglé' of the local priests gave him little rest. Jesuits, supported by the French Crown, frequently exchanged blows, over who should hold services in the consulate, with monks from the rival orders of Franciscans, Capucins, Carmelites and Cordeliers.[14] Consuls were also required to settle disputes involving merchants and protégés or *beratlis* of their own nationality. In return for payments, some Aleppines connected to foreign consulates acquired rights to their legal protection.[15]

Ottoman officials were generally polite. However, d'Arvieux found that they needed 'decent and often repeated little presents' – in a steady flow, not simply at the moment of arrival: 'However much Turks appear to be good friends to Christians, they never forget their interests and defend them very well.'[16] D'Arvieux also found that one governor, called Kara Bekir Pasha as he was dark-skinned (*kara* is Turkish for black), 'had the eyes and physionomy of a marauding wolf and that was assuredly his character'. In Aleppo people complained of the current pasha or consul, but missed him when he was gone.[17]

The English consulate, also in the Khan al-Gumruk (one room of which served as an Anglican chapel), also functioned as a research centre.[18] Edward Pococke, English chaplain in Aleppo from 1630, learnt Hebrew, Syriac and Arabic and bought manuscripts for Oxford when he returned in 1636 to be first Laudian Professor of Arabic and Hebrew. English merchants from Aleppo were the first Europeans to rediscover the ruins of Palmyra, mounting two expeditions there, in 1678 and 1691 (the latter, led by a chaplain called William Halifax, resulted in the first picture of Palmyra, now in the Allard Pierson Museum in Amsterdam).[19] Later English scholars in Aleppo would include Henry Maundrell, chaplain from 1696 until his death there at the age of thirty-one in 1701, author of *A Journey from Aleppo to Jerusalem at Easter AD 1697* (1703): like other Christians in Aleppo, English merchants frequently went on pilgrimage to Jerusalem at Easter.[20]

Whereas in Constantinople, Smyrna and Alexandria, Europeans often wore Western dress, in Aleppo, to avoid insult, they wore local costume, with European hats and wigs.[21] European merchants generally conducted business with local traders through Jewish or Christian interpreters, to whom they talked Italian – probably in the simplified form, known in the Levant as lingua franca. In 1780 an English traveller called John Griffiths wrote that 'the language of the city [meaning the people he knew in it] is chiefly Italian'. In the evening, Europeans shut themselves in their khans, 'after the manner of colleges'.[22]

Foreign merchants had long claimed they could never obtain a fair hearing in a local Muslim court. By capitulations renewed in 1675 English merchants (and the local Christians they protected) for the first time – largely through changes in clause LXIX not noticed by the Sublime Porte (the Ottoman government) – won the right to appeal to their ambassador in all commercial cases involving sums of over 4,000 *akçes*. Thus all such disputes became foreign policy issues rather than local commercial ones.[23] The fortunes made by Europeans in Aleppo, however, were less spectacular than those won in India. In 1673, after twelve years in Aleppo, John Verney returned to London with only £6,000.[24] Nathaniel Harley, brother of Robert Harley, the Tory Lord Treasurer of England 1710–14, arrived in 1685. He died there in 1720, after thirty-five years without a break, still relatively poor.[25] Until their 'factory' declined in the mid eighteenth century due to French competition, there were usually thirty or forty English merchants in the city; their ships were called *Levant Merchant*, *Levantine* or *Aleppine*.[26]

The Natural History of Aleppo (1756), by Alexander Russell, the most complete account of an Ottoman city in a Western language, is as informative as d'Arvieux's memoirs. A revised second edition, published by Russell's brother Patrick, also a doctor, in two volumes in 1794, added further information. Russell describes at length, and with many illustrations, the diseases prevalent in the city, in particular the plague and a boil caused by the bite of the sand-fly, known as the 'mal d'Alep', or 'the Aleppo button', which affected most inhabitants of the city until the twentieth century. He also analyses the people, fauna, flora and climate of the city, praising the 'perfect tolerance' of the government, and 'the salubrity of the air and the solidity and elegance of its private buildings as well as the convenience and neatness of its streets'. With his help Alexander Drummond, later British consul in the city, established a Masonic lodge there on St Andrew's Day 1747. Little is known of its subsequent history, but it too may have contributed to the city's spirit of coexistence.[27]

Like d'Arvieux seventy years earlier, Russell showed how a consul's audience with the governor solemnised the Ottoman Empire's relations with foreign powers:

> Soon after the Consul enters the audience chamber, the Bashaw [pasha] makes his appearance, supported by two officers, and proceeds immediately to his place on the Divan, without taking notice of the company as he passes. The Consul sits down at the same time with the Bashaw, a chair of state having been previously brought from his own house. Two of the principal officers stand near the Bashaw; the gentlemen of the Factory stand behind the Consul's chair; they sometimes, but not always, are invited to sit down on the Divan. As soon as the Bashaw is seated, he begins by welcoming the Consul in very polite terms, and then enters into a routine of questions, and professions of regard for the English [or another nation] which, with the compliments made by the Consul in return and his recommendation of the nation to the protection of His Excellency, fill up the quarter of an hour usually devoted to an audience. During the conversation the Consul is entertained successively with sweetmeats, coffee, tobacco, sherbet and perfume: all which are, by other pages, presented at the same instant to the Bashaw. Towards the end of the audience he orders the Consul to be invested with an ermine fur. The gentlemen in his suite are entertained with the same refreshments, tobacco excepted.

Similar audiences were given by the *kadi* and the *mohassil*, or chief tax farmer.[28] A few janissaries, from the Empire's elite corps, escorted the consul outside his consulate, beating trouble makers with sticks or swords; one janissary alone, d'Arvieux had written, could keep 'one thousand of these *canailles* in respect'.[29]

At a crossroads of trade routes, Aleppo was a natural destination for travellers. They were drawn by general curiosity and particular fascination with the classical ruins in the region. The Ottoman Empire, moreover, had fewer bandits or robbers than many regions of Europe.[30] According to Alexander Russell, 'the gentlemen of the British Factory at Aleppo' were treated by the pashas, and therefore by the people, with 'civility and respect', 'so that we live among them in great security in the city and can travel abroad unmolested by Arabs or Curds where the natives dare not venture'.[31] It was easy to purchase, through ambassadors in Constantinople, or local consuls, firmans or decrees from the Ottoman government which gave foreigners permission to travel in the Empire. Kept in embroidered bags, they were shown when needed. One such firman, issued for two English officers, asked Ottomans to allow them

> to be conveyed in a hospitable manner with a courier for known purposes and to be provided on their journey with necessaries for travelling and the customs of hospitality to be observed towards them [...] Our divan has written and issued this command and sent it by a courier [...] God willing [...] they pass in safety and with despatch to their intended place.[32]

Aleppo was visited by North Africans, Iranians, Arabs and Indians as well as Europeans – and was often used as a resting-place on the way to or from India.[33] In Aleppo travellers could find shops, guides, doctors and caravans with which to continue their journey. The number, variety and chronological range of the travellers' books describing Aleppo – collected in a magnificent 2,000-page, three-volume book published by Olivier Salmon in Aleppo in 2011, *Alep dans la littérature de voyage européenne pendant la période ottomane (1516–1918)* – made it better known in Europe in the seventeenth and eighteenth centuries than later.[34] That is why so many travellers' accounts can be quoted in Part II of this book. Illustrated with prints, drawings and maps, such books make a vital contribution to Aleppo's history. The most accurate early panorama of the city, recently bought by the Musée des Beaux-Arts in Tours, is by Louis-François Cassas. He worked for the French ambassador in Constantinople, the Comte de Choiseul-Gouffier, travelling through the Ottoman Empire in 1784–6 to draw its cities and monuments. The best early map was by a local French merchant called Vincent Germain, prepared in 1811 at the suggestion of the French consul-general, and published in 1825.[35]

As Britain became a world power, British officers and merchants, who wanted to avoid the long sea journey to or from India round Africa, often travelled via Aleppo and the Gulf, as their Portuguese equivalents had long been doing.[36] Many took 'the Great Desert route' directly through the desert from Basra to Aleppo, rather than the slower route

along the Tigris to Baghdad and then west along the Euphrates. The
desert route was also used by postal services and despatch bearers of
the Ottoman government and the East India Company. In 1780 the
Dutch painter Jan van der Steen, after ten years working for the Swedish
embassy in Constantinople, passed through Aleppo on his way to India,
where he died a lieutenant in the Bombay Artillery in 1784.[37] On his
way from London back to India in 1786, another painter, Tilly Kettle,
painted his last portrait in Aleppo – then died, probably resisting robbers, outside the city.[38]

Chapter Four

Entertainments

How did the inhabitants of Aleppo amuse themselves? The wealthy played *jirid* outside the walls – throwing sticks at rivals on horseback, to see who could first unhorse the other. The Portuguese traveller Pedro Texeira, who visited Aleppo in 1605, said that every Friday evening 1,000 horsemen practised *jirid* outside the walls.[1] Men also enjoyed hawking. Hunting boars, hares, partridges and rabbit in the neighbouring countryside, and cricket (described in 1676, the first certain mention of the game being played abroad[2]) were popular with foreigners. At one time the English went hunting with hounds twice a week. The Dutch traveller Cornelis le Bruyn, who visited the city in 1683–4, wrote that they would drink the health of their hunt master or 'capo', shouting 'hurray!' 'à la manière des Anglais dans ces sortes de réjouissances'. Hunts would end with a picnic in a marquee by a river.[3] A portrait of the English merchant Henry Lannoy Hunter in a version of Turkish dress, painted in the 1730s by Andrea Soldi, now in the Tate Gallery, shows him in the desert surrounded by the game he had shot (see Plate 2).

During the carnival season, as if they were in a Mediterranean port, consuls organised 'balls and masquerades [...] in one continued circulation of entertainments', according to Francis Vernon, a naval officer who visited it in 1785. Such parties allowed foreigners, and some local Christians and Jews, to enjoy 'the sweets of Aleppo'. Vernon claimed that it was easy to meet Turkish ladies ('veiled coquetts') in the houses of their Jewish friends.[4]

Mosques and schools contained libraries. In the courtyards of the Great Mosque, notables held teaching circles. Cafés appeared soon after the introduction of coffee from Yemen in the sixteenth century. Rauwolff's travels contain one of the first European descriptions of coffee – 'a very good drink [...] almost as black as ink and very good in illness especially of the stomach'. Thirty years later Texeira found 'coffee houses well built and furnished, adorned with numerous lamps, for their chief custom is at night'.[5] Some cafés could accommodate several hundred customers. A surviving example was the lavishly decorated, many-domed café of Ipshir Pasha, built in the suburb of Judayda in 1654.

The great Ottoman traveller Evliya Celebi, who visited Aleppo in 1671, claimed there were 105 cafes in the city. Of the café of Arslan Dede, he wrote that it was as near to heaven as it was possible for a mortal to find in the world.[6] Customers played draughts, chess and backgammon, or, according to Alexander Russell, declaimed plausibly on the decay of religion, the follies of private life, the perversion of public justice and the corruptions of government'.[7]

Some cafés also acted as theatres and music halls, where customers could listen to poetry or music, and watch puppet-shows or dancing boys, performing with what the seventeenth-century French traveller Jean Thévenot called 'abominable lasciviousness'. Visiting Aleppo a hundred years later in 1786, John Griffiths listened to drums, tambourine, flute and guitar being played in cafés. Sometimes there was singing; he preferred the puppet-shows, despite the many 'indecorous sallies' of the hero/villain, Karagöz.[8] Occasionally the governor closed cafés for 'immorality'.[9]

Alexander Russell noted that in one area prostitutes were licensed by the governor. Often visited by soldiers, they were 'dressed in a flaunting manner in the highest degree impudent and profligate [...] no person of any character can have any decent pretence to approach them'. Venereal disease was called 'the Frank disease'.[10]

Perhaps because of its trading spirit, Aleppo was distinguished by its manners – another factor which kept the machinery of the city in working order. An Aleppo proverb enjoined, 'If you do business with a dog, you should call him sir.' Throughout its Ottoman centuries, travellers and inhabitants agreed: 'halabi chalabi' – 'a man from Aleppo is a gentleman' – whereas, some added, a man from Damascus is a thief. D'Arvieux, who had travelled throughout the Empire, wrote: 'What is good and extraordinary and which advantageously distinguishes this people from all those of the Ottoman Empire, is that they are the gentlest, the least malicious and the most tractable of all this vast empire.'[11]

Later writers also praised Aleppo's manners: 'Aleppo is the choicest of places on earth: no other locality matches it in the excellence of its climate, people and food.'[12] Even later Haim Sabato recorded:

[T]he people of Avram Zova [Hebrew for Aleppo, derived from the name of Abraham's half-nephew Aram] are proud of their city and unstinting in its praise. They are as proud of its air and its fountains as of the acumen of its tradesmen. The manners of Aleppo brook no deviation: one is obliged to begin with certain words and conclude with certain words. The conventions are rigid: who asks and who answers, and when. According to the etiquette of Aleppo, you are not asked why you have come and you do not say why you have come. Everything must be explained by way of allusion.[13]

Chapter Five

Muslims, Christians, Jews

At a time when almost all European cities excluded or penalised religious minorities, Aleppo, like other Ottoman cities, contained Muslims, Christians and Jews. Most lived among their own community, near a mosque, church or synagogue. Some rarely, or never, ventured into the rest of the city. Before the nineteenth century, of the ninety-nine quarters of the old city, fifty were entirely Muslim, one was 91 per cent Jewish, eighteen were more than 80 per cent Christian and thirty were mixed.[1] There were no legally enforced ghettoes like the ghetto in Venice, into which Jews were obliged to lock themselves every night and to pay the Christians who guarded it, from 1506 until the French conquest in 1797. The Ottoman Empire was more relaxed about minorities than other Muslim regimes such as the Mamluk sultanate or the empire of Morocco. It needed the revenue from the special taxes they paid. After the Ottoman conquest, throughout the Levant the proportion of Christians in the population rose from about 6 per cent in 1516 to about 20 per cent by 1700.

Conditions varied from decade to decade and governor to governor. There were occasional incidents, often arising from the law making apostasy from Islam punishable by death. During a quarrel over allegedly unpaid taxes, Da'ud, an Orthodox Christian cobbler, had placed a Muslim's turban on his head. This was interpreted as a sign that he had become Muslim. When he refused to abjure Christianity after two months in prison, he was executed on 18 July 1660. Some Christians considered him a martyr.[2] In 1693 the green slippers worn by the wife of a Dutch merchant called Richard Verschuer almost provoked a riot. It was considered insulting for a Christian to wear shoes of a colour which many Muslims considered sacred, as was shown by the green turbans worn by descendants of the Prophet. Her husband had to pay local officials 500 *kuruş* to save her life.[3]

For most of the time in Aleppo, however, Christians and Jews enjoyed a mixture of marginality and prosperity. The long periods of coexistence, although less likely to provide events to record, were more characteristic of the city than moments of violence. Christians were generally allowed to ride horses, which was not the case in Constantinople. Dress regulations – by which non-Muslims were obliged to wear dark colours like black and blue, while bright colours were reserved for Muslims – were a means of raising revenue as well as imposing visual segregation. They could be relaxed by special payments.[4] Properties were bought and sold without difficulty between members of different communities.[5] Old churches were renovated, new ones (despite a theoretical ban by the Ottoman government) built. Priests wore their robes in the street. In the seventeenth century a school of brilliant local icon painters flourished.[6]

If a governor made outrageous demands, Christians would close their churches until he reduced them. Not only could Christians win legal cases against Muslims, they often preferred Sunni Muslim to Christian law courts. The former were generally quicker and cheaper, and allowed daughters to inherit a greater share of their property; they were also used in marriage disputes.[7] Islamic courts accepted the oath of a Christian on the Gospels, and of a Jew on the Torah.[8] In the 1750s women made up 40 per cent of the people buying and selling houses. Some worked in the marketplace.[9] At times they were allowed to enter cafés. In 1797–9, the twice-widowed Luisa Vernon, member of a wealthy and long-established family of Levant merchants, acted as agent in Aleppo for both the Levant and the East India companies, also conducting business on her own behalf 'with great spirit'.[10]

Muslim courts also provided a neutral battleground on which Christians from different sects could conduct their internecine disputes. Christians and Muslims went to the same shops and worked in the same guilds, although some guilds were dominated by members of one religion. Around 1600, for example, gold and silver smiths were Jews, silk-spinners tended to be Christians.[11]

According to one Aleppo proverb: 'the greatest blessing is in things concealed from view'.[12] Indeed some of the finest old houses in the city, such as the Ghazaleh house, built for the family of that name around 1600 and later enlarged, in Judayda the 'new' area outside the city walls built from the sixteenth century, are hidden from the street. Only after walking down a featureless alley do you find a door opening onto a courtyard lined with majestic rooms.

Architecture and decoration can be as revealing as documents. These merchant mansions, built in the same style and on the same scale, by Muslims and Christians, are signs of status, wealth, taste and coexistence as revealing as documents. They shared spectacular courtyards, and domed *iwans* or open halls with intricately painted wooden panels on the walls and ceilings, decorated with flowers and Arabic inscriptions. Among them are, or were, Beit Basil; the Beit Dallal and the Beit Atchikbash; and Beit Wakil.

The Aleppo Room in the Islamic Museum in Berlin comes from Beit Wakil. It is perhaps the finest, and certainly the oldest, surviving Aleppo interior. Built in 1009–12/1600–3 for "Isa bin Butros' (Jesus son of Peter), its swirling multicoloured decor of flowers and leaves painted on wood contains inscriptions from the Psalms; scenes from the Old and New Testaments, including Salome's dance and Jesus and Mary; portraits of the Arab lovers Layla and Majnun; and hunting scenes. A room built by and for Christians, dated according to the Muslim calendar, and painted in mixtures of Ottoman and Persian styles, it is a visual expression of Aleppo's diversity. Probably no house built for a Muslim, however, would have been decorated with human figures, owing to the prejudices against human representations (some frescoes in eighteenth-century Istanbul *yalis* show boats without people). The room's presence since 1912 in Berlin is another sign of Aleppo's international character, in this case the alliance between the Ottoman and German empires. It was purchased for the museum through a German living in Aleppo called Martha Kohl.[13]

The Beit Ghazaleh, built for the Christian family of that name, is distinguished not only by its size – there are six courtyards – but also by its sculpted stonework panels in the courtyard and by the finest private hammam in the city. In Beit Ghazeleh wooden panels from 1691 (now stolen) were decorated with fruit and flowers; inscriptions in Arabic, such as Psalm 91; popular maxims; and poems condemning excess and praising God, honour and wisdom. Another poem, perhaps composed for the reconstruction of the main room in 1747, honours the beauty and generosity of the master of the house:

> In glasses he appears handsome and shining to the guests like lightening in the middle of clouds.
> He inspires passions in the heart of men. He softens the hard hearted whom nothing can touch [...]
> [...] let the eye of God protect him from the greed of enemies and preserve him from their envious eye.
> He who has tasted his freshness is smitten with him, assured that he is the source of joy.[14]

Probably musicians would sing the words carved on the walls as entertainment for the owner's guests.

Aleppo also contained an ancient community of about 5,000 Jews, living in their own quarter.[15] In 1605 the Portuguese traveller Pedro Texeira wrote 'Many of them are rich, most are merchants, some brokers or craftsmen, such as lapidaries, silversmiths and of the like trades.'[16] The oldest, most complete and most authoritative Hebrew manuscript of the Torah, preserved in the city since the fourteenth century, was called the Aleppo Codex. Guarded in the Great Synagogue, it was invested by pious Jews with a unique sanctity. A curse was believed to afflict 'he who steals it, sells it or mortgages it. It may never be sold or redeemed'.[17]

Coexistence was also practised in the city's forty or fifty hammams, although in theory Christians, Jews and Muslims wore different robes in them and were sometimes obliged to attend on different days.[18] An English officer on his way to India in 1789, Major John Taylor, wrote of Aleppo hammams: 'They are large and elegant and resorted to by all ranks of people.'[19] Men generally went in the morning, women in the afternoon. Both sexes applied 'the Dowa or depilatory to the pubes and armpits', according to Dr Patrick Russell, brother of Alexander Russell, before being washed and massaged. Baths were places of entertainment, where women took picnics and often spent four or five hours at a time, enjoying 'gaiety, decent freedom and youthful frolic'.[20]

Aleppines shared the same language as well as the same baths. Christians as well as Muslims were scholars of Arabic literature and grammar. Christians contributed to the Arabic literary revival for which the city became famous in the early eighteenth century. Germanos Farhat, the Maronite bishop of the city, wrote famous works of grammar, poetry and religious polemic, and translated the Gospels into Arabic.[21] Another Maronite from Aleppo supplied Antoine Galland with some of the stories in his French translation of the *One Thousand and One Nights*.[22] There were Muslim elements in the writings of the eighteenth-century Maronite nun from Aleppo, Hindiyya. Her mystic visions of Mary and Jesus brought her many followers; but the Order of the Sacred Heart of Jesus, which she founded in 1750, was dissolved by the Pope in 1779.[23]

John Barker, from a great Anglo-Levantine family with branches in Smyrna and Alexandria, served as British consul in Aleppo from 1803 to 1826. He claimed that most of the time, 'men of different creeds live in perfect peace and not infrequently in relations of the closest friendly intercourse'. He noticed more antipathy between Sunni and Shi'a Muslims than between Muslims and Christians.[24] Indeed in Aleppo, conflicts were generally more lethal within religions than between them.[25]

The relative ease of coexistence between Christians, Jews and Muslims shows that Aleppo once had sufficient dynamism to counterbalance the oppression, or weakness, of the government and the lure of religious hatreds. Legal cases were settled promptly. Violence was unusual. Streets were clean. Evliya Celebi saw 'night and day rubbish collectors are busy tidying the streets with their baskets'.[26] The explorer John Lewis Burckhardt from Basel, who lived in Aleppo to study Arabic in 1809–12, wrote:

> It is necessary to have lived for some time among the Turks, and to have experienced the mildness and peacefulness of their character, and the sobriety and regularity of their habits, to conceive it possible that the inhabitants of a town like Aleppo should continue to live for years without any legal master, or administration of justice, protected only by a miserable guard of police and yet that the town should be a safe and quiet residence.

One in which, moreover, Europeans were 'rigidly respected'.[27]

This 'mildness and peacefulness' of Aleppo was helped by the absence of major religious shrines. As Thackeray wrote of Smyrna, in Aleppo there was no 'fatigue of sublimity'. Damascus, in contrast, was a religious city, which the Prophet himself had compared to paradise. Its economy was dominated by the annual arrival of Muslim pilgrims on their way to Mecca and Medina. Aleppo had the further advantage that it was not a port, like Smyrna, Alexandria or Beirut, open to attack by the navies of Christian powers, thereby increasing tensions between Muslims and Christians.[28]

Chapter Six

❋

Catholics against Orthodox

If Aleppo was a base in the Ottoman Empire's wars against Iran, it was also on the front line in an even older war, that between Catholics and Orthodox. Catholic orders had long been present in Aleppo. Franciscans arrived in 1560, later joined by Capucins (1623), Jesuits (1625), Carmelites (1627) and Cordeliers. Local Christians – Orthodox, Syriac, and Armenian – who rejected the authority of the Pope were the targets of these Catholic orders, rather than the Muslims who were forbidden to convert by law. Maronites, a local Christian sect widespread in Aleppo and Mount Lebanon, had acknowledged the supremacy of the Pope since the twelfth century. In 1649 – without informing his ally the Ottoman sultan – the King of France took all Catholics in the Empire under his 'protection'. By 1660 Aleppo had become 'the flower of the missions' for the entire region. Encouraged by the French consul, many local Christians such as Syriacs and Armenians, while keeping their own rites and liturgy, submitted to the authority of the Pope.[1]

In 1674 the French ambassador in Constantinople, the Marquis de Nointel, visited Aleppo on his way to Jerusalem, to publicise the French capitulations of 1673 which guaranteed, among other privileges, the freedom and safety of Catholic pilgrims to Christian sites. In Aleppo he went in state to the Syriac and Maronite churches, as he wrote to his foreign minister Pomponne,

> to the sound of trumpets and drums, surrounded by my household and followed by more than a hundred horsemen who composed the French nation [i.e. Frenchmen living in Aleppo]. All the streets were lined with an extraordinary concourse of people, not only Christians but also Turks [Muslims].

In the church the Syriac patriarch preached a sermon in praise of Louis XIV.[2] Syriac, Armenian and Orthodox patriarchs, as well as the chief of the Yezidis, urged a French invasion of the Empire – religious hierarchies could be more militantly anti-Muslim than their flocks.[3]

In the early eighteenth century, encouraged by the French consul, most Orthodox Christians in Aleppo became Catholic, acknowledging the authority of the Pope while keeping local rites and traditions. Their conversion was a means to assert a local identity, independent of Orthodox church authorities in Constantinople and Damascus; to obtain less corrupt, better-educated and Arabic-speaking priests; and, crucially, to win French diplomatic protection and its legal, economic and educational benefits. Greek Catholics, as they were called later, claimed to be the true Rum, loyal to both Pope and sultan: their Orthodox former co-religionists accused them of 'turning Frank'. After 1724 there was a formal schism between Orthodox and Catholics in the city. The Orthodox patriarch of Antioch, responsible for Aleppo's Orthodox Christians, denounced the Catholics to the Ottoman government for building new churches contrary to Sharia law.[4] Hatred between Catholics and Orthodox, often expressed in riots and excommunications, lasted into the twentieth century.[5]

The great Aleppo Dispersion, which has drained the city of some of the most enterprising inhabitants, began at this time. Some priests from Aleppo went to Rome for training. Partly to escape the hostility of the local Orthodox, many Aleppo Catholics emigrated to Egypt, where they grew rich through trade and jobs in the customs and tax administration: the first of the Syrians and Lebanese who would help to modernise Egypt.

Chapter Seven

Janissaries against Ashraf

After 1650, while its internal trade with the rest of the Ottoman empire prospered, Aleppo's external trade with foreign countries, and relative importance in the global economy, diminished. The malaria-infested marshes surrounding the port of Iskenderun (not finally drained until the 1890s), made it a graveyard. Wars with Iran, both in the early seventeenth century and in 1723–47, further diminished Aleppo's trade; the population, which had risen from 80,000 around 1600 to 115,000 in 1683, had fallen back to 80,000 by 1800.[1] The number of Christians paying the poll tax fell from 8,120 in 1740 to 5,200 in 1792.[2]

Conservatism accelerated Aleppo's decline. In 1722 the governor refused an offer by the English Levant Company to build, at its own expense, a bridge across the Euphrates to lure more trading caravans to Aleppo (the first bridge across that river would not be built until 1915, for the railway line to Baghdad).[3] Showing a similar mentality, until the early nineteenth century outbreaks of plague, when more than 10,000 might die in one year, were regarded by many Muslims, both educated and uneducated, as a blessing and an opportunity for martyrdom. Only

God and good conduct could save them. Unlike local Christians, they did not try to avoid catching plague by isolating themselves during outbreaks.[4]

A further reason for Aleppo's decline was the power struggle, after 1770, between groups called janissaries and *ashraf*. The janissaries, originally soldiers stationed in the city, were by the late eighteenth century generally shopkeepers and artisans, who claimed to be soldiers in return for tax privileges. By then 15,000 Aleppines called themselves janissaries. The *ashraf* (plural of sharif, meaning noble), claimed descent from the Prophet. According to Burckhardt they represented 'the landed interests, all the Aleppo grandees of ancient families, and all the Ulema and Effendis', and owned many of the villages round the city. Each group had its own militia.[5] Janissaries tended to live in the suburbs, *ashraf* in the centre of the city. Janissaries wore red 'Barbary caps' and daggers in their belts. The *ashraf* wore green turbans as a sign of descent from the Prophet – hence Russell's name for them of 'Greenheads'.[6] They were better educated but more fanatical than the janissaries.

From 1770 the city was also plagued by tax riots. The central government was losing control; unpopular or oppressive governors were dismissed or expelled due to popular pressure in 1775, 1784, 1791, 1804, and 1819. After a governor's expulsion, janissaries and *ashraf* often united to rule the city until the arrival of a new one. One wealthy grandee known as 'Çelebi effendi' 'obliged several Pashas who would not yield to his counsels and designs to quit the town', according to Burckhardt.[7] John Barker, the British consul, wrote: '[T]he townspeople of Aleppo were always ready to revolt against the Pashas (but not against the Porte) [...] whenever the tyranny and rapacity of these Pashas became unbearable.'[8]

In addition, until the 1850s the countryside was prey to what Alexander Russell called 'plundering Kurdeens' – local Kurdish tribes. They often controlled the road to Iskenderun and attacked pilgrims as well as pigeons flying from Aleppo to Iskenderun.[9] There was a decline in the number of villages around Aleppo. Desertification increased.[10] Yusuf al-Halabi wrote in 1788 – when another war between the Ottoman Empire and Russia had broken out – 'all authority has ceased to exist. There is no longer a leading figure in Aleppo capable of imposing his will.' In 1789 Major John Taylor found: 'of forty large villages that formerly surrounded the city, not one is left now inhabited'. In 1791 the British factory closed, and the British consul departed, not to be replaced until the arrival of John Barker in 1803.[11] Many Aleppines, then and later, were convinced that the Ottoman Empire – defeated by Russia in the wars of 1768–74 and 1787–91 – was doomed.[12] In addition, in the last years of the eighteenth century the city began to be threatened by raids from the extremist sect of Wahhabis, who would later help found the Kingdom of Saudi Arabia.

In 1805 the *ashraf* were defeated by the janissaries. The latter remained dominant, ruling through monopolies, extortion and fear. According to Burckhardt, however, most Aleppines

> do not wish for the return of a Pasha. In the Pasha's time living was cheaper and regular taxes not oppressive; but the Pasha would upon the most frivolous pretexts order a man of property to be thrown into prison and demand the sacrifice of one fourth of his fortune to grant him his deliverance.[13]

In 1813, the leaders of the janissaries were massacred by the pasha on the orders of the Porte. The city, however, remained hard to control. In 1818, during riots between Catholics and Orthodox, eleven Catholics were killed.[14] The Ottoman government, and Aleppo Muslims, often preferred local Catholics, judged more loyal than Orthodox, who might sympathise with the Orthodox Tsar of Russia. High prices, the governor's plans to raise taxes to improve the water system and dislike of his corrupt and immoral officials ('dubious behaviour with bad boys in the stalls', in the words of one judge) led to a popular revolt on 23 October 1819.[15] Aleppo was then bombarded by the Ottoman army. Finally, showing their importance in the internal politics of the city, the consuls, including John Barker for Britain, Henri Guys for France and Elias de Picciotto for Russia, arranged for a provisional surrender of the city on 1 February 1820. Janissaries who had helped the rebels were executed.[16] Adding to the disasters afflicting Aleppo, an earthquake on 13/14 August 1822 destroyed about a quarter of it, including the walls and the governor's palace near the citadel: the notables asked the French consul to intervene with the Porte, so that the city could be exempted from taxes for five years.[17] Five years later 30,000 people died of the plague.

Nevertheless, despite such cataclysms, Aleppo continued to do business. A leading family, the Jabiri, for example (who would later provide a deputy for Aleppo in the first Ottoman parliament in 1876, and a prime minister of Syria in the 1940s), owned houses, shops, orchards and gardens and equipment to make soap from olive oil. They were famous, among other notables of the city, for choosing Turkish, rather than local wives.[18] Manufacturing was carried out 'with great spirit both by Christians and Mussulmans; silk and cotton form the chief articles', according to the English traveller W. G. Browne in 1797. Caravans from India with shawls, carpets and 'Indian goods' still numbered 2,000 or 3,000 camels, as did the three or four caravans leaving every year for Constantinople.

Wealthy families in Aleppo sometimes commissioned a bride's trousseau in India. Wedding parties revealed the city's social hierarchy. The consuls 'and the first class of European residents' would be invited on the first day; landowners on the second; Muslim and Christian merchants on the third; on the last, shopkeepers, Jews 'and such people'.[19]

Aleppo also remained a centre of the horse trade. The French government sent missions to Aleppo to buy stallions to improve the stock of French horses in 1760, 1819 and 1849.[20] In 1818 Count Waclav Rzewuski came from Poland to buy horses, for himself and for some royal studs, and – like Seetzen and Burckhardt before him – to learn Arabic. His book *Impressions d'Orient et d'Arabie* (2002) is a brilliant account, with drawings, of Arab horse-breeding and horsemanship, bedouin tribes and the revolts and riots in Aleppo in 1818–20. John Barker, however, was not impressed by Taj el-Fakir, as Rzewuski called himself. For Barker he was one of the growing number of travellers passing through Syria during and after the Napoleonic Wars who gave him 'an immense deal of trouble' by demanding help and hospitality (another was Lady Hester Stanhope, the first Englishwoman to settle in the Middle East). Rzewuski gave 'balls and garden parties and made presents to the ladies of valuable cashmere shawls', but left without paying his bills.[21]

John Barker returned after an interval as consul in Alexandria, and built a house with a famous garden at Samandag on the banks of the Orontes, where he would die in 1849. His family was famous for 'collecting in their house the best native and only European society in the city', in the words of Henry Layard, the discoverer of Nineveh.[22] Barker also helped change local agriculture. At a time when Mohammed Ali Pasha was revolutionising the landscape of Egypt by introducing oranges, mangoes, bananas and improved strains of cotton, Barker was introducing, among many other plants, tomatoes,

greengages, plums and Chinese quince to Syria – and Syrian nectar-
ines to England.[23]

Consuls were used by Aleppo factions as intermediaries with the
Ottoman authorities, and with other local factions, as well as with the
foreign government they represented. Sometimes, by complaining
to the Porte in Constantinople, consuls could engineer the dismissal
of government officials in Aleppo.[24] Showing the growing power of
European embassies, one governor of Aleppo province asked the French
and British consuls in Aleppo to praise him in despatches to their ambassadors in Constantinople.[25]

No family in Aleppo supplied more consuls for more foreign governments than the Picciottos, Jews who had arrived from Livorno in
1738. Living in the Khan al-Gumruk, they provided the first consul
for the Holy Roman Empire in Aleppo in 1784, and in 1806 were
among the first Jews to be ennobled by the Austrian Empire which
replaced it. In Vienna, Jews suffered many kinds of discrimination; in
Aleppo, Esdras de Picciotto, as Austrian consul-general, presided over
Catholic services, such as the enthronement of the Apostolic Vicar of
Syria on 13 January 1818. In that year Esdras de Picciotto's brother
Eliahu was vice-consul of Denmark; a third brother Raffaele was
consul of Russia (the choice of a Jew by a government as anti-Jewish
as Russia was another sign of Aleppo's flexibility). Other members
of the family would be consuls of Sweden, the Netherlands, Prussia,
Spain and the USA. Their power and wealth – many citizens of
Aleppo owed them money – enabled them to win 'great consideration' for the Jews of the city. Every Saturday they received 'visits
of ceremony', conducted with 'the utmost form and state'. Remarks
addressed to the consul would always begin and end with the words
'Signor Console Generale'.[26] A few decades later, Moise de Picciotto
was able to wear the diplomatic uniform of five different countries,
since he was consul in Aleppo for Austria, Prussia, Denmark, the
Netherlands and Belgium.[27]

Chapter Eight

Ottoman Renaissance

In early 1831, like Burckhardt twenty years earlier, Francis William Newman, brother of the future cardinal, came to Aleppo to learn Arabic; he was planning to work in the region as a missionary. He found that much of the city still bore the marks of the earthquake of 1822, while the countryside was depopulated and badly cultivated. Compared with previous centuries, religious tensions were growing, no doubt encouraged by Ottoman defeats and European interference. Newman considered that 'in such an imbroglio of peoples there seems to be no nation, no union, no strength [...] Each man's church is here his country: he has no other country [...] fanaticism is indistinguishable from patriotism.' Staying with a local Levantine family, he found 'a painful sense of emptiness'. Some Europeans talked freely of 'the necessity of Turkey being governed by the European nations [...] [W]ho can live here and not wish for a revolution?'[1]

Later that year, however, the troops of Mohammed Ali Pasha, the modernising governor of Egypt, occupied Syria. A more efficient administration was introduced, as well as the detested novelty of conscription.

On 24 June 1839 Ibrahim Pasha defeated an Ottoman army at the Battle of Nezib (now Nizip in Turkey), north of Aleppo. Due to pressure by Britain, Austria, Russia and Prussia, however, and a revolt in Mount Lebanon, Egyptian forces withdrew in 1840. Their most lasting legacy was a large red-brick barracks outside the city, said to be able to house 8,000 soldiers.[2] To the relief of most inhabitants, the Ottoman Empire recovered control.

In 1838 the liberal treaty of Balta Liman with Britain, lowering customs rates, had opened the Empire to European goods. The number of looms working in Aleppo dropped sharply. Local Christians and Jews, with more contacts with European merchants and greater knowledge of European languages, prospered. No longer needing Muslim business partners, these minorities began to adopt Western dress.[3] Tensions between communities increased.

Returning from Constantinople in August 1849, with a firman from the Ottoman sultan officially recognising the Greek Catholics as a separate community, the Greek Catholic patriarch Mgr Mazloum made a formal entry into the city. Crosses were held high, lavish vestments were worn and guns fired in the air. Churches could now be repaired and extended without special permission from the Porte. One year later, on 17 October 1850, partly due to minorities' growing prosperity and claims of equality with Muslims, but also to resentment of the reintroduction of conscription for Muslims (but not non-Muslims) by the Ottoman government, Aleppo witnessed its principal outbreak of violence, before 2012, between Muslims and Christians.

Rioters attacked outward signs of Christian power. They demanded that Christians be forbidden to ring church bells (until recently they had used only wooden clappers to announce church services) or to own slaves. They should not hold crosses high in processions 'above the heads of Muslims', and should treat them with 'respect'. Many Christians hid in the houses of Muslim or Jewish friends (Mgr Mazloum, for example, hid in the house of Edgar de Picciotto, before fleeing to Beirut). Riots left twenty Christians dead (the head of Naoum Homsy was exposed on a tree by the Church of Saint George), six churches, thirty-six shops and 688 houses gutted. The governor – Murad Pasha, formerly General Josef Bem, a hero of the risings of 1830 in Poland and 1848 in Hungary who had fled to the Ottoman Empire and converted to Islam – and his small garrison of 500 withdrew from the city.[4]

Another reason for the rebellion had been the Ottomans' dismissal from office of the veteran janissary leader, and tax farmer, Abdullah

Bey Babilsi, who commanded thousands of armed followers and was the only person capable of maintaining order in the city. He was described by Andrew Paton, in *The Modern Syrians* (1844) as 'of low extraction, rough exterior and destitute of education but possessed of unbending energy, inflexible attachment to his own people and generosity in pecuniary matters'. He had good relation with the local bedouin as well as 'all the canaille of the Pashalic [...] no man in Syria concentrated so much power in his hands'. Both Ibrahim Pasha and the Ottoman government found him useful, although the Ottoman governor Assad Pasha, to emphasise the distance between them, 'never allowed him to sit on the divan and gave him coffee but never a chibouque [pipe]'. Seeing himself as the city's natural leader, he wore the sheepskin jacket of the local butchers as a gesture of solidarity.[5]

Thousands of Muslims were killed in retaliation by Ottoman forces after the city had, as in 1820, been bombarded into submission.[6] That year Abdallah bey el-Babilisi, according to an English resident of Aleppo called Frederick Arthur Neale, died while being taken prisoner to Constantinople, 'very shortly after partaking of some coffee, which, report said, contained something more than dregs at the bottom of the cup'.[7]

The next governor, Mehmed Kibrisli Pasha, had recently been Ottoman ambassador in London. He compensated Christian victims of the revolt, banished notables who had joined it and enlarged the city council to include representatives of other classes.[8] The Ottoman army had acted in Aleppo as the outside force restoring order and restraining inter-community conflict, which in the current cataclysm neither the Syrian government nor the United Nations has been able to provide.

Thereafter the city experienced a renaissance. Religious tensions, which had risen in the early nineteenth century, were partly defused. Sultan Abdulmecid, a young man in favour of reforms who reigned from 1839 to 1861, gave money for the construction of an Armenian Catholic church. A new Orthodox church was built in 1861, a Maronite church (with a musical clock in the belfry playing *Ave Maria* every fifteen minutes) in 1873. The governor would attend ceremonies at Christian schools and walk through Christian districts to ensure law and order.[9] In 1860, when thousands of Christians were massacred in Damascus and Mount Lebanon, Aleppo was relatively calm. Many in the city considered Ottoman rule the best guarantee against communal violence.[10] There was less unrest and bloodshed in Aleppo than in

Constantinople itself, where riots helped overthrow Sultan Abdulaziz in 1876 and Abdulhamid in 1908–9.

Meanwhile in the countryside, since the arrival of Ibrahim Pasha's forces in 1831, many abandoned villages had been resettled and new ones built. Cotton and wheat production boomed. Public security improved. Travellers remarked on the increase in wealth and traffic and in the number of inhabited villages in the country around Aleppo. The desert receded.[11]

Maronites brought a printing press to the city in 1857 – the first since the first Arabic printing press in the region had been established in Aleppo by the patriarch of Antioch in 1705, printing nine religious books before moving in 1711 to Mount Lebanon.[12] The first news-paper was published, in Turkish and Arabic, in 1867. In 1877 the city obtained an elected council. From 1883 a new quarter called Jamiliye, west of the citadel, with a new house for the governor, was laid out. In another quarter called Aziziye, after Abdulmecid's successor Abdulaziz (1862–76), many consuls built palatial new houses, and new schools were built. In 1900 the population of these prosperous new suburbs was 73 per cent Christian.[13]

A leading historian of the city, Bruce Masters, writes:

> In the diaries of both Yusuf al-Halabi and Na'um Bakhash, mention of a sultan's name is followed by the obligatory prayers for his long life and prosperity, but it is hard to infer any degree of political com-mitment to the sultanate beyond that. Rather, it would seem that as the leading families of Aleppo were unable to form a political base to challenge the Porte, they acquiesced in its legitimacy. It served their interests and the alternative was rule by the street mobs [...] While the Ottomans were on the defensive throughout so much of their territories, Aleppo thanks to a myriad of local conditions and political currents, had been reclaimed for the empire by the end of the nineteenth century.[14]

However, the opening of the Suez Canal in 1869 had made Aleppo an economic backwater. More Syrians moved to Egypt, to benefit from its economic boom. European competition began to ruin Aleppo's trade in silk and gold and silver thread. In 1890 the British consul reported that trade was 'almost exclusively in the hands of Christians and Jews'.[15]

At the same time Aleppo's French connections grew stronger. The Ottoman language bound the governing class to the Empire. Arabic linked the city to the Empire's Arab provinces. French connected it to the Western world. By 1831, according to Francis William Newman, it had replaced Italian as the dominant language for Europeans.[16] It spread through Christian and Jewish schools, such as those run by the Franciscaines Missionaires de Marie and the Alliance Israélite Universelle, which could also be attended by Muslims. For the next hundred years, some educated Aleppines not only spoke French – sometimes to the exclusion of Arabic at home – but wrote, read and thought in it as well. Elvire, the name of a Lamartine heroine, became a popular girls' name. 'Bonjour', 'au revoir' and 'pardonnez-moi' were used in Arabic conversation. The governor, like other Ottoman officials, often spoke French.[17] By the 1870s French clothes were common among Christians and Jews.[18]

For some, France and Paris became synonymous with culture. I have heard an elderly lady from Aleppo, Elena Makzume, born Girardi (a family which had arrived from Venice in the nineteenth century), and known to her friends as 'la belle Hélène', praise Iskenderun – which she called by its French name Alexandrette – as 'un petit Paris'.

While losing some of its cultural hegemony, the Ottoman Empire retained military control. The governorship of Jemil Pasha after 1881 was described as a 'reign of terror' by British officials. Sultan Abdulhamid (1876–1909), an autocrat who wanted to concentrate power in his own hands, appreciated his skill in increasing imperial properties and revenues around Aleppo, and in limiting the influence of foreign consuls. Jemil Pasha persecuted indiscriminately: villagers, Aleppo notables and Nigoghos der Markarian, the Armenian dragoman of the British consul. Accusations and counter-accusations went by telegram between Aleppo, the Sultan's palace and the Constantinople embassies. In 1886, after the Sultan had been sent more than 200 petitions against Jemil, he was dismissed and sent to govern the Hejaz.[19]

In 1898, as part of the 'clock tower boom' throughout the Empire, a clock tower was erected at Bab el-Farraj in honour of Abdulhamid II's jubilee. Its different faces showed both modern European time, starting at midnight, and the region's traditional time, starting at sunset. If many in Aleppo looked to Paris, most still preferred Constantinople. The most famous Aleppine of the day, Abul Huda al-Sayyadi, born in a nearby village in 1850, rose to be *naqib al-ashraf*, or head of the corporation of *ashraf*, of Aleppo in 1873. He then moved to Constantinople, became chief judge of Rumeli, head of the Rifai brotherhood of Sufi Muslims and one of Abdulhamid's chief religious advisers, living near his palace of Yildiz. Intelligent and ambitious, as an apologist for the Sultan's autocracy he was detested both by the notables of Aleppo and the Young Turk opponents of the Sultan. Between 1890 and 1908 he published more than 200 pamphlets defending the Sultan and his claim, as the most powerful Muslim ruler, to be caliph of the Muslims and to receive their absolute obedience. Those who criticised the caliph, he wrote, were enemies of Islam. His magnificent family house, built near the citadel in the Ottoman baroque style of Constantinople, is now the seat of the mufti of Aleppo. Beside it Abul Huda's tomb (he died soon after Abdulhamid's deposition in 1909) was, until recently, visited by devotees.[20]

The city was becoming modernised. In 1899 Mark Sykes wrote: 'Aleppo is so frequently visited by tourists that I will not detain my readers by saying much about it.'[21] Public health improved. A Neapolitan called Michele Corrado, a specialist on the 'Aleppo button', which he began to eradicate, was sanitary inspector of the Aleppo *vilayet* and chief physician of the military hospital in Aleppo.[22] A modern hospital, the Hôpital Saint-Louis, opened in 1907; another had already been started by an Armenian from Anatolia called Assadour Altounyan – he chose Aleppo rather than his native Antep as it was cleaner and richer.[23] In 1910 another Armenian family, the Mazloumians, built the first comfortable hotel, the Baron Hotel ('Unique hôtel de Première classe à Alep. Chauffage central partout. Confort parfait. Situation unique', as a poster proclaimed). It became popular with visiting archaeologists like Leonard Woolley and T. E. Lawrence.[24]

After 1890 railway lines connected the city to Beirut and Damascus. Aleppo was also destined to be a major junction on the German-built line from Constantinople to Baghdad, which started construction in 1900.[25] The Homsi and Picciotto families established their own banks. One money-lender called Rizkallah Ghazeleh was so rich that in 1912, when the director of the Ottoman Bank branch in Aleppo expressed doubts about his credit-worthiness, Ghazeleh drew a cheque so large that it would have been bankrupted. To save it, the director was obliged to come in person to Ghazeleh's office in the Khan al-Gumruk and present his apologies. The Franciscaines' girls' school was later financed out of the remains of Ghazeleh's fortune.[26]

However, many in Aleppo were discontented with Ottoman autocracy. Ibrahim Pasha Milli, a Kurdish leader and head of the Hamidiye cavalry founded by the Sultan to control eastern Anatolia, despite his loyalty to Abdulhamid, also dreamt of a Kurdish state, perhaps including Aleppo. A photograph shows him meeting the European consuls in Aleppo, all in full uniform, in 1904 – doubtless to discuss the city's future.[27]

Abdul Rahman al-Kawakibi, born into a prominent family in Aleppo around the same time as Abul Huda, had very different ideas. He edited the local newspaper *Furat* (Euphrates) in 1875–80. After a short period as mayor of Aleppo, in 1898 he moved to the freer atmosphere of Egypt. There he urged Arabs to embrace modernity and challenge Ottoman tyranny. 'If I had an army at my command I would overthrow Abdulhamid's domination in twenty-four hours', he wrote. Whereas Abul Huda wrote that God and the Prophet demanded obedience to the sultan caliph in Constantinople, al-Kawakibi believed that the rightful caliph should be, like the Prophet himself, an Arab from the Quraysh tribe – the tribe of the sharifs and emirs then ruling Mecca under Ottoman suzerainty. He died, possibly poisoned by the Sultan's agents, in Cairo in 1902.[28]

The Young Turk Revolution against Abdulhamid which finally broke out in July 1908, and subsequent gains in personal freedom, were received with joy in Aleppo. 'Men were obsessed with a sense of change', wrote Gertrude Bell.[29] After the first raptures, however, tensions grew. The Ottoman Empire's defeats in the Tripolitanian and Balkan Wars in 1911–13 confirmed its vulnerability. Some foreign diplomats launched the idea that, having lost the Balkans, the Empire should move its capital to Aleppo, far from the corruption of Constantinople.[30] T. E. Lawrence had been helping Woolley on his excavations for the British Museum at a Hittite site at Carchemish on the Euphrates. In February 1913, in the first intelligence mission of his career, he helped bring ammunition, revolvers and rifles, landed near Beirut by British warships, to the British consulate in Aleppo 'for its protection and for that of British subjects'. The British consul, Raphael Fontana, feared attacks on the city by Kurdish and Arab tribes, and foretold the end of the Empire.[31]

However, Lawrence would later remember Aleppo as a city of coexistence rather than conflict. Deals took precedence over ideals. In *The Seven Pillars of Wisdom* (1922) he called it:

[A] point where the races and creeds and tongues of the Ottoman Empire met and knew one another in a spirit of compromise. The clash of characteristics which made its streets a kaleidoscope imbued the Aleppine with a lewd thoughtfulness which corrected in him what was blatant in the Damascene. Aleppo had shared in all the civilizations that had turned about it and the result seemed a lack of zest in its people's belief. Even so they surpassed the rest of Syria.

Like other visitors, Lawrence felt that in Aleppo 'more fellowship should rule between Christian and Mohammedan, Armenian, Arab, Turk, Kurd and Jew than in perhaps any other great city of the Ottoman Empire, and that more friendliness, though little licence, should have been accorded to Europeans'.[32]

Chapter Nine

The French Mandate

Aleppo escaped most of the fighting in the First World War. The Ottoman governor of Syria was Cemal Pasha, with Enver and Talaat one of the Young Turk triumvirate who in November 1914 had dragged the Empire into the war on the side of Germany and Austria. In Beirut and Damascus he had Arab nationalists condemned for treason and hanged in public. In Aleppo, however, he attended tea parties, as is shown by the following invitation – which also confirms the continued cultural hegemony of France, even when it was fighting the Ottoman Empire:

> Mme et M. Albert Homsy prient Monsieur Guillaume Poché de leur faire le plaisir de venir prendre le thé chez eux demain à 4 h. de l'après-midi. Son Excellence Djemal Pacha nous fera l'honneur de sa visite. L'on fera de la musique. Mardi 21/12/15.

Before entering Madame Homsy's salon, Cemal Pasha always removed his sword.[1]

Guillaume Poché, the Homsys' guest, descended from a merchant who had arrived from Bohemia in 1806 and married the daughter of the last Venetian consul. His descendants became Austrian consuls and businessmen. The Poché family collection of pictures, photographs, textiles, ceramics and antiquities housed in the Khan al-Nahasin, formerly home to the Venetian consulate, was a time machine from the nineteenth and early twentieth centuries. Before the outbreak of the civil war it was said to include 500,000 pages of documents in sixteen languages: its present fate is unknown.[2]

Aleppo could escape fighting, but not the Ottoman government's destruction of Armenians. True to the spirit of the city, one governor called Celal Bey at first defied orders to deport Armenians. He was moved to another post in June 1915. Armenians in the city tried to hide deportees or help their widows and orphans.[3] Geography, however, which had made Aleppo a commercial crossroads, also made it a crossroads for death marches. Armenian deportees from Anatolia were housed in camps and trains on the edge of the city, or driven through the streets, on their way to death in the Syrian Desert or the Euphrates valley.[4] The region was also devastated by outbreaks of typhus and cholera, plagues of locusts and famines partly caused by the blockade of the coast by the Royal Navy. Walter Rössler, the German consul, lamented the 'indescribable misery 'of Armenians in and around Aleppo. The total number of deaths in the city has yet to be established.[5] The Altounyan Hospital, however, survived. The only hospital with an X-ray machine, it was used by Ottoman officers, including Mustafa Kemal himself, and was allowed to employ Armenian refugees.

By autumn 1918 Ottoman defeat was certain. The advancing British army was helped by Arab forces under Emir Faisal, from the family of the sherifs of Mecca; in 1916 they had, as Kawakibi had advocated, started a revolt against the Ottoman Empire, and on 1 October 1918 had helped take Damascus. The Ottoman commander in Aleppo was the hero of Gallipoli, Mustafa Kemal Pasha. He had been recovering from a kidney complaint in the Altounyan Hospital, which he found so convenient that for a time he used it as his headquarters. On 23 October 1918, avoiding Ottoman forces to the south, Arab troops under Nuri Bey broke in from the east. There were risings in the city. Looting began. Australian troops were reported to be advancing. After taking part in street fighting, Mustafa Kemal ordered his troops to withdraw.[6]

On 25 and 26 October 1918, 402 years after Ottoman forces had arrived under Yavuz Selim, they left under Mustafa Kemal. They were replaced by Arab, Indian, Australian and British soldiers. Aleppo had proved more pro-Ottoman and less sympathetic to the Arab revolt than Damascus. However, allied troops were 'met with wild demonstrations of joy and support'.[7]

The British army remained in overall control until 11 November 1919 when forces loyal to Emir Faisal took over the city. Faisal had visited Aleppo on 6 November 1918, showered with flowers and rose-water. Tolerant of Christians and Jews, as well as Shi'a Muslims, on 11 November he made a famous, over-optimistic speech, repeated the following June. He proclaimed his faith in coexistence: 'The Arabs were Arabs before Moses and Jesus and Muhammed. All religions demand that their adherents follow what is right and enjoin brotherhood on earth. Anyone who sows discord between Muslim, Christian and Jew is not an Arab.'[8]

The governor of Aleppo, Jafar al-Askari, who had joined the Arab secret society al-Ahd while at Officer Training College in the city before the war, also devoted himself to defusing tensions between Muslims and Christians (especially Armenians, 200 of whom had been killed in February 1919). 'Banquets and visits between the different ethnic groups began to be organised', he remembered. He frequented 'the pre-eminent Christian families' and the heads of each denomination.[9]

However, France, in accordance with its ambitions since the seventeenth century and the mandate it had been awarded by the League of Nations, was determined to rule Syria. On 23 July 1920, French forces entered Aleppo. Many inhabitants had been so terrified of massacre and looting by bedouin and 'freedom fighters' that they were relieved. The US consul, J. B. Jackson, reported that 'rifle shots were heard from every part of the town and threats were made against the Christians'. Without being consulted, against its will, Aleppo changed geographical direction and political masters. It was no longer ruled from the north by the Ottoman sultan in Constantinople, but from the south by the French High Commissioner in Damascus.[10] The French mandate established Syria's capital and principal institutions in Damascus. Aleppo was left subordinate and resentful.[11] Like other pre-1914 international cities such as Trieste, Salonica and Constantinople itself, its horizons had narrowed.

From the start, the French mandate was crippled by economic problems. Aleppo was cut off by brutal post-war frontiers from its former

hinterlands. Turkey had been awarded Arabic-speaking areas formerly
in the province of Aleppo; Iraq, including Aleppo's former trading part-
ner Mosul, was now a separate state, under a British mandate. Turkish
sympathies in Aleppo remained strong.[12]

Insurgents against French rule, often helped by Turkey under Mustafa
Kemal, reached within a few miles of the city. In May 1921 the British
consul wrote:

> Commerce is stagnant. Aleppo which before the war traded with the
> greater part of Asia Minor lying to the north and north-east is now
> limited to the district lying within a radius of some 20 miles from
> the town.[13]

In 1923 the British consul again reported:

> Feeling in Aleppo is on the whole favourable to the Turks and
> anti-French. The Muslims favour the Turks because they think that
> the native Christians [...] are bound to prosper to their detriment
> under a European power, which would maintain security and a cer-
> tain degree of equal opportunity.[14]

In 1938 Aleppo lost its port as well as its hinterland, when the 'Sanjak of
Alexandretta' [Iskenderun] was ceded by France to Turkey.

Despite the brutal new frontiers, one form of communication
improved. From 1928 the *Taurus Express* connected Aleppo directly
by rail to Istanbul (and from 1940 to Baghdad). Passengers left Aleppo
at 5 a.m. and arrived at Haydarpasha station, on the Asian side of the
Bosphorus, at 6.55 p.m. the next day. Agatha Christie, who herself first
arrived in Aleppo on the *Taurus Express*, begins her detective story *Murder
on the Orient Express* (1934) with Hercule Poirot leaving Aleppo by the
same train. Like T. E. Lawrence, she often stayed at the Baron Hotel after
an excavation season (her husband was the archaeologist Max Mallowan,
many of whose finds ended in the city's National Museum). For her the
city meant: 'Alep! Shops! A bath! My hair shampooed! Friends to see!' For
a time in 1938–9 you could, like the British historian Steven Runciman,
book a berth in a sleeper carriage going directly from London to Aleppo.[15]

In Aleppo most Muslims disliked the mandate; anti-French demonstrations and elections were frequent. In December 1931, writes Philip
Khoury, Aleppo was a scene of repeated violence, its bazaars and shops

'closed tight as all economic life came to a halt'.[16] Christians, however, often supported the mandate. Their feelings were reflected in verses by a local poet, Zoe Ghadban:

> Et nous attendons là, tout pleins de confiance,
> Ton sourire divin, o grande, o noble France!

Their fervour reflected belief in France's *mission civilisatrice*, as well as desire to use it in their own interests. Balconies collapsed under the weight of Christians applauding French military reviews on the feast-day of St Joan of Arc.[17]

At a time when Constantinople and Smyrna were losing their Christian populations due to Turkish persecutions, Aleppo remained distinctively multi-denominational. So many Armenian, Assyrian, Syriac and Orthodox survivors of massacres and deportations by Turks and Kurds in Anatolia moved to Aleppo that it became more Christian than at any time since the Arab conquest: a 'Noah's Ark for Christians', as William Dalrymple has called it.[18] In 1930, out of a population of around 220,000, approximately 52 per cent were Muslim, 16 per cent Christian (mainly Catholics, but excluding Armenians), 4 per cent Jewish and perhaps 28 per cent Armenians – many still living in refugee camps on the edge of the city.[19] Central Turkey College, an American missionary school in Antep (since its resistance to French forces in 1921, Gaziantep) serving the Armenian population, reopened in Aleppo in 1924. As Aleppo College, it became one of the best schools in Syria.[20]

Chapter Ten

❁

Independence

In the Second World War as in the First, Aleppo was spared almost all fighting. The French mandate, increasingly opposed by Syrian and Lebanese nationalists, remained in control. In April and May 1941 the Vichy French administration allowed German planes to use the Aleppo aerodrome on their way to support the anti-British Rashid Ali government which had taken power in Iraq. German supplies also reached Iraq via the *Taurus Express*.

Allied forces, however, invaded Syria and Lebanon from Palestine on 8 June. By 14 July they had defeated the Vichy French army, which was then allowed to embark for France. Thereafter Aleppo, although nominally under French authority, had a second British period: British troops and officials held the balance of power between the French authorities and local nationalists. While Turkish officials told British officers they regarded Aleppo as a 'glittering jewel that has fallen out of reach but can be gathered up again with only little effort', General Sir Edward Spears, British minister to the Levant States, encouraged local populations' dreams of independence.[1] Christopher Summerhayes, from the legendary Levant Consular Service which trained many British diplomats, was both consul and political officer for Aleppo. Another British officer, Richard Pearse, was smitten by Aleppo's 'display of feminine beauty' at dusk. 'These Oriental women walk with a superb gait and carriage that make European women look like cripples [...] The West has scarcely touched them except in their dress and coiffure.'[2]

The *Taurus Express* enjoyed a golden age as the most important route from allied-held territory, via neutral Turkey, into Axis Europe. It became a sealed train, with a British sentry at every carriage door. Popular with diplomats, foreign students attending German universities, Turkish businessmen and Kurdish farmers, it was called 'le bordel ambulant'.[3] Some Kurds were trained in Aleppo by British officers, to act as guerrillas in Turkey in case it joined, or was invaded by, Germany. On the *Taurus Express* in September 1941, one British officer told me, the great singer Asmahan, Druze princess, Egyptian actress and British propaganda agent during the allied invasion of Syria, fought like a tigress at the last stop before the Turkish frontier, to avoid arrest by British soldiers: she was trying to escape to Turkey, to sell military secrets, acquired from one of her admirers in the British army, to the German embassy. That night, however, after her interrogation, they all dined together at the Hotel Baron.[4] A wagon-lits attendant on the express, 'acquired through the good offices of Turkish intelligence', served as a British double-cross agent 'for the purposes of deception' with the code name Doleful.[5]

Full Syrian independence was reluctantly granted by France on 1 January 1944, although the last French troops did not leave until April 1946. The end of the German occupation of France in 1944 led to the *épuration*, in which thousands were killed or imprisoned. Showing the tolerance and resilience of Syrian society, the end of the French occupation in 1946 was followed by no such horror – although local Christians had prospered under the French mandate.[6] By the revulsion it inspired, French rule had succeeded in uniting Syrians. The British consul in Aleppo reported that the French were generally hated: 'Most Christians, however, while rather nervous with respect to the future, seem determined to support Syrian Muslims in their present dispute with the French.'[7] In Aleppo there was less violence than in 1919 and 1920 – and less than in Damascus, bombarded by French forces in 1946 with many casualties. The city had successfully survived both French imperialism and its end.

Independence was, however, followed by the first anti-Jewish riots in Aleppo, on 1 December 1947, sparked by the imminent creation of the State of Israel. *Halabiyah*, as Aleppo Jews were called, began to leave their native city in large numbers (the last left in 1997) – as a few had long been doing for economic reasons. Many were reluctant to go and kept happy memories of Aleppo. In New York, Jack Ciary, remembered: 'Don't believe that the Muslims did not like the Jews in Aleppo. They treated us with courtesy and consideration. The Muslims were very nice to the Jews', implying that Christians, long the Jews' business rivals, were not.[8]

Many chose to settle in Beirut, New York or Buenos Aires, rather than Israel. The Banque Picciotto for example, belonging to the famous Aleppo family of that name, is now based in Geneva; Edgard de Picciotto, founder of the Union Bancaire Privée, is one of Switzerland's most prominent bankers. Other members of his family live in Paris, Brussels and Montreal. Members of the Safra family, from Aleppo, settled in São Paolo and Monte Carlo, including the wealthy brothers Edmond and Joseph Safra. Their father, 'attached to every house, every stone, every alley' of their native city, had been reluctant to leave.[9]

The legendary Aleppo Codex, damaged in the 1947 riots, was smuggled out via Turkey in 1958. It now contains only 295 of the original 487 leaves, the others having been lost or stolen – during the riots, the journey or in Israel itself. The surviving section is in the Ben-Zvi Institute in Jerusalem, under the guardianship of representatives of the former Jewish community of Aleppo.[10] The curse said to afflict anyone who damaged the codex was remembered by some Aleppines when Edmond Safra, whose family was alleged to have helped to organise the codex's journey from Aleppo, died in a mysterious fire in his flat in Monte Carlo in 1999. His brother Joseph, however, flourishes to this day, the second richest person in Brazil.[11]

Syrian independence was marked by growing tension between Aleppo and Damascus. In the Syrian Arab Republic some Aleppines disliked new rules imposing, from 1954, Arabic as the language of signs in shops, cafés and hotels, and quotas for Muslims in all inter-communal organisations.[12] There were complaints about the small number of cabinet ministers from Aleppo. Some Aleppo politicians proposed that Aleppo become capital of Syria, or that Syria join Iraq in one large state uniting the Fertile Crescent. Aleppines remembered that France had briefly divided Syria into five small states, including 'states' of Aleppo and Damascus in 1920–4.[13] However, Damascus remained the capital and union with Iraq a dream.

In the 1950s the city flourished. These were the golden years of the Club d'Alep/Nadi Halab, favoured by businessmen and their wives, who enjoyed whist and cocktails. No longer, as had been usual before the war, did husbands and wives eat separately and rarely share their social life.[14] Food became a form of communication – of wealth, status or character – as well as a necessity and an entertainment. Travellers had long praised the quality of the ingredients in Aleppo: the 'perfection' of the fruit and 'the finest mutton, I think, that I ever tasted', according to Bartholomew Plaisted.[15] 'Superb vegetables, solid, delicate and cheap to the poorest', wrote Francis Newman.[16]

Aleppo's exaltation of food continued in the twentieth century. 'The people of Aleppo', wrote Haim Sabato in *Aleppo Tales* (2004), 'extol the food of their city and its delicacies. They do not eat to excess but they expend inordinate effort and employ meticulous precision in the preparation of dishes. The saying goes: "If you want to judge the quality of someone from Aleppo, uncover his pot and inspect his food." '[17] In the 1970s, remembered Marie Mamarbashi, author of the novel *Les corbeaux d'Alep* (1988), a guest's disparaging comment on a dish could send her mother to bed with a headache – knowing that the remark had a hidden motive. Like jewellery, a recipe could be valued as a family heritage, never to be shared with outsiders. A dinner menu might be discussed for a month.[18] There are said to be at least twenty-six versions of *kebab halabi* or Aleppo kebab, including kebab cooked with cherries; with aubergine; with chili, parsley and pine-nuts; and with truffles from the desert. Aleppo was also famous for being the capital of 'pistachiomania': any dish could be decorated with pistachios – meat, chicken, cakes. *Kibbe* was another speciality: Aleppo was known as the city of 1001 *kibbe* – fried, boiled, whitened, flavoured with coriander, spinach, truffles, apricots or quince. Poems were written to *kibbe* as to a beloved.[19]

However, Syria also experienced nationalisations (first land, then large businesses) and military coups. In 1958–61, Syria joined Egypt in the United Arab Republic, under the presidency of the hero of the Arab world, Gamal Abdul Nasser. In February 1959 Nasser came to Aleppo, stayed at the Hotel Baron and was received like a god; in their enthusiasm, students carried the President on their shoulders through the city – in his Cadillac.[20] The union with Egypt was more popular in Aleppo than Damascus. Aleppo University was founded in 1958. Revisiting Aleppo in 1959, however, Taqui Altounyan, daughter of the legendary Dr Ernest Altounyan and his English wife, noted the growing fear of the secret police: '[F]or the first time in all my years in Syria I noticed the sudden frightened silence that fell, in the middle of a conversation, when a servant or even a small child entered the room.' The Altounyan hospital was nationalised and, like the Altounyans' house, later demolished.[21]

Ernest Altounyan, a friend of T. E. Lawrence and Arthur Ransome (his children, who often took holidays in the Lake District, were the models for the children in *Swallows and Amazons*, which was dedicated to them), had worked all his life in the family hospital in Aleppo. Son and husband of Englishwomen, educated in England, he regarded himself as entirely English – his friend Cecil Hourani remembered there was always bacon, and toast and marmalade, for breakfast. Although sometimes 'filled with gloom' by Aleppo, he had advanced the cause of Syrian independence, and advised Syrian politicians, when working in British headquarters in Cairo before 1945. Nevertheless, he had to leave his city and died in England in 1963.[22]

The Aleppo Dispersion became a flood. After the Jews, Muslims and Christians also began to leave. Private ambition, and desire for security and prosperity, were stronger than loyalty to city or nation. Aleppo was twice a world city: through the trade it attracted in the sixteenth century, and the people it exported in the twentieth. To take a few examples, Mustafa Akkad, the producer of the films *Muhammad Messenger of God* (1976) and *The Lion of the Desert* (1980) in the USA, had been born in Aleppo in 1930 – as were the first president of independent Armenia, Levon Ter-Petrosyan (1991–8), in 1945, and Tony Rezko, an early supporter of Barrack Obama in Chicago, now in prison for fraud and corruption, in 1955. Mohammed Hayder Zammar, born in Aleppo in 1961, left at the age of ten and later became a recruiter for al-Qaeda.

Despite, or because of, Aleppo's character as a trading city, it inspired attachment just as passionate as 'holy cities' such as Jerusalem or Mecca, or famous capitals like Paris or Rome. According to a famous joke, one Aleppo lady replies to another, who has asked about her summer holiday: 'Paris, c'est joli, mais ce n'est pas Alep!'[23] Emigrants left Aleppo; Aleppo did not leave them. Many continue to choose spouses and neighbours from other Aleppo families. Crossing frontiers and continents, Aleppo survives in districts of New York, São Paolo and Jerusalem – a virtual Aleppo, outside the city, which is now larger than the real

Aleppo in Syria. Putting city before country, many people will say they are from Aleppo, rather than Syria.[24]

Emigrants also continue to cook the food of their city, long after they had left it. The food writer Claudia Roden was born a Douek, member of a famous Jewish family which had left Aleppo in the previous century. When she published Passover recipes in an article showing her photograph with her daughters, she at once 'received phone calls from Milan, New York, Mexico and Rio de Janeiro from people of Syrian origin asking for my daughters in marriage on behalf of their sons'.[25] Aleppines proved the truth of 'The City', the poem by the poet of Alexandria, Constantine Cavafy:

> You said: 'I'll go to another country, go to another shore,
> find another city better than this one.'
> [...]
> You won't find a new country, won't find another shore.
> This city will always pursue you. You will walk
> the same streets, grow old in the same neighborhoods,
> will turn grey in these same houses.
> You will always end up in this city. Don't hope for things
>   elsewhere:
> there is no ship for you, there is no road.
> As you've wasted your life here, in this small corner,
> you've destroyed it everywhere else in the world.

Most Aleppo lives, however, were far from wasted.

Chapter Eleven

❀

Years of the Assads

After five coups in the 1960s, from 1970 the Ba'ath government of Syria was dominated by President Hafez al-Assad and his family, from the Alawi community. Based in the mountains behind Syria's Mediterranean coast, the Alawi were a partly Shi'a minority. After centuries of poverty and humiliation, they had begun to prosper during the French mandate – which in 1919, unlike almost all other Syrians, they had supported. Many had entered the armed forces. Apparently secular socialists, in reality the Assads ruled with the support of other minorities and some Sunni Muslims. Religious tensions began to fester again.[1]

On 16 June 1979 thirty or more cadets at the Aleppo Artillery School, mainly from the Alawi minority, were separated from their comrades and murdered by members of the militant Fighting Vanguard of the Mujahideen. The following year 8,000 'suspects' were arrested in Aleppo and 25,000 troops and tanks used to 'clear' the city. House-to-house searches were common. For two weeks the souks were shut.[2] In retaliation, between 1979 and 1982 the government demolished many traditional districts.[3] In 1987 the writer Charles Glass found soldiers 'everywhere – off duty, in uniform, milling among the crowd, many of them country boys looking for excitement in the city'. He considered Aleppo 'a city of memories', and compared it to a decaying actress.[4]

Thereafter, although Syria remained a dynastic dictatorship, Aleppo began to experience a commercial and cultural renaissance, particularly after Bashar al-Assad succeeded his father in 2000. He visited the city more often than his father, who had preferred Damascus and Latakia. People determined to preserve the city's monuments could occasionally defeat planners and developers. In 1993 the Syrian and German governments signed the Project for the Restoration of the Old City of Aleppo, which had been listed as a UNESCO World Heritage Site in 1986. The Aga Khan Foundation also helped in restoration of Aleppo buildings.

Aleppines could be recognised not only by their accents, and their relative openness, but also by their dress, usually smarter and more modern than that of Damascenes. The population rose from 340,000 in 1946 to 900,000 in 1970 and 2,132,000 in 2004. Exhibitions and books about the history, monuments and cookery of the city were organised by, among others, Hussein el-Mudarris, whose father Ismet had been the first Muslim in Aleppo to become consul of a European country (of the Netherlands in 1982, succeeded by his son in 1997). Georges Antaki, formerly consul-general of Italy and consul of Portugal, who inherited the archives of the Marcopoli family (who had arrived from Chios after 1822), assembled a magnificent collection of Aleppo clothes, portraits, documents, books and photographs.[5] Historic houses like Beit Wakil and Dar Zamaria, Mansouriya Palace and Beit Salahieh were transformed into luxury hotels.

The book *My Aleppo* (2011) is a record of a vanished city. People interviewed in it praised Aleppo's hospitality, friendliness and gentleness. The architect Adly Kudsi described the historic centre as 'a living, breathing being that gives us an endless abundance'.[6] Said, a young souvenir seller, called the souk 'a world theatre, like a sea with waves of different people continuously floating through the souk'.[7] This was not nostalgia, but people speaking at the time, about the city where they worked.

With 6,000 shops (often exchanging hands for very high prices), the souk remained an economic hub. Three sounds dominated: the rattle of the sewing machines and shuttle looms making textiles; the braying of donkeys carrying goods for sale; and the voices of people bargaining.[8] The Aleppo souk retained its role as a place where you could buy 'everything of the East and almost everything of the West'. Into the 1970s people from nearby districts in Turkey continued to travel to Aleppo to buy goods which they could not obtain at home.[9]

Aleppo was known as 'the cradle of Arab music'. There were three traditional requirements for an Aleppo bride. She should be plump and pretty. She should cook well. And she should play the oud. In Aleppo, Sufi brotherhoods maintained traditions of poetry and music, both classical and popular: *qasida*; *mawwal*; *taqasim*; and others. Aleppines acquired the reputation of being the boldest improvisers, and most critical audiences, in the Arab world. If you had not performed in Aleppo, it was said, you had not passed the test.[10]

The musician Sabah Fakhri, born in Aleppo in 1933, was proud to have studied in his native city, rather than in Cairo like other Arab musicians. Famous throughout the Arab world, he popularised traditional Aleppo music forms like *qudud halabiya*, singing poems of al-Mutanabbi as well contemporary works. His record-breaking performance in Caracas, when he sang for ten hours or longer, shows the global reach of Aleppo: most of the audience must have had Aleppo roots.[11] Another famous Aleppo musician, Sami Shawa, came from a family of violinists. Described as a musical miracle, he was famous for helping to introduce Western notation to Arabic music.[12]

Chapter Twelve

Death of a City

During the Lebanese Civil War of 1975–90, however, one Syrian prophesied to this author: 'Lebanon is the engagement party. Syria will be the wedding.' A portent of Aleppo's fate can be found in the novel *In Praise of Hatred* (Damascus, 2008, English edition London, 2012) by Khaled Khalifa, a self-styled 'prisoner of Aleppo', born near the city. It describes the regime's repression in Aleppo and Hama in the 1970s and what he calls the 'one-party culture and its sycophantic ideology'. For years pupils of both sexes attended school in military-style uniforms. Many see this novel as prophetic of the horrors experienced since 2011.[1]

Growing numbers of textile, furniture and pharmaceutical factories on the outskirts of the city helped keep it relatively prosperous. Foreign investment was starting to modernise Syria's economy. However, some rural areas suffered economically. Droughts led to desertification, growing economic disparities and resentments.

Finally, triggered by forty years of dynastic autocracy, growing economic dislocation and the examples of the Arab Spring, civil war began in Syria in 2011. Crowds shouted:

No Maher [...] No Bashar,
No to this barbaric gang [...]
Syria is longing for freedom,
Syria is demanding freedom.[2]

Aleppo has been drawn into the wars between Sunni and Shiʻa – Salafis
and other Muslims – secularists and clericalists – dictators and liberals –
armies and civilians – the city and the country – which are destroying
the Muslim world from Mali to Malaysia. The Syrian government is
supported by Iran, the insurgents by Sunni countries: Syria is enduring a horrific re-enactment of the wars which before 1750 had raged
between Iran and the Ottoman Empire. At first Aleppo had been slow
to join anti-Assad insurgents; since July 2012, they control half the city.
The souk and the mosques have become battlefields. Beit Wakil and Dar
Zamaria have been destroyed.[3]

What is left of Aleppo has become a city of bread queues, electri-
city and water cuts, rationing and road-blocks. Rubble and rubbish fill
the streets. Looting, hunger and sleepless nights are normal. Medical
services have collapsed.[4] Lebanon has become a refuge for Syrians, as
Syria had been a refuge for Lebanese during their civil war. Factories
and people have relocated to Turkey. After New York and São Paulo,
Gaziantep in south-east Turkey now contains another 'Aleppo in exile'.
Alawis have fled to the coast, Armenians to Yerevan.

Mixed Ottoman cities such as Aleppo, inhabited by different races
and religions, had survived for centuries. After 1900, however, they
were transformed. Salonica was Hellenised; Constantinople and Smyrna
Turkified; Alexandria Egyptianised; Nicosia, Sarajevo and Baghdad
sectarianised; Beirut gutted by civil war. Of them all, Aleppo had survived the longest. Indeed, in the twentieth century its proportion of
non-Muslims increased. Since 2012 Aleppo too has been destroyed: by
the lethal coincidence of the Assad regime, popular fury and fundamen-
talist forces armed and financed from abroad. Aleppo had once carried
a message: that different races and religions can coexist in the same city.
Switching from tolerance to terrorism, almost overnight, Aleppo has
changed its message: it shows that the twenty-first century can be as
destructive as its predecessors.

For cities depend on force. Cities need armies. As Voltaire wrote,
God is on the side of the big battalions, or at least of those which shoot
best. If the state supports a mixed city, it can flourish, as Ottoman cities

did before 1914, and London and Dubai do today. If the state weakens or turns hostile, or outside forces attack, cities are vulnerable. This is just as true of mono-national cities, for example, Paris in 1871 or Madrid in 1939, as it is of a mixed city like Aleppo after 2012. Commerce and *convivencia* are no protection against armies. Power comes from the barrel of a gun.

Newspapers report the hell into which Aleppo has descended. On 13 September 2012 the *Daily Telegraph* (p. 22) stated that sniper positions and check-points had appeared among the boutiques in Judayda. 'Christian militias', in alliance with Armenians and the Syrian army, were fighting the rebel 'Free Syrian Army': 'Everybody is fighting everybody'; 'the battle for Aleppo has become bitter with militant jihadist groups playing a more prominent role than in any other city'. They are shouting 'the Alawites to the grave and Christians to Beirut'. Others said: 'the Free Syrian army are all a bunch of thugs and thieves'. Some districts are controlled by Kurdish militias. The city has become a battle-ground for fanatics. Ideals have triumphed over deals.

On 20 December 2012 Charles Glass reported in the *New York Review of Books* that – for the first time – no soap was being made in Aleppo, as the soap factories in the souk had been burnt. Social, economic and legal collapse were imminent. The poor suburbs supported the 'freedom fighters' from the countryside, some of whom denounced the corrupting effects of city life.[5] In March 2013, following government bombardments of insurgents, the minaret of the Great Mosque, dating to 1095, collapsed. Many churches have also been destroyed. Aleppo is now surrounded by another ring of 'dead cities', in addition to those from the Roman Empire: wastes of smashed factories and burnt chemical plants in former industrial estates. As the war continues, Aleppo itself is becoming a 'dead city'.

'A thousand years of civilization have been reduced to wreckage in a few months' fighting', said 'Abdurrahman' in July 2013. 'This war is taking our history as well as our lives.'[6] On 2 January 2014 the *New York Times* (p. 5) wrote of Aleppo's 'growing sense of helplessness'. The population feels besieged by attacks from the Syrian air force and insurgents in the city and 'abandoned by the world outside'. Barrel bombs are a speciality: devices, made from old oil drums or gas bottles, packed with explosives, nails, petrol, chlorine and other substances. They are tossed out of helicopters by Syrian airmen onto targets in insurgent-held areas, including mosques, markets, schools and hospitals.[7] The chop-chop-chop of helicopter blades causes panic every time they pass over the city. President Assad's denials that his forces are using barrel bombs are absurd – 'we are living through a hurricane of barrel bombs', says one inhabitant – and only emphasise their monstrosity.[8] Lacking aircraft, insurgents use 'hell cannons' against government-controlled areas. All sides are destroying indiscriminately; the government has more means of destruction. Every day Aleppo is experiencing what Amnesty International calls 'unthinkable atrocities'. The city has become a nightmare.[9]

Fouad Mohammad Fouad, a poet of the city, wrote in 'Aleppo Diary':

> I sit on the balcony. Aleppo spread before me black and deserted [...] No sound save sporadic gunfire from somewhere, then a single shell preceded by a peculiar whistle. Someone is leaving this planet with a dry throat. Aleppo before me black and still [...] No oud plucked. No 'Swaying Silhouette'. No drinks in The Nightingale.[10] No drinkers. No song.
>
> One by one they awaken the beasts of darkness.

In a recent interview the novelist Khaled Khalifa said:

> Right now in Aleppo, the everyday question is how not to die [...] When a place gets wrecked it does not become ruined alone, it ruins its people also [...] It's a sad, soulless city at the moment, and its people have lost all of their dreams. One of the major crimes of the Arab regimes is robbing and destroying this deep memory. You know the city I told about in my novel is another city, a city that does not exist, but it's defending itself and its memory.[11]

The Aleppo Dispersion has further accelerated. By August 2014 the population was reported to have been reduced from 2 million to 500,000: the Syrian army prepared to besiege the insurgent-held east of the city. 'The noose is tightening around Aleppo', admitted Houssam Marie, spokesman for the Free Syrian Army.[12]

The rapidly expanding 'Islamic State in Iraq and the Levant' (ISIL), born out of the US–UK occupation of Iraq, is imposing a reign of terror on Muslims and Christians alike. Its self-appointed caliph Abu Bakr al-Baghdadi is a gruesome contrast to the caliphs of the past. Hating what he calls 'shameful peace' and 'blasphemous democracy', he has made ISIL a killing machine. Some Syrian enemies of the regime believed ISIL's expansion was 'a tool made by Assad', in order to make Syrians support him.[13] By May 2015 ISIL controlled most of the region between Baghdad and Aleppo – finally realising, in the most brutal way, the dream of uniting the Fertile Crescent which had been popular in the 1950s. Marj Dabiq, where Yavuz Selim defeated the Mamluk army 500 years ago, is now an ISIL stronghold, where it hopes, in accordance with a prophecy attributed to the Prophet Muhammad, to win final victory over Christian invaders. The contrast between Aleppo's past and its current catastrophe is a warning to other cities. Even the most peaceful cities are fragile.

States and religions are killing Aleppo. People and monuments are dying. Satellite imagery shows that there are now almost no lights at night in the city. In the twenty-first century, Aleppo has entered its dark ages.

PART II

Through Travellers' Eyes

Chapter Thirteen

A Collection of Curious Travels and Voyages containing Dr. Leonhart Rauwolff's Itinerary into the Eastern Countries (1693)

Leonhard Rauwolff *(1535–96) was a doctor and botanist from the south German trading city of Augsburg. He visited the Levant and Mesopotamia in 1573–5 in search of medicinal herbs. He published not only this travel account (English translation 1693 by John Ray, from a German edition of 1583), but also a herbarium describing the medical use of the herbs he had found. He died while serving as a doctor to Austrian troops, during a war against the Ottoman Empire.*

PART I
CHAPTER VI

Of the situation of the potent city of Aleppo, of the buildings thereof, and also of the delicate fruit and fine plants, that grew there within and without the gardens.

The town of *Aleppo* (which is the greatest and most potent in *Syria*, anciently called *Nerea*) is in some places well fortified with ditches and walls, only they are not quite round it, so that one may (the same it is with *Tripolis*) at any time of night go in and out; neither are the gates, as used in our country, chiefly in cities of account, beset with soldiers but you will only see two or three waiting at the head-gates, where the highways go through, which are rather there to take custom, than to keep the gates, neither have they any arms. But in the middle of the city there is a castle on a high hill, which is strong, large, surrounded with walls and ditches, and well beset with a good guard. Concerning their other buildings (which are flat at the top, and covered with a sort of pavement, that one may walk on the tops of them) they are like unto them of *Tripolis*. Amongst the rest there is a very magnificent building, which they say hath cost a great deal of money, which hath for its entrance a very low and small door, so that one must bend himself very low that will go into it, but when you come in, you find there delicate large halls, high open arches, very pleasant and cool to sit underneath in the summer, water-works, orchards, and kitchen-gardens, where among the rest was one of these *Ketmy's*: besides these there was also some fine mosques with steeples, which were round and small, but very high; some of them had a balcony at the top, like unto a garland, where-upon the waits are, and their priests go about at the time of prayers, to call people in. But for other stately buildings, that might be erected for the memory of some potent king or prince, there is none.

Without the city they have here and there some country-houses, among the rest one built for the *Turkish* Emperor, at four miles distance from the city, where he used to be sometimes, chiefly when he is at war with the *Sophy*, King of *Persia*, that he may presently assist his army, in case of necessity; this is very large, but not built so stately as so great a monarch deserveth. In the great garden is a chappel built by the river that runs through it, upon pillars, where the *Great Sultan* used to hold conferences with his privy-counsellors and vizier-Bashaws. It happened in the reign of *Solyman the Great* (as the gardiner did relate to us) that when they were assembled, to consult whether it was more profitable to him, to suffer the *Jews* in his provinces, or to root them quite out; after every one had given his opinion, and the most of them were of the opinion, that they ought not to be tolerated, because of their insufferable usury, wherewith they oppressed his subjects; and after the Emperor had heard every ones sentiment, he gave them also to understand his, and that in this instance, *viz*. He bade them look upon a flower-pot, that held a quantity of fine flowers of divers colours, that was then in the room, and bid them consider whether each of them in their colour, did not set out the other the better and that if any of them should decay, or be taken away, whether it would not somewhat spoil the beauty of the rest. After every one had heard the *Sultan*'s opinion, and did allow of it to be true; the Emperor did begin to explain this, and said, The more sorts of nations I have in my dominions under me, as *Turks*, *Moors*, *Grecians*, &c. the greater authority they bring to my kingdoms, and make them more famous. And that nothing may fall off from my greatness, I think it convenient, that all that have been together so long hitherto, may be kept and tolerated so still for the future; which pleased his council so well, that they all unanimously agreed to it, and so let it remain as it was.

Without the city of *Aleppo*, are abundance of quarries, where they dig great free-stones of a vast bigness, almost as white and soft as chalk, very proper for building: There are also about the town some walks or grottos under ground, which are above an *English* mile long, which have the light let into them by holes made near the highway, so that a man must be very careful (chiefly at night) that he may not fall into them, or that he may not be trapann'd by the *Moors* that live in them in great numbers. The ground about it being very chalky, it causeth to the soles of our feet, chiefly at night, although one be very well provided with strong shoes, a very considerable dryness and heat, as one may also see by the *Moors*, that, for the most part, go bare-foot, which causeth the soles of their feet to be so shrifled, that into some of their crevises you may almost put your little finger. Yet notwithstanding that, *Aleppo* is surrounded with rocky hills, and the valleys thereof are chalky; they have no want of corn, as barley, wheat, &c. but rather it is very fruitful, and their harvest beginneth commonly in *April* or *May*: But they have but few oats, and less grass or hay for the dryness is great, and it is so sandy, and the hills are so rough and full of bushes, that they make but very little hay. Wherefore they feed their cattel with barley, and with straw, which is broken in pieces by threshing waggons, that are drawn by oxen. The valley is also full of olive-trees, so that yearly they make several thousand hundred weight of oil for to make soap. There is also a great quantity of tame and wild almond-trees, of figgs, of quince, and white mulberry-trees, which are very high and big: *pistacies*-trees, which they call *Fistuc*, are hereabout very common; they have underneath very strong stems, which have outwardly an ashen coloured bark, and are adorned with handsome leaves of a sad green colour, like unto their *Charnubis*, and behind them grow many small nuts like grapes in clusters together. In the spring when they first put out, they send forth long shoots, which the *Moors* gather in great quantity for their sallad, and dress them as we do asparagus. There are also abundance of delicate orchards, that are filled with *oranges, citrons, lemons, Adams-apples, sebesten, peaches, morelloes,* and *pomgranates,* &c. and amongst them you find sometimes apples and pears, but very few, nor so many sorts, nor so big, nor so well coloured as ours. There grow many mirtles, which bear roundish berries of the bigness of our *Sorbus* or services, of a blewish grey colour, very good to eat, which have white seeds of the shape of our jumping cheese-magots, they propagate them diligently, because they are beautiful, and remain long green to put about their graves. Moreover there are many *sumach*-trees, which they plant for their seeds sake, which is much used by them; but *cherries, amelanchier* and *spenleny* I have not seen there, and very few gooseberries, or currans; *weychseln* they have, but very few, wherefore they esteem them, and keep them choice, as a foreign plant, to shew them to others, and to present great persons with them. This may suffice of trees.

Concerning their garden plants, those that are common, are endives, lettice, keal or coleworts, colliflowers, *Caulorapa Rauckelen, Apium, Tarcon* whereof *Rhasis* describeth two sorts, one with long small leaves, by us called taragon, and the other with broad leaves, which I reckon to be our *Lepidium,* by the inhabitants called *Coziriban. Ravos Serap;* or our artichokes. But beyond all they plant *Colocasia* in such plenty, as we do turneps, whereof they have also great plenty. They are also very well provided with horseraddishes, garlick and onions, which the inhabitants still call bassal. Of *Pumpions, Citruls,* and *Cucumis anguinus* (which they call *Gette*) they plant as many as they have occasion for; but many more *Angurien* and Indian Muskmillion, (watermellons) which they call *Batiechas,* but *Serap. Dullaba,* they are large, of greenish colour, sweet and pleasant to eat, and very cooling, wherefore they esteem them to be their best fruits: but chiefly those, which have more red than white within, they are very innocent and harmless, and keep so long good, that they sell them in their

Batzars all the winter long. Moreover, there are three sorts of those plants which the Arabians call *Melanzana*, *Melongena's* and *Beudengian*, as ash-coloured, yellow and flesh-coloured, which are very like one another in their crookedness and length, and like unto the song gourds. There are two other sorts, which are called *Bathleschain*, *viz.* oblong and round ones, which are much bigger, of a black colour, and so smooth and glazed, that they give a reflection. They eat these oftener, boiled (chiefly after the way which *Averrhoes* mentioned) than raw. Without their gardens are two other strange plants, which also (being they eat them commonly with others) may be reckoned among the kitchen herbs: whereof one is called by them *Secacul*, which I found about the town in shady places, and among trees, and in the corn, its roots are of an ashen colour without, and white within, smooth, mellow, or tender, of one inch thick, and one and a half long, it hath instead of fibers, little knobs like unto warts, and a sweet taste, not unlike to our carrots in stalk, herb or head, saving only the flowers which are yellow; the herb-women carry them strung upon strings about the streets to sell them. The other sort is also very plentiful, and is found in dry and rough places, which the inhabitants to this day with *Serapio* called *Hacub*, whereof he maketh mention in his 295th chapter, under the name of *Hacub Alcardeg*, whereof they cut in the spring, the young shoots or sprouts that grow round about it, boil and eat it as we do *asparagus*, corruptly called *sparrowgrass*; the whole plant is very like to our carlina, only this hath bigger, higher and more prickly heads, whereon appear flesh-coloured flowers. It being that it is every way like it, and that also the root hath the same virtue, for if you steep it in water, and drink of it, it maketh you vomit and fling up; therefore I am of opinion, that without doubt it must be, the true *Silybum Dioscorides*; besides this there grow also in the road, and on old walls, such plenty of capers, that they are not at all esteemed; they take these flowers before they open, and pickle them, and eat them for sauce with their meat. I had almost forgot another herb, which I found in their gardens, that beareth roundish smooth stalks about two foot high, the leaves are two and two equally distant from one another, and one above the other, they are long, crenated at the sides, like unto our mercurialis; between them sprout out in harvest time yellow flowers, which produce long aculeated cods, which open themselves when they are ripe, within them are six distinctions, and in each of them little black seeds placed in very good order: the herb is of a sower taste, like sorrel, wherefore it is to every body (chiefly the *Jews*) known, which boil the leaves thereof with their meat to eat them; wherefore some take it to be *Olus Judaicum Avicenna*, and others take it for *Corchorum Plinii*, whether it be or no I suspend my judgment.

They have abundance of pulses in these countries, which they feed upon, so that you see several in their *Batzars* which sell nothing else but them. Among the rest you will find abundance of *Phaseoli*, or kidney beans, little and great ones, very white and many sorts of *Cicer*, which they call *Cotane*, and with *Avicenna*, *Hamos*. Whereof they have as many as we have pease in our country, and boil them for their daily food, and oftentimes they eat them raw, chiefly if they be roasted till the outward shell falls off, they often call for them thus dressed, when they are a drinking in their coffee-houses, and have them brought to table with cheese after their meals instead of preserves, or fruit, as citrus, haselnuts and the like, for they eat very mellow, and have a fine saltish taste! They dress the *Orobus* after the same manner, which they call now *Ades* and *Hades*, but whether right or no I leave to the learned; they are somewhat less and rounder, and not unlike the *Cicers* in their colour, only that these are reddish and white, and the other white and yellow. These put me still in mind of another strange plant, by the *Arabians* called *Mas*, whose leaves and cods are pretty like our *Phaseolus*, and the cods contain little round seeds something less than our pease, of a dark green colour, and are so smooth and shining that they reflect again. *Serapio* maketh mention of them in his 116th chapter under the name of *Mes*. And *Avicennas* in his 488th chapter under the name *Meisie* and the very learned and experienced botanist *Carolus Clufius* calleth it in his *Epitome* of the *Indian* plants by the name of *Mungo*. The Turks love these pulses very well, chiefly to eat them among their rice. So much I thought convenient to mention here of their kitchen-herbs and fruits that grow in gardens and about *Aleppo*; of others that belong not to the kitchen I shall make mention hereafter.

In this city of *Aleppo* the merchants buy great store of drugs, brought from several parts by the caravans, as *Rheubarb*, *Galbanum*, *Opoponax*, *Styrax*, *Laser*, *Sagopenum*, *Scammony*, &c.

CHAPTER VIII

Of the great trading and dealing of the city of Aleppo and also of several sorts of their meats and drinks, of their ceremonies and of their peculiar way of sitting down at meals.

Having heretofore treated of the buildings and situation of that excellent town of *Aleppo*; and of the customs, manners, and offices of the *Turks* as much as I could apprehend of it, I cannot but speak, before I leave it of the dealings and merchandisings that are daily exercised there, which are admirably great. For great caravans of pack-horses and asses, but more camels arrive there daily, from all foreign countries, *viz.* from *Natolia*, *Armenia*, *Ægypt* and *India* etc., with convoys, so that the streets are so crouded, that it is hard to pass by another. Each of these nations have their peculiar champ to themselves, commonly named after their master that built it, *viz. Champ Agemi*, *Champ Waywoda*, *Champ Abrac*, *Sibeli*, *Mahomet's Bashaw*, and which are kept for them, that they may make them their inns, and live in them, and to keep or sell their merchandises according to their pleasure. So among the rest of the nations there are *Frenchmen* and *Italians*, &c. which have also there their peculiar buildings (which as is before said, are called *Fundiques*) wherein some live together, and others (chiefly the *Italians* that are married) live without in lodgings; they have very, small habitations, and live sparingly like the *Turks*. In these *Champs* you meet with several sorts of strange merchandises, before all in the *Champ Agami*, where you have all sorts of cotton-works, *viz.* handkerchiefs, long fillets, girdles, which they roll about their loins and heads and other sorts, by the Arabians called *Mosselini* (after the country *Mussoli*, from whence they are brought, which is situated in *Mesopotamia*) by us *Muslin*; with these do the *Turkish* gentlemen cloath themselves in summer. There is delicate tapestry, artifficially wrought with all manner of colours, such as are sometimes brought over by us. From *Persia* they bring great quantity of an unknown as *Manna* in skins by the name of *Trunschibil* which is gathered from a prickly shrub, called by the *Arabians Agul* and *Albagi*, which is the reason that it is mixt with small thorns and reddish chaff. This *Manna* hath grains something bigger than our *coriander* seeds, so that, to all appearance, it is very like unto our *Manna*, which we gather from the *Larix*. It might also very well be taken to be the same that the *Israelites* did eat, had not God the Almighty fed his people and maintained them miraculously and supernaturally. But that it falls upon thorns, is also attested by *Serapio* and *Avicen* in those chapters where they treat of *Manna*, which they call *Theceriabin* and *Trangibin*, and that very learned and experienced botanist *Carolus Clusius* saith the same in his epitome of *Indian* plants. I found some of these shrubs that grew about *Aleppo*, which were about a cubit high, which shout out into several roundish stalks, and divide and spread themselves from the stem into several sprigs like unto a flower (part whereof were quite over-grown with *Epithymum*, as *Thymus* used to be) and had an abundance of long thin and soft prickles, from whence grew out flesh-coloured reddish flowers, that bore small red cods, very like, and of the same shape with the cods of our *Scorpioides* (whereof I have found many at *Montpelier*) wherein are seeds of the same colour. The root thereof is pretty long, of a brown colour, its leaves long, like unto those of *Polygonum*, of an ash colour; those that grow at the bottom of the thorns are of a warm and dry quality. The people use the herb for a purge, they take a handful thereof and boyl it in water. Besides this they have another *Manna* like unto that, that cometh to us from *Calabria* by the way of *Venice, and is the concreted Saccarine Exudation of the* Ornus.

Among the rest they also shew costly stones, by the *Arabians* called *Bazaer*, which are oblong and roundish, and smooth without, and of a dark green colour. The *Persians* take these from a peculiar sort of bucks, and use the powder against mortal and poisonous distempers. There are some that are very like unto these in form and figure, but not to be compared for goodness: wherefore a man must have great care that he be not cheated. But there are some proofs to know whether they are good or no, which a merchant communicated to me as infallible. Take quicklime and mix it in powder with a little of this stone, and with water make them up into a paste, when that is dry grind it, if it then remaineth white it is esteemed false, but if it turns yellow it is good, and brought from *Persia*. They also bring hither *Turkey* stones, that grow almost only in their country, and their king the *Sophy* has an incredible treasure of them together: lately so many of them were brought to us that the prices fell very much, but when the king heard of this, he immediately forbid that any should be exported in seven years time, that so they might come to their former price again, which seven years as I am informed are now expired. There are also put to sale many chains of delicate Oriental pearls, which are for the greatest part taken or found in the *Persian* Seas, near to the island called *Bahare*, situated not far from that great trading city of the *Turkish Batzora*, or *Balsara*.

From *India* they bring hither many delicate spices, *cinnamon, spicnard, long pepper, turbith, cardamoms, nutmegs, mace,* and *China roots,* which the *Arabians* make more use of then of *Guajacum,* and delicate *China* cups and dishes, *Indico*: and in very great quantity they bring that noble root called *rhubarb*. And moreover, they sell several sorts of precious stones, *viz. garnats, rubies, balasios, saphirs, diamonds,* and the best sincerest *musk* in little cods. These precious stones are hid by the merchants in the great caravans that come from *India*, and they bring them secretly, because they dare not pay custom for them, that the

Bashaws, *Sangiachs* and others, may not rob them of them on the high-ways, for they use to do so if they find any. I will cease to discourse any longer of these and other drugs, and several merchandises, which the merchants convey thither from foreign places daily, and from thence to other places again, because it is none of my business to deal in them. With the spices are sometimes by the merchants brought from the *Indies* delicate canes, which are very long, solid, or full within, flexible and bright without, of a yellowish colour, they are almost everywhere alike thick, only a little tapering; but few joynts, far distant from one another, and are hardly seen in them. There are two sorts of them, great and small ones; the great and stronger ones are used by old and lame people instead of crutches to walk with, but the lesser (which are very like the former) are made into arrows and darts, for which they are very fit, the *Turks* wind them about with silk of many sorts of colours, which they are very proud of when they make their entries. You find also in the shops another sort of canes to be sold, which are small and hollow within, and smooth without, a brownish red colour, wherewith *Turks*, *Moors*, and the *Eastern people* write, for to write with goose-quills is not in use with them; wherefore these may be esteemed to be the true *Syringas* or *Fistularis* of *Dioscor*. Besides these there is another bigger sort of canes, almost of the same colour, but full of joynts; the pilgrims that go to see their *Mahomet* bring these with them, from *Mecca*, and the people of that country carry them along with them on horseback instead of short pikes, chiefly the *Arabians* for they are long, strong, and light, and yet solid or full within, with these they come running on upon their enemies, or else they (lifting it up above the middle in one of their hands) fling it at them, with such force, that they pene-trate deeper with their sharp iron (wherewith they are tipt before and behind) then their arrows. *Theophrastus* maketh peculiar mention of them in his fourth book and the 11th chapter, and *Pliny* in his sixteenth book and the 36th chapter.

We see very few of these in our country, for the Christians are for-bidden under great penalties to carry any of them (the same it is with any other arms that they make use of in their wars) out of the country, if any doth and is found out, he exposes himself to infinite troubles and dangers, as did happen to one in my time, which after a scimiter was found about him, was very highly accused, and fined seventy ducats to be paid in two days time, and if he had not paid it they would certainly have circumcised him and made him a *Turk*.

Besides these above-mentioned *Champs*, there are a great many more without and within the city, where also all sorts of merchandises are sold, *viz. Quibir* the Great, *Sougier* the Little, *Gidith* the New, *Atich*, Old, *&c.* And besides all these they have a great exchange called *Batzar* by the inhabitants, which is in the middle of the town, and is bigger than *Friberg* in *Bavaria*, in it there is many alleys, and each of them divided for several wares and handycraft trades; first the grocers and mercers, then those that sell tapestry and other soft woollen cloths, and also *Turkish macbyer, camlet, taffetty,* and other silks and cottons delicately wrought. There are also good *cardavon*, delicate furrs of *Martins* and chiefly *wild cats*, whereof abundance runs about in these countries.

There are also jewellers that sell all manner of jewels, precious stones, pearls, *&c.* All sorts of handy-craft tradesmen, as shoe-makers, taylors, sadlers, needle and pin-makers, painters, goldsmiths, brasiers, locksmiths, &c. that have their shops in the *Batzar* where they work, but their work, chiefly that of the goldsmiths, painters, and locksmiths, is so silly, that it is by no means to be compared with ours. There are also turners, fletchers that make arrows and darts, and bow-makers, that have besides their shops small butts, that anybody that goes by may exercise himself, or try his bow before he buyeth it. These bows are sometimes plain work, and some inlaid with ivory, buflers horns, *&c.* which maketh them of a differing price. The archers wear a ring upon their right thumbs, as our merchants wear their seals wherewith they draw the string on when they are going to shoot, these are made of wood, horn, or silver, and some are set with precious stones. Besides these you find in great *Batzars* some barbar-surgeons, which, (when they have no body to trim) use to go about the streets with their instruments and a flask of lather to look out for work; if they find any that will be trimed they do not come back to their shops but go to work in the streets, or in the next *Champ* if any be near, and there begin to lather him, and shave all the hair of his head, save only one long lock which he leaves to hang down his back. There are also places where they sell slaves of both sexes, old and young, which are sold dearer or cheaper, according to their strength or handsomeness, *&c.* But in all these countries I saw neither wheel-wright nor cart-wright, because neither waggons nor carts are in use with them: Neither could I find (for all it is so great a city) a gunsmith that understood how to mend the least fault in a gun-lock. Because there is a great trade daily driven in these *Batzars*, you shall find there at all times of the day a great number of people of several nations walking up and down, which makes a crowd as if you were in a fair. Amongst them you will often see drunken *Turks*, which use to push people that do not give them the way immediately, chiefly if they be Christians; but the Christians are not afraid of them for all that, but prepare themselves (when they perceive some of them to approach among the people) and stand upon their guard to be even with them, and when the *Turks* come and push them; they make them rebound again to one side, or to one of the shop-boards. Sometimes also the *Turks* will lean themselves backwards against the shops, and when they see a Christian go by they let him fall over their legs, and so laugh at them, but then the Christians again when they perceive this, they kick up the other leg of the *Turk* whereon he rests and so make him fall down himself. For it is usual with the *Turks* to try the Christians what metal they are made of, whether they have courage or no, wherefore they oftentimes before they are aware of them, assault the Christians with rough words, and if they find them to be affraid they laugh at them to boot, but if they resist them they give over immediately as soon as they find them in earnest (just like some dogs that sooner bark than bite) and esteem him afterwards the more for it, and call them brave people that are fit for the war.

You find also in this crowd several that are in orders, called *Sacquatz*, (which commonly are pilgrims that have been at Mecca) that go about with skins full of water, and for charity give to any, nay, even to the Christians that desire it: (because the *Mahumetans* are forbid to drink wine in their *Koran*.) Wherefore you see many in their peculiar habits (moved thereunto by devotion) that go all day long among the people to exercise a work of love and charity to those that are thirsty. They have in one hand a fine gilded cup wherein they power the water out of their skins, wherein they have commonly laid chalcedonicks, jaspirs, &c. Sometimes also delicate tasted fruit, to keep the water fresh, and to recreate the people. When they give you to drink out of it they reach you also a looking-glass with this admonition, That you shall look yourself in it, and remember that you are mortal and must die. For this service they desire nothing of you, but if you give them anything they take it and thank you, and spout into your face and beard (to shew their thankfulness) some fragrant water which they have in glasses, in a great pouch tip'd with many brass clasps. The *Turks* and *Arabians* also esteem it to be a great charity and love, if they let their marble troughs or great pots that stand everywhere about their doors be filled up with fresh water every day, that travellers or any that are dry may quench their thirst as they pass by; in it hang little kettles to drink out of: if one goes to it, others that see him go also, and drink rather for companies sake then to quench their thirst: So you find often a whole multitude about a pot. If you have a mind to eat something or to drink other liquors, there is commonly an open shop near it, where you sit down upon the ground or carpets and drink together. Among the rest they have a very good drink, by them called *Chaube* (coffee) that is almost as black as ink, and very good in illness, chiefly that of the stomach; of this they drink in the morning early in open places before everybody, without any fear or regard out of *China* cups, as hot as they can, they put it often to their lips but drink but little at a time, and let it go round as they sit. In this same water they take a fruit called *Bunru*, which in its bigness, shape, and colour, is almost like unto a bayberry, with two thin shells surrounded, which as they informed me are brought from the *Indies*; but as these in themselves are, and have within them, two yellowish grains in two distinct cells, and besides, being they agree in their virtue, figure, looks, and name, with the *Buncho* of *Avian*, and *Bancha* of *Rafis ad Almans* exactly; therefore I take them to be the same, until I be better informed by the learned. This liquor is very common among them, wherefore there are a great many of them that sell it, and others that sell the berries, everywhere in their *Batzars*: they esteem it as highly as we do in our country wormwood wine, or that that is prepared with several herbs and drugs: yet they love wine better if their law would allow them to drink it, as we have seen in the reign of the Emperor *Selymo*, when he gave them leave to drink it, that they met together daily in drinking-houses, and drunk to one another, not only two or three glasses of strong wine not mixed with water, but four or five of such as came from *Venice* to them so quickly one after another with such eagerness, as I have often seen it that they would not allow themselves to eat a morcel or two between it and so as you may easily guess, they become to be sordid presently, and so hoggish, that they excel all other nations in it. But after *Selymus* was dead, and his son *Amurah* succeeded him in his right, he immediately forbad them to drink wine in the very beginning of his reign, and looked after it with such severity, that anybody that did but smell of wine was imprisoned immediately, put out of his place, and a great fine put upon him according to his capacity, or for want of it, punished severely with many blows under his soals. During this prohibition, it happened, that when the *Bashaw* of *Aleppo* had a mind to go abroad and met in the courtyard one of his men that was drunk, and perceived it by his staggering, he drew his scimeter and

cut off his head, and so left him dead upon the place. But yet notwithstanding all this severity, and be it never so peremptorily forbid, they do
not only not mind such prohibition, chiefly the renegadoes, being very
much used to it, but long and linger the sooner after it with that eagerness, that in the summer time they use to carry in privately, just like
the ants, great quantities of wine, and lay up good stores that they may
meet at night and drink together until they have their bellies full, and
so rest after it all night that they might not smell of wine the next day.
In that time when they were prohibited to drink wine we Christians
fared very well and bought our wine very cheap, until afterwards they
had leave to drink it again: Their wines are generally red, very good and
pleasant, they keep it in skins; they are brought to *Aleppo* from several
places, but chiefly from a famous town called *Nisis*, which lieth two days
journey distant from it upon the borders of *Armenia*: The use of skins is
still very great with them as it was in former ages, as we may see by the
similitude of Christ, when in *St. Matthew* Chap. ix. verse 17 he says, *No
man put new wine into*, &c. Seeing that the Christians have leave to drink
wine, therefore they sell and buy most of it, they also plant it, and have
whole villages in their possessions, with abundance of vineyards. But
the *Turks* not being allowed to drink wine by their laws do not keep
or cultivate many vineyards, and if they do they press the grapes after
several ways, for some they make into *Cibebs*, chiefly these people that
live in and about *Damascus*, where indeed the best groweth; others boil
the juice of the grapes up to the consistence of honey which they call
Pachmatz, chiefly these that live at *Andeb*, a town between *Bir* and *Nisis*.
They have two sorts of this rob, one very thick, and the other somewhat thinner, the former is the best, wherefore they put it up into little
barrels to send into other countries, the latter they use themselves, mix
it sometimes with water and give it to drink (instead of a julep) to their
servants, sometimes they put it into little cups, to dip their bread in it, as
if it were honey, and so eat it. Besides these they have other sweet drinks
which they prepare out of red berries called *Jujubes*, or of *Cibebs*, which
when boiled in water with a little honey the inhabitants call *Hassap*, and
others called still by the old name of *Berberis*, of which they bring great
quantities down from mount *Libanus*. Among other liquors they have a
special one called *Tscberbeth*, which boiled of honey tasteth like unto our
mead; they have another made of barley or wheat, by the ancients called
Zychus and *Curmi*: These two last make the *Turks* so merry and elevated,
that as our clowns do when they drink beer, they sing and play on their

hautboys, cornets, and kettle-drums, which their musicians make use of every morning when the guards are relieved: All these liquors are sold in their great *Batzars* where they have baskets full of ice and snow all the summer long, whereof they put so much into the drink that it maketh their teeth chatter and quake again. Thus much I thought convenient to mention of their liquors or drinks.

Concerning their food, their bread is nourishing and good, and so white, chiefly at *Aleppo* that none is like it in all *Turkey*: so they have several sorts of it, of several shapes and mixtures, whereof some are done with yolks of eggs, some mixt with several sorts of seeds, as of Sesamum, *Romish* coriander, and wild garden saffron, which is also strowed upon it; meat is cheap with them and very good, by reason of the precious herbs that grow there about, chiefly upon mount *Tauri*, which extendeth itself very far eastwards, from whence they have abundance of cattel, as rams, weathers, and sheep with broad and fat tails, whereof one weigheth several pounds. They have also great store of goats which they drive daily in great numbers through that city to sell their milk, which every one that hath a mind to it drinks warm in the open streets; among them there are some that are not very big, but have ears two foot long, so that they hang down to the ground and hinder them from feeding, when one of them is cut off which is commonly done, they turn themselves always upon that side that the other ear may not hinder them from feeding. They have no want of beefs and buffles, for they are very common there, and the butchers kill the beasts in the fields without town, where they have their slaughter-houses; thereabouts are a great many dogs that live of the offels, and have their young ones in holes and cliffs where they bring them up, and these become so ravenous and wild, that they run about in the night after their prey, as I am informed, like wolves in our country. And this may very well be, for the *Turks* do not only not kill any dogs but rather carry them home when they are young, and there feed them till they are grown up and able to shift for themselves, and they believe that they do a deed of charity that is very acceptable to God Almighty; like unto the divines in the *Indies*, called *Banians*, which serve the birds in the same manners these do the dogs and cats. These wolves are more like to our dogs both in shape and bigness and so says *Pliny*, that the wolves in *Ægypt* are less and lasier then these towards the north. Being there are no inns in *Turkey*, where, as with us, travellers may lodge and have their diet, therefore there is a great many cakeshops kept in the *Batzar*, where all manner of victuals are cleanly dressed *viz.*

butchers meat, fouls, and all sorts of sauces, and broth, and soups, where everybody buys what he hath a mind to, according to the capacity of his purse. Among the rest nothing is so common as rice, which they boil up to such a stiffness, that it crumbleth. A great many other sorts you shall see in copper basons, upon their shop-boards, prepared after the same way, amongst the rest peculiarly a very common one, called *Bnuhourt*, made of barley and wheat, which were first broke on a mill, and perhaps dryed, and so boyled with or without milk, into a thick pap. *Dioscorides*, in the 83rd chapter of his second book, maketh mention of this by the name of *Crimnon*; and also *Avicen.* and *Rhasas ad Almans* in *Synonymis* calleth it *Sanguick* and *Savick.* The *Turks* provide themselves with good store of this, chiefly in war-time, by water and by land, that when they want provision, they may make use of it instead of bread. Besides these, they have more dishes amongst them; I remember one called *Trachan*, when it is dressed, it is so tough, that you may draw it out like glue; this they make up into little pieces, which being dryed, will keep good a great while, and is very good and pleasant food after it is boiled; wherefore they lay up great stores of this in their strong fortifications, as we do of corn, that in case of necessity they may eat it instead of bisques, or other food. That such sorts of foods, by the Latinists called *Puls*, have been very well known to the ancients, and that in case of necessity they use to make a shift with it, *Pliny* testifieth in his eighteenth book, and the eighth chapter.

They have also all manner of poultry in great plenty, *viz.* pullen, snipes, partridges with red bills, woodcocks, &c. but very few fishes, because they have only a small rivulet, which is full of turtles, so that at *Aleppo* they are very scarce; neither do they esteem them much, because most of them drink water instead of wine, which is prohibited by their law, wherefore there are but very few brought thither from foreign places, as *Antiochia*, and the great River *Euphrates*, &c. distant from thence two or three miles. Besides this, they have little by-dishes as keal, colliflowers, carrots, turneps, French-beans, besides trees and codded fruits, and many more; but yet they are not so well skilled in the dressing of them, as we are in our country.

Lastly, they put also up with their cheese, cibebs, almonds, dryed cicers, pistachios, and crack'd haselnuts, which, although they are carried thither from our country, are better tasted, and pleasanter than ours. They have many sorts of preserves, very well done with sugar and honey, very artificially, chiefly those, they carry about to sell upon plates very well garnish'd, made up and set out with several colours and shapes very beautiful to behold. For the rest, they live very sparingly, and bring the year round with small and little expences, for they do not make so great feasts, nor have so many dishes, nor bestow so great cost as we do in our country.

In these Eastern countries they eat upon the plain ground, and when it is dinner-time they spread a round piece of leather, and lay about it tapestry, and sometimes cushions, whereupon they sit cross-leg'd before they begin to eat, they say grace first, then they eat and drink hastily, and every one taketh what he has a mind to, and do not talk much. The rich have fine cotton-linnen about their necks, hanging downwards, or else hanging at their silk-girdles, which they use instead of napkins; their wives or women do not eat with them, but keep themselves in their peculiar apartments. After they have done, they rise altogether with a jerk, swinging themselves about, which our countrymen cannot easily imitate, till after they have been there a long while, for the limbs are numbed in sitting cross-legg'd, so that one hath a great deal to do to bring them to themselves again. At last they take up the leathern table, with bread and all, which therefore serveth them also instead of a table-cloth and bread-basket, they draw it together with a string, like a purse, and hang it up in the next corner.

Chapter Fourteen

The Six Voyages of Jean-Baptiste Tavernier ... through Turkey into Persia and the East Indies (1678)

Jean-Baptiste Tavernier *(1605–89) was a French traveller and merchant. Between 1630 and 1668 he made six journeys to the Levant and lands to the east, once getting as far as Java, mainly in search of jewels to sell to clients in Europe. One of his jewels, a 116-carat blue diamond later called Le Bleu de France, was bought in 1669 by Louis XIV, who wore it in his cravat pin (it now belongs to the Smithsonian Institute). At the instigation of Louis XIV, Tavernier published* Les six voyages *in two volumes in 1676–7. Intended to act as a guide to other merchants, it was translated into German, Dutch, Italian and English. Since he was a Protestant, Tavernier left France after the revocation of the Edict of Nantes in 1685. He died in Moscow in 1689 at the age of eighty-four, on his way to Persia. Here he describes Aleppo in 1638.*

BOOK II
CHAPTER II

The description of Aleppo, now the capital city of Syria.

Aleppo is one of the most famous cities in all *Turkie*, as well for the bigness and beauty of it, as for the goodness of the air, and plenty of all things, together with the great trade which is driv'n there by all the nations of the world. It lyes in 71 deg. 41 min. of longitude, and 36 deg. 15 min. of latitude, in an excellent soil. With all the search that I could make, I could never learn how it was anciently call'd. Some would have it to be *Hierapolis*, others *Beroea*: and the Christians of the country agree with the latter. The *Arabian* historians that record the taking of it, call it only *Aleb*, not mentioning any other name. Whence this observation is to be made, that if the *Arabians* call it *Aleb*, others *Alep*; the reason is, because the *Arabians* never use the letter P in their language. This city was tak'n by the *Arabians* in the fifteenth year of the *Hegyra* of *Mahomet*, which was about the Year of CHRIST 637, in the reign of *Heraclius* Emperor of *Constantinople*.

The city is built upon four hills, and the castle upon the highest that stands in the middle of *Aleppo*, being supported by arches in some places, for fear the earth would tumble and moulder away from it. The castle is large, and may be about five or six hundred paces in compass. The walls and towers, though built of free-stone, are of little defence. There is but one gate to enter into it from the south, over a draw-bridge, laid over certain arches cross a moat about six or seven fathom deep. There is but one half of it full of water, and that a landing puddle to boot, the rest is a meer dry ditch: so that it cannot be accounted a wholsom place. However there is water brought into the castle through a large pipe from the fountains in the city: and there is a strong garrison kept in it.

The city is above three miles in circuit, and the best half of it is unmoated; that moat there is not above three fathom deep. The walls are very good, and all of free-stone with several square towers, distant one from the other about fourscore paces, between which there are others also that are less. But these walls are not all of them of an equal height, for in some places they are not above four fathoms from the ground. There are ten gates to enter into the city, without either moat or draw-bridge, under one of which there is a place that the *Turks* have in great veneration where they keep lamps continually burning, and report that *Elijia* the Prophet liv'd for some time.

There is no river that runs through *Aleppo*; and but only a small one without the city, which the *Arabians* call *Coïc*. However, though indeed it be but properly a rivulet, yet it is very useful to water the gardens, where grows an abundance of fruit, particularly pistaches, much bigger, and better tasted than those that comes from the parts near *Casbin*. But though there be no river, yet there are more of fountains and receptacles of water, which they bring from two places distant from the city.

The edifices, neither public nor private, are not very handsom, but only within-side; the walls are of marble of several colours, and the ceiling of foliage fret-work, with inscriptions in gold'n letters. Without and within the city there are six and twenty *Mosquees*, six or seven whereof are very magnificent, with stately *Duomos*, three being cover'd with lead. The chiefest and largest of all, was a Christian church which they called *Alhha*, or *Listen'd unto*: which is thought to have been built by *St. Helen*. In one part of the suburbs also stands another *Mosquee*, which was formerly a Christian church. In that there is one thing worthy observation. In the wall upon the right side of the gate, there is a stone to be seen two or three foot square, wherein there is the figure of a handsom chalice, and a sacrifice over the hollow of it, with a crescent that covers the sacrifice, the two horns whereof descend just upon the brims of the mouth of the chalice. One would think at first that whole figures were in *Mosaïc*-work: but it is all natural, as I have found with several other *Franks*, having scrap'd the stone with an iron instrument, when the *Turks* were out of the way. Several consuls would have bought it, and there has been offer'd for it 2000 crowns, but the *Bashas* of *Aleppo* would never suffer it to be sold. Half a league from the city lyes a pleasant hill, where the *Franks* are wont to take the air. On the side of that hill is to be seen a cave or *grotto*, where the Turks report that *Haly* liv'd for some few days and for that there is an ill-shap'd figure of a hand imprinted in the rock, they farther believe it to be the hand of *Haly*.

There are three colleges in *Aleppo*, but very few scholars, though there be men of learning that belong to them, who have salaries to teach grammar, and their odd kind of philosophy, with the grounds of their religion, which are the principal sciences to which the *Turks* apply themselves.

The streets of the city are all pav'd, except the *Bazar's*, where the merchants and handicraft-tradesmen keep their shops. The chiefest artists, and the most numerous, are silk and chamlet-weavers.

In the city and suburbs there are about forty inns; and fifty public baths, as well for women as for men, keeping their turns. 'Tis the chiefest pastime the women have to go to the baths; and they will spare all the week long to carry a collation, when they go at the weeks end to make merry among themselves, in those places of privacy.

The suburbs of the city are large and well peopled, for almost all the Christians have their houses and churches there. Of which Christians there are four sorts in Aleppo, I mean of Eastern Christians, that is to say, *Greeks, Armenians, Jacobites* or *Syrians,* and *Maronites.* The *Greeks* have an archbishop there, and are about fifteen or sixteen thousand in number; their church is dedicated to St. *George.* The *Armenians* have a bishop, whom they call *Vertabet;* and are about twelve thousand in number; their church is dedicated to the Virgin. The *Jacobites* being about ten thousand, have a bishop also; and their church is likewise dedicated to the Virgin, as is that of the *Armenians.* The *Maronites* depend upon the Pope, not being above twelve hundred, their church being consecrated to St. *Elias.* The *Roman* Catholics have three churches, serv'd by the *Capuchins, Carmelites,* and *Jesuites.* They reckon that in the suburbs and city of *Aleppo* there are about 250000 souls.

There is a vast trade at *Aleppo* for silks and chamlets, but chiefly for gall-nuts, and *Valanede,* which is a sort of acorn-shell without which the curriers cannot dress their leather. They have also a great trade for soap, and for several other commodities; the merchants repairing thither from all parts of the world. For not to speak of the *Turks, Arabians, Persians, Indians,* there are several *English, Italians, French,* and *Hollanders,* every nation having their consul to carry on their interests, and maintain their priviledges.

Nor does this place happ'n to be so great a mart, through the convenience of the two rivers of *Tigris* and *Euphrates,* as some have writt'n; by which they say such vast quantities of commodities are transported and imported out and into the city. For had that been, I should never have cross'd the desert, coming from *Bagdat* to *Aleppo;* nor at another time, going from *Aleppo* to *Balsara.* And as for *Euphrates,* certain it is, that the great number of mills built upon it, to bring the water to the neighbouring grounds, have not only render'd it unnavigable, but made it very dangerous.

I must confess, that in the year 1638 I saw a great part of the Grand *Signor's* army, and several boats full of warlike provisions fall down the stream, when he went to besiege it: but then they were forc'd to take away all the mills that are upon the river, which was not done without a vast trouble and expence. As for *Tigris,* it is not navigable 'till beyond *Babylon* down to *Balsara* where you may take water, and be at *Balsara* in nine days. But the voyage is very inconvenient, for at every town which the *Arabs* have upon the river, you must be hal'd, and be forc'd to leave some money behind you. Sometimes indeed the merchants of *Moussul* and *Bagdat*, and others that come out of *Chaldea* to trade at *Balsara*, carry their goods by water from *Bagdat*; but in regard the boats are only to be tow'd by men, it takes them up a voyage of seventy days. By this you may judge of the time and expence of carrying goods by water up the River *Euphrates* to *Bir*, where they are to be unlad'n for *Aleppo*.

In short, if the convenience of *Morat-sou* (for so the *Turks* call *Euphrates*) were to be had, and that goods might be transported by that river, the merchants would never take that way; for the *Arabian* Princes, with their people and their cattel, lying all the summer long upon the banks of the river, for the sake of the water and the grass, would make the merchants pay what toll they pleas'd themselves.

I saw an example of this, coming one time from *Babylon* to *Aleppo*. In all which road we met but with one of those *Arabian* Princes, who lay at *Anna*: yet he made us pay for every camel's load forty *Piasters*. And which was worse, he detain'd us above five weeks, to the end his subjects might get more of our money by selling us their provisions. The last time I pass'd the desert, I met another of these *Arabian* Princes together with his brother, both young men: He would not let us go a step farther, unless we would exchange two hundred *Piasters* in specie for *Larins*, the money of the country, and he forc'd us to take them, whatever we could urge to make it appear how much we should lose by them. And indeed we said as much as we could, for the dispute lasted two and twenty days to no purpose; might overcoming right. By this you may guess what the other *Arabians* would do, who are not a jot more civil; and whether the merchants would get by taking the road of Euphrates.

The city is govern'd by a *Basha*, who commands all the country from *Alexandretta* to *Euphrates*. His guard usually consists of three hundred men, and some years ago he was made a vizier. There is also an *Aga* or captain of the cavalry, as well within the city as without it who commands four hundred men. There is another *Aga* who has under him seven hundred *Janizaries*, who has the charge of the gates of the city, to whom the keys are carry'd every evening, neither has he any dependance upon the *Basha*. The castle is also under another commander sent immediately from *Constantinople*, who has under him two hundred musketeers, and likewise the charge of the cannon; of which there are about thirty pieces, eight great guns, the rest of a small size. There is also another *Aga* or captain of the city, who commands three hundred Harquebuzes; beside a *Sou-Bashi*, who is a kind of provost of the merchants, or captain of the watch, going the round every night with his officers through the city and suburbs. He also puts in execution the sentences of the *Basha*, upon criminal offenders.

In civils there is a *Cadi*, who sits sole judge, without any assistants, of all causes as well civil as criminal, and when he has condemn'd any man to death, he sends him to the *Basha*, together with his accusation, with whom the *Basha* does as he pleases. This *Cady* makes and dissolves all contracts of marriage, all acts of sale and purchase pass in his presence. He also creates the sworn matters of every trade, who make their inspection that there may be no deceit in the work. The Grand *Signor's* duties are receiv'd by a *Testerdar*, or treasurer-general, who has under him several receivers in divers places.

In matters of religion, the *Mufti* is the chief, and the interpreter of the law, as well in relation to the ceremonies, as in all ecclesiastical differences. Among these interpreters of the law there is a *Chieke* or doctor, appointed to instruct those that are newly converted to *Mahumetanism*, and to teach them the maxims and customs of their religion.

Three days after I arriv'd at *Aleppo, Sultan Amurat* made his entry, going to his army, which was upon its march to the Siege of *Babylon*. Now you must take notice, that not far from *Aleppo*, toward the east, there stands a house inhabited by the *Dervies*, which are a religious order among the *Turks*; though it formerly belong'd to the monks of St. *Basil*, and was a fair covent. It is still in good repair, the walls of the chambers, halls, and galleries being all of marble. All the *Dervies* of this house went half a league from the city, as far as mount *Ozelet*, to meet the Grand *Signor*; and the superiour, at the head of the rest, having made a speech to his highness, two *Dervies* came and made their obeisance in particular. Which being perform'd, from that place to the castle of Aleppo, for half an hours march together they went just before the Grand Signer's horse, turning round continually with all their might, 'till they foam'd again at the mouth, and dazl'd the eyes of those that beheld them. There are some of these *Dervies* that will turn in that manner for two hours together, and glory in that which we account folly.

While the Grand *Signor* staid at *Aleppo, the Basha* of *Cayro* came thither with a thousand *Janizaries*: And indeed, there never was a sight of men more active, or better order'd. Every one of them had scarlet breeches that reach'd down to their ancles, with a *Turkie*-robe of *English* cloth, and a wast-coat of Calicut painted with several colours. The most part had buttons of gold and silks and as well their girdles as their scimitars were adorn'd with silver. The *Basha* march'd at the head of this magnificent regiment in a modest garb; but the harness of his horse was as rich as his habit seem'd to be careless, having spar'd for no cost to appear before the Grand *Signor* in a stately equipage.

There is a necessity for a man to stay some time at *Aleppo*, as well to dispose of his affairs, and in expectation 'till the caravan be ready, unless he will venture himself alone without a guide, which I have done more than once. And thus much for *Aleppo*, next to *Constantinople* and *Cayro*, the most considerable city in all the *Turkish* Empire.

Chapter Fifteen

The Natural History
of Aleppo (1756)

Alexander Russell (c.1715–68). *Educated as a doctor in Edinburgh, he sailed
to Iskenderun in 1740 and became physician to the English merchants in Aleppo.
Russell learnt Arabic and was also consulted by the governor and notables of the
city. In 1754 he returned to England and two years later published his* Natural
History of Aleppo, *dedicated to the British consul Alexander Drummond, with
a diary of the progress of the plague in 1742–4. The work is a detailed account
of the life of the city and the animals, birds and plants of the surrounding region,
with a large number of prints. Thereafter he worked as a doctor at St Thomas's
Hospital. A second, enlarged edition was published in two volumes by his brother
Patrick, who had also lived in Aleppo, in 1794. This extract is from the first
edition.*

A DESCRIPTION OF THE CITY OF ALEPPO, AND
THE PARTS ADJACENT
PART I

HALEB, or, as we call it, *Aleppo*, the present metropolis of Syria, though greatly inferior to the cities of *Constantinople* and *Cairo* in extent, number of inhabitants, riches, and perhaps several other circumstances, yet, in respect to buildings, yields to none in the *Turkish* empire.

This city and suburbs stand on eight small hills or eminences, none of them considerable, except that in the middle of the place, on which the castle is erected. This mount is of a conic form, and seems, in a great measure, to be artificial, and raised with the earth thrown up out of a broad deep ditch that surrounds it. The suburbs, called *Sheih il Arab*, to the N.N.E. are next in height to this, and those to the W.S.W. are much lower than the parts adjacent, and than any other parts of the city.

An old wall not a little decayed, and a broad ditch now in most places turned into gardens, surround the city, the circumference of which is about three miles and an half; but, including the suburbs, which are chiefly to the north east, the whole may be about seven miles.

The houses are composed of apartments, on each of the sides, of a square court all of stone, and consist of a ground floor which is generally arched, and an upper story which is flat on the top, and either terraced with hard plaster, or paved with stone. Their ceilings are of wood neatly painted, and sometimes gilded, as are also the window-shutters, the pannels of some of their rooms, and the cupboard doors, of which they have a great number: these, taken together, have a very agreeable effect. Over the doors and windows within the houses of the *Turks*, are inscribed passages out of the Koran, or verses either of their own composition, or taken from some of their most celebrated poets. The *Christians* generally borrow theirs from scripture.

In all their houses the court yard is neatly paved, and, for the most part, has a bason with a jet d'eau in the middle, on one or both sides of which, a small spot is left unpaved for a sort of garden, which often does not exceed a yard or two square; the verdure, however, which is here produced, together with the addition of a few flowers in pots, and the fountains playing, would be a very agreeable sight to the passenger, if there were openings to the street through which these might be discovered, but they are entirely shut up with double doors so contrived, as that, when open, one cannot look into the court yard; and there are no windows to the street, except a very few in their upper rooms; so that nothing is to be seen but dead walls, which make their streets appear very disagreeable to *Europeans*.

Most of the better sort of houses have an arched alcove within this court open to the north, and opposite to the fountain; the pavement of this alcove is raised about a foot and an half above that of the yard, to serve for a divan. Between this and the fountain the pavement is generally laid out in mosaic work, with various coloured marble; as is also the floor of a large hall with a cupola roof, which commonly has a fountain in the middle, and is almost the only tolerably cool room in their houses during the summer.

The people of fashion have in the outer court but one or two rooms below stairs for themselves, the rest are for servants and stabling; the pavement of this is but rough, as their horses stand there all the summer, except a few hours in the middle of the day. Above stairs is a colonade, if not round the whole court, at least fronting the west, off from which are their rooms and *kiosks*; these latter are a sort of wooden divans, that project a little way from the other part of the building, and hang over the street; they are raised about one foot and an half higher, than the floor of the room, to which they are quite open, and, by having windows in front and on each side, there is a great draught of air, which makes them cool in the summer, the advantage chiefly intended by them. Beyond this court is another, containing the women's apartments, built much in the same manner that I have described the other houses; some few of them have a tolerable garden, in which, as well as in the outer yard, there is generally a tall cypress tree.

The mosques in *Aleppo* are numerous, and some few of them magnificent; before each is a square area, in the middle of which, is a fountain for the appointed ablutions before prayers, and behind some of the larger mosques there is a little garden.

Besides these open spaces there are many large *khanes* or (as most travellers call them) *caravan seraijs*, consisting of a capacious square, on all sides of which are built on the ground floor a number of rooms, used occasionally for stables, warehouses, or chambers. Above stairs a colonade occupies the four sides, to which opens a number of small rooms, wherein the merchants, as well strangers as natives, transact most of their business.

The streets are generally narrow, but, however, are well paved, and kept remarkably clean.

The market places, called here *bazars*, are properly, long, covered, narrow streets, on each side of which are a number of small shops just sufficient to hold the tradesman (and perhaps one or two more) with all the commodities he deals in about him, the buyer being obliged to stand without. Each separate branch of business has a particular *bazar* allotted them, and these, as well as the streets, are all locked up an hour and an half after sun-set, and many of them earlier, which is a great security from house-breakers. It deserves to be remembered, how odd soever it may appear, that though their doors are mostly cased with iron, yet their locks are made of wood.

In the suburbs, to the eastward, are their slaughterhouses, in a very airy place, with a large open field before them. The tanners have a *khane*, where they work, in the south west part of the town near the river.

To the southward, just without the walls in the suburbs, they burn lime; and a little way further is a small village, where they make ropes and catgut, which last manufacture is, at some seasons, extremely offensive.

In *Mesherka*, which is part of the suburbs on the opposite side of the river to the westward, is a glasshouse, where they make a coarse kind of white glass, but they work only a few months in the winter, the greatest part of this manufacture being brought from a village called *Armenafs* about thirty-five miles to the westward, from whence also they bring the sand used in their glass-house at *Aleppo*.

The city is supplied with very good water from some springs near the banks of the river at *Heylan* about five miles to the north north east, which is conveyed from thence by an aquæduct, and distributed to the different parts of the town by earthen pipes. There is a tradition, that this aquæduct was the work of the empress *Helena* and that from her the springs took their present name: this water is sufficient for the necessary purposes of drinking, cookery, &tc. Besides this, almost every house has a well, but the water of these, being brackish, is only employed for washing their court yards, and filling the reservoirs for their fountains.

The fuel, used in their houses, is wood and charcoal; for heating their bagnios, they burn the dung of animals, leaves of plants, parings of fruit, and such like, which they employ people to gather and dry for that purpose.

The markets are well supplied with provisions, of which we shall have occasion to give a more particular account.

For at least four or five miles round *Aleppo*, the ground is very stony and uneven, having a number of small eminences, most of which are as high as any part of the city. From the west south west to the north west by west, this sort of country continues for at least twenty miles, with a number of small fertile plains interspersed. To the northward and southward, after about six or seven miles, the country is level and not stony. To the eastward a vast plain commences, which, though it is called *the desart*, yet for a great many miles beyond *Aleppo*, affords a fine fertile foil.

In clear weather, the top of mount *Cassius*, bearing west by south, and part of the mountains, called *Amanus*, are to be seen from several places in the city; but, as the nearest of these, viz. that part of *Amanus*, which stretches to the eastward and approaches to *Killis*, is at least thirty miles distant from *Aleppo*, they can be supposed to have but very little influence upon the air of the place, any more than a small conical rocky hill, called *Sheih Barakat*, at about twenty miles to the west by north, and a narrow chain of low rocky hills, usually named the *Black Mountains*, to the south south east, at about ten miles distance.

The river *Coic* (if a stream scarce six or eight yards wide deserves that name) passes along the western part of the city within a few yards of the walls, and barely serves to water a narrow slip of gardens upon its banks, reaching from about five miles north to about three miles south of the town. Besides these gardens, there are a few more near a village called *Bab Allah* about two miles to the north-east, which are supplied by the aquæduct.

The rising-grounds above the gardens, to which the water cannot be conveyed, are in some places laid out in vineyards interspersed with olive, fig, and pistachio trees, as are also many spots to the eastward, where there are no gardens.

Inconsiderable as this stream and these gardens may appear, yet they contain almost the only water and trees that are to be met with for twenty or thirty miles round, for the villages are all destitute of trees, and most of them only supplied with water by what rain they can save in cisterns.

The latitude of *Aleppo*, as fixed by a French mathematician who was there in the year 1753, is thirty-six degrees twelve minutes N. latitude, which, though some minutes different from the observations of others, yet is probably the most exact, as he was not only a man of eminence in his profession, but was also furnished with the best instruments, an advantage which perhaps the other observators had not. The longitude is said to be 37 D. 40 M. east from *London*. Its distance from the sea, in a direct line is about sixty miles, and its height from thence is considerable, but not yet accurately ascertained.

Having thus finished what was thought necessary concerning the situation of *Aleppo*, with respect to the parts adjacent, let us now take a general view of the face of the country throughout *Syria*.

The coast in general is bordered by very high mountains, except near *Seleucia* and there from mount *Pieria* to mount *Cassius* which is ten or fifteen miles, is quite level, leaving a passage for the river *Orontes* to empty itself into the *Mediterranean*. Those mountains are covered with trees, shrubs, and a number of plants; so that, different from the plains, they retain their verdure all the summer. As they abound with springs these collect into little rivulets, and in a few places on that side next the sea rivers, which plentifully irrigate the plains that are between them and the sea. Behind them, on the land side, are generally extensive plains which receive great benefit from the streams that descend from the mountains, nigh to which they are well cloathed with myrtle, oleander, and other shrubs. The opposite boundaries of those plains are for the most part low, barren, rocky hills, and behind them other large plains, which though they have no water but the rain which falls in the winter, yet are exceeding fertile; and this is not improbably occasioned by the quantity of soil which must necessarily be washed down into them from the surrounding little rocky hills, by the violent rains of the winter. This intermixture of rocky eminencies and plains reaches within land about sixty or seventy miles, after which the country is generally level, from what I have been told, all the way to *Bassorah*, and is properly *Arabia Deserta*.

In all *Syria* there is but one river, (the *Orontes*) that having its rise on the land side of the high mountains, finds its way to the sea; the rest, which indeed are but few and inconsiderable, being soon absorbed by the thirsty plains through which they run, more especially as they receive but very few supplies in their passage: and even the *Orontes*, though it be swelled by a number of little brooks from the high mountains behind which it runs, and derives a farther supply from the lake of *Antioch*, yet seems as considerable a great many miles above *Antioch*, as where it empties itself into the *Mediterranean*.

The seasons in this country, generally speaking, are exceeding regular, particularly at *Aleppo*, where the air is usually very healthy, and so pure and free from damps that all the inhabitants, of what rank soever, sup and sleep in their court-yards, or upon the house tops, exposed to the open air, from the end of *May* to the middle of *September*, without suffering any inconveniency from it. However, as I shall hereafter have occasion to be more particular on this subject, I will at present only mention in general the changes of the seasons as they appear to our senses.

The natives reckon the severity of the winter to last but forty days, which they call *Maarbanie*, beginning from the twelfth of *December*, and ending the twentieth of *January*; and in fact this computation comes near the truth. The air, during this time, is excessively piercing, particularly to strangers, even though they are but just come from a cold climate. In the thirteen years that I resided there, it happened not above three times that the ice was of sufficient strength to bear a man, and that too with caution, and only in a situation where the sun-beams never reached it. The snow, excepting three years, never lay above a day, and even in the depth of winter, when the sun shines out and there is no wind, it is warm, nay sometimes almost hot, in the open air. Narcissus's are in flower during the whole of this weather, and hyacinths and violets at the latest appear before it is quite over.

As *February* advances, the fields which were partly green before, now by the springing up of the later grain become entirely covered with an agreeable verdure, and though the trees continue in their leafless wintery state till the end of this month, or the beginning of *March*, yet the almond, when latest, being in blossom before the middle of *February*, and quickly succeeded by the apricot, peach, &c. gives the gardens an agreeable appearance. The spring now becomes extremely pleasant, and has no defect but its short duration, for as *March* brings it on with rapidity, so *April* advances with like haste towards summer, and the gay livery that the fields wore in those two months, and indeed most of the winter, fades before the middle of *May*; and before the end of this month the whole country puts on so parched and barren an aspect, that one would scarce think it was capable of producing anything but the very few robust plants which still have vigour enough to resist the extreme heats. From this time not so much as one refreshing shower falls, and scarce a friendly cloud appears to shelter us from the excessive heat of the sun till about the middle of *September*, when generally a little rain falling, either in *Aleppo* or the neighbourhood, refreshes the air greatly.

From these first rains till the second, an interval of at least between twenty and thirty days, the weather is temperate, serene, and extremely delightful, and if the rains have been at all plentiful, though but of a few hours duration, the country soon assumes a new face; after the second rains the weather becomes variable, and winter approaches by degrees, not with so swift a pace as the summer, for the greater part of the trees retain their leaves till the middle of *November*; the most delicate never make fires till about the end of this month, and some few pass the whole winter without them.

It is seldom that *Aleppo* is troubled with very hard gales of wind; the coldest winds in the winter are those that blow from between the north west and the east, and the nearer they approach to the last-mentioned point, the colder they are during winter and part of the spring. But from the beginning of *May* to the end of *September*, the winds blowing from the very same points bring with them a degree and kind of heat which one would imagine came out of an oven, and which, when it blows hard, will affect metals within the houses, such as locks of room doors, nearly as much as if they had been exposed to the rays of the sun; yet it is remarkable that water kept in jarrs is much cooler at this time than when a cool westerly wind blows. In this season the only remedy is to shut all the doors and windows, for though these winds do not kill as the *fumyel* (which are much of the same nature) do on the desart, yet they are extremely troublesome, causing a languor and difficulty in respiration to most people. Many summers pass without any of these winds, and, during my stay, in no summer have there been more than four or five days of them; for though the easterly and northerly winds reign most in the winter, yet providence has wisely ordered it that the westerly winds are the most frequent in the summer, without which, considering the intense heat of the sun's rays, and the reflection from a bare rocky tract of ground, and from the white stone walls of the houses, the country would scarcely be habitable.

Where the town is situated it is, as most of the other rising grounds, rocky, and the soil just round it a white light earth, very stoney, and not fertile; but in most other parts of the country, the soil is a redish, or sometimes blackish light mold, and produces the fruits of the earth in great abundance.

A considerable part of the country lies uncultivated, from the tyranny of their government, the insecurity of property, and the consequent indolence of the inhabitants; but very little is allowed to lie fallow with a view to culture nor do they use much manure.

They begin to plough about the latter end of *September* and sow their earliest wheat about the middle of *October*. The frosts are never severe enough to prevent their ploughing all the winter, so that they continue to sow all sorts of grain to the end of *January* and barley sometimes after the middle of *February*. No harrow is used, but the ground is ploughed a second time after it is sown, in order to cover the grain; in some places where the soil is a little sandy they plough but once, and that is after sowing. The plough is so light, that a man of a moderate strength may easily carry it with one hand: a little cow, or at most two, and sometimes only an ass, is sufficient to draw it in ploughing, and one man both drives and holds it with so much ease that he generally smokes his pipe at the same time.

Besides *Turkey* wheat, barley, and cotton, they sow in the fields cicers, lentils, beans, chickling, small vetch, sesamum, ricinus, hemp, a green kidney bean called by the natives mash, and much wheat; musk melon, water melon, a small sort of cucumber called ajour, fennel-flower, fænugreek, bastard-saffron, *Turkey* millet.

About *Aleppo* they sow no oats, their horses being all fed with barley; but near *Antioch* and on the coast of *Syria* I have seen some few fields of them.

Near the city tobacco is planted in the gardens only, but in the villages about ten or fifteen miles off a large quantity is planted in the fields, and all the hills from *Shogre* to *Latachia* produce such plenty of this vegetable that it makes no inconsiderable branch of trade, particularly with *Egypt*.

The harvest commences with the barley about the beginning of *May* and that, as well as the wheat, is generally all reaped by the twentieth of the same month.

The more wet the spring the later the harvest and the more plentiful the crop. As soon as it is cut down or rather pluck'd up, (for this is their more usual way) it is carried to some neighbouring spot of hard even ground, and there dislodged from its husk by a machine like a sledge, which runs upon two or three rollers, drawn by horses, cows, or asses. In these rollers are fixed low iron wheels, notched like the teeth of a saw, and pretty sharp at once cutting the straw and separating the grain.

Their granaries are even at this day subterraneous grottos, the entry to which is by a small hole or opening like a well, often in the high way, and as they are commonly left open when empty, they make it not a little dangerous riding near the villages in the night.

The cotton is not gathered till *October*, and such spots as are sown with it yield a pleasant verdure when everything else seems to be burnt up. In the neighbourhood of *Aleppo* there is no great quantity.

The olives produced about the city are, as I apprehend, very little more than sufficient for pickling for the use of the inhabitants. But at *Edlib*, about thirty miles to the south west, and the other villages near it, they have large plantations affording yearly abundance of oil, with which, and the ashes brought by the *Arabs* from the desart, a very considerable quantity of soap is annually made, some at *Aleppo* but the greatest part at *Edlib*.

When proper care is taken, the oil is very good, but as the people of the country are not nice in their taste, they are less disposed to be attentive about it.

The ricinus furnishes an oil which serves the common people for burning in their lamps, and from the sesamum an oil likewise is extracted called seerage, consumed chiefly by the *Jews*.

The vineyards round the city produce several sorts of tolerably good grapes, sufficient for the supply of the markets. I need scarce mention that the *Turks* make no wine, but the *Christians* and *Jews* are allowed to make sufficient for their own use, upon payment of a certain tax; and the grapes for this purpose, as well as raisins, are all brought from some distance. Their white wines are palatable, but thin and poor, and seldom keep sound above a year. The red wine is deep coloured, strong, and heady, without any flavour, and much sooner produces sleep or stupidity than mirth and elevation of spirits.

From the raisins, usually mixed with a few aniseeds, they draw an ardent spirit; which they stile arrack, and of this the *Christians* and *Jews* drink pretty liberally.

The inspissated juice of the grape, called here dibbs, is brought to the city in skins, and sold in the public markets; it has much the appearance of coarse honey, is of a sweet taste, and in great use among the people of all sorts.

Though use seems the chief thing consulted in the laying out of their gardens (except in a few where they have small summer-houses) and they have not either fine walks, or any sort of ornament, yet, after what has been said of the country, it will be easily imagined how agreeable their verdure and shade must be in the hot weather, and consequently how much they must be resorted to at that season. But this is not the only refreshment they afford the inhabitants, for the markets are from them plentifully supplied with several sorts of fruits, pot-herbs, roots, and sallading; though, as they are obliged to use a great deal of water (which they raise with the *Persian* wheel) it must be owned that their fruits in general have very little flavour, nor do they often stay till they are ripe before they gather them.

[...]

The people in general are of a middle stature, rather lean than fat, indifferently well made, but not either vigorous or active. Those of the city are of a fair complexion; but the peasants, and such as are obliged to be much abroad in the sun, are swarthy. Their hair is commonly black, or of a dark chesnut-colour; and it is very rare to see any other than black eyes amongst them. Both sexes are tolerably handsome when young; but the beard soon disfigures the men; and the women, as they come early to maturity, fade also as soon, and in general look old by the time they reach thirty. The greater part of the women are married from the age of fourteen to eighteen, and often sooner. The tender passion of love can have very little share in promoting matrimony among them, for the young folks never see one another till the ceremony is performed. A slender waist, far from being admired, is, on the contrary, rather looked on as a deformity in the ladies of this country; so that they do all they can to make themselves plump and lusty.

The men are girt very tight round the middle with a sash. The women's girdles are not only very slight and narrow, but loosely put on; which, with the warmth of the climate, and frequent use of the bagnio, is probably one principal reason why their labours are much easier than those in Britain; the most delicate being seldom confined above ten or twelve days, and those of the villages are rarely hindered from going about their usual employments the next day. Women of all conditions suckle their own children, and seldom wean them, till either the mother is again with child, or they arrive at the age of three, and sometimes four years.

The people of distinction in *Aleppo* may justly be esteemed courteous and polite, if allowance is made for that superiority which the *Mohammedan* religion teaches those who profess it to assume over all who are of another faith. And as this prejudice is observed to encrease among the people in proportion to their vicinity to *Mecha*, the natives of *Aleppo* have still a much greater proportion than those of *Constantinople*, *Smyrna* and other parts at a greater distance; though, even here, it has greatly declined within these few years, insomuch that several *bashaws* have conferred many public honours and civilities on the *Europeans* that formerly would have caused great popular discontent. As to the common people, an affected gravity, with some share of dissimulation, is too much their characteristic. And though few in the world are more given to harsh language and quarrelling, yet none are less guilty of fighting. One can seldom pass a few yards in the street without being witness to some noisy broil; yet in many years you may perhaps never see one blow struck, except the person who gives it is very well assured that it will not be returned. But though they are so prone to anger upon the most trifling occasions, yet no people in the universe can be more calm when it is their interest so to be. This, I am sorry to say, is but too generally a true representation: but it would be very ungrateful, as well as unjust in me, not to acknowledge that there are many amongst them of all sects who deserve a much better character, and whom I know, from repeated experience, to be persons of the utmost honour and integrity.

Their usual bread is of wheat flour, not well fermented, made into thin flat cakes ill-baked, and for the most part ate soon after it comes out of the oven. The better sort have small loaves of a finer flour, well fermented, and well baked. Besides these, there are a variety of rusks and biscuits, most of which are either strowed on the top with the seeds of sesamum or fennel-flower. The *Europeans* have very good bread, baked in the *French* manner.

Coffee made very strong, and without either sugar or milk, is a refreshment in very high esteem with everybody; and a dish of it, preceded by a little wet sweet-meat (commonly conserve of red roses, acidulated with lemon-juice), and a pipe of tobacco, is the usual entertainment at a visit. If they have a mind to use less ceremony, the sweet-meat is omitted; and, if they would shew an extraordinary degree of respect, they add sherbet, (some syrup, chiefly that of lemons, mixed with water) a sprinkling of rose or other sweet scented water, and the perfume, with aloes-wood, which is brought last, and serves as a sign that it is time for the stranger to take his leave. This is looked upon as an entertainment sufficient for the greatest men in the country, only that such have a piece of embroidered or flowered silk thrown over their knee when they drink the coffee and sherbet: and if it is a visit of ceremony from a *bashaw* or other person in power, a fine horse, sometimes with furniture, or some such valuable present, is made him at his departure. People of inferior rank (or even others, if they have any favour to ask) commonly bring a small present (a flower is frequently thought sufficient) when they visit.

Tobacco is smoked to excess by all the men, and many of the women. Even the labourers or handicraft tradesmen have constantly a pipe in their mouths, if they can afford it. Those pipes are made of the twig of a rose-bush, cherry-tree, &c. bored for that purpose: those of the better sort are five or six feet long, and adorned with silver. The bole is of clay, and often changed; but the pipes themselves last for years. Many who are in easy circumstances have lately adopted the *Persian* manner of smoking the nargeery; which is an instrument so constructed, that the smoke of the tobacco passes through the water before it comes into the mouth. The method of drawing it is different from that of a pipe; and a good part of the smoke seems to descend some way into the breast. The *Persian* tobacco is what they use in this instrument, which has an agreeable flavour; attended with this further advantage, that, when smoked in this way, neither the taste or smell of it remain after washing the mouth.

The vulgar, in imitation of their superiors, have at the coffee-houses an ordinary instrument of the same construction: in this they use the common tobacco, wetted a little with dibbs and water, or an infusion of raisins, adding at times *sheera*, to make it intoxicating; and they will draw in such vast quantities of smoke, that when they throw it out again at the mouth and nostrils, it appears surprising where they found room to contain it.

Opium is not of so high esteem with the inhabitants of Aleppo as at Constantinople, and some other places; nor could I ever find the taking it so general a practice in Turky as is commonly apprehended, being chiefly practised only by debauchees. They who take it to excess are commonly stiled *teriaky* and the *Theriac.Andromach* is called in *Turkish teriack* which perhaps may countenance a conjecture that this was the original form they used it in. At present they not only use it in that form, but have various other electuaries or confections wherein it is mixed with aromatics. Some few use it pure; and the greatest quantity I ever knew taken was three drachms in twenty-four hours. The immediate effects that I observed it to have upon such as were addicted to it was, that their spirits were exhilerated, and, from a dosing, depressed state which they fell into after passing the usual time of taking their dose, they became quite alert. The consequences of a long use of it are, that they soon look old and besotted, like such as in *Europe* have ruined their constitutions by hard drinking. And it may be considered as point of fact, that they but seldom live to a good old age: though they are rarely carried off by dropsies, or such other diseases, the usual consequences of hard drinking amongst us; but rather having first lost their memory, and most of their intellectual faculties, they decline, in all appearance, in the same way as those who sink under the weight of years.

In *Aleppo* there are a number of public bagnios, which are frequented by people of all sects and conditions, except those of a very high rank, who have mostly baths in their own houses. The first entrance in the public bagnio is a large, lofty room; in the middle of which is a fountain, with a bason, which serves for washing the linen, that hangs upon lines at a considerable height all over the room. In this first apartment are broad benches, where they dress and undress; and the air is here not at all influenced by the heat of the bath, except it be just at the door, by which you pass into a small room, which is pretty warm, and from thence into a larger very hot. About the sides of these two rooms are placed round stone-basons, of about two feet and a half diameter, with two cocks, one of hot, and the other of cold water; so that you may temper it according to your own pleasure, and there are copper-bowls for you to lave it upon your body. In the corners of the inner room there are small retiring-chambers; in one of which there is frequently a cistern of warm water, about four feet deep, and large enough for bathing the whole body. All these rooms are surmounted by cupolas; and the inner receive their light from small openings in their domes, which are covered with glasses. The outer room receives its light, not only from the lanthorn of its dome, but also from windows. Some few bagnios are solely for the men, others are appropriated to the women only; yet the generality of them admit both sexes, though at different times; that is, the men in the forenoon, and women in the afternoon.

When a man goes into the hot room, the first thing he does is to apply the *dewa*, (or medicine for taking off the hair), to the pubis and armpits. This is suffered to remain till the hair is quite loose, and then must be immediately washed clean away with great care. After this, one of the servants of the bagnio begins with chaffing, or kneading violently, first the tops of the shoulders, and then by degrees the whole body. When he comes to the hand, he pulls the joints of the fingers, so as to make each crack separately; then laying the person on his back, with his arms across his breast, he raises him forcibly by the back part of the neck, so as to make the greatest part of the vertebrae crack. He then chaffs the back a little more, and, throwing a quantity of warm water over the whole body, rubs him hard with a bag made of a sort of coarse camelot, which is drawn over the servant's hand, for some time. He is next rubbed over with a soap-lather and the whole being washed clean off, he puts one towel round his middle, another round his head, and perhaps a third over his shoulders; in which manner he goes out to the great room, where he generally smokes a pipe, drinks coffee, and perhaps eats some fruit, before he dresses.

The women having the additional trouble of combing and washing, as well as unplaiting and plaiting their hair, besides very frequently that of a number of children to wash, remain generally in the hot room for a considerable time; but refresh themselves at intervals, by going out into the other rooms, where they smoke, converse, and drink coffee, with one or other of the various parties that are commonly there. Every company of two or three are attended by an old woman, whose business it is to rub and wash them; but do not chaff and crack their joints as the men, and their bag for rubbing is much finer. They also use the *dewa*.

Each company, generally speaking, has its collation, which they eat in the middle room before dressing: and as the bagnio is the principal place where they have an opportunity of showing their fine cloaths, seeing a number of company, or enjoying the freedom of conversation, though with their own sex only, it is not to be wondered that they are very fond of it, though their entertainment may not be so elegant as *Europeans* might expect.

The first time a woman of the country (whether *Christian*, *Turk*, or *Jew*) goes to the bagnio after child-bearing, she must have what they call the *shdood*; which is thus performed. She is set down in one of the washing-places of the inner room, and the midwife rubs her over with a composition of ginger, pepper, nutmegs, and other spices, made into a sort of ointment, or rather electuary, with honey. In this manner she sits for some time, the other women in the mean while singing and warbling with their voices in a particular tone, which is their usual way of rejoicing in this country. After this the lady is washed clean, and the ceremony finished. This they imagine strengthens them, and prevents a great many disorders that would otherwise ensue after delivery; and they use it also after recovery from any very severe fit of sickness.

The people here have no notion of the benefit of exercise, either for the preservation of health, or curing diseases; and it is with reluctance that they use much, either for business or pleasure. To walk or ride to the gardens once or twice a-week at the proper seasons, is as much as most of them do for the last mentioned purpose; and the other is different, according to the nature of their employments.

The people of condition, and their dependents, should however be excepted in some instances, they being commonly very active on horse-back, and in sporting, or the *jareed*, using very violent exercise. This however is but seldom, and hardly compensates for the time they spend in that indolent indulgence, of lolling on their divans, which is the way the generality pass much the greatest part of their time.

As they have no coaches, persons of condition ride on horseback in the city, with a number of servants walking before them, according to their rank; which, though it may not be so convenient in bad weather, has certainly a more manly, if not a grander appearance, than our coaches. The ladies, even of the greatest figure, are obliged to walk on foot, both in the city, and when they go to any garden, if it is but at a moderate distance. In longer journies, the women of rank are carried by mules in a litter, close covered up; and those of inferior condition on these occasions are commonly stowed one on each side of a mule, in a sort of covered cradles.

Most of the natives go to bed in good time, and rise early in the morn-ing. They sleep in their drawers, and at least one or two waistcoats, and some of them in winter in their furs. Their bed consists of a matrass laid on the floor, and over this a sheet (in winter a carpet, or some such woollen covering), the other sheet being sowed to the quilt. A divan-cushion often serves for a bolster and pillow; though some have a bolster and pillow as we have. When the time for repose draws nigh, they sit down on this matrass, and smoke their pipe, till they find themselves sleepy; then they lay themselves down, and leave their women or servants to cover them when asleep; and many of the people of station are lulled to rest by soft music, or stories told out of the *Arabian Nights Entertainment* or some other book of the same kind, which their women are taught to repeat for this purpose. If they happen to wake in the night, they sit up, fill their pipe, have a dish of coffee made, and sometimes, especially in the long winternights, eat some of their sweet pastry, and so sit till they drop asleep again. In the summer their beds are made in their court-yard, or on the house-top; in the winter they choose for their bed-chamber the smallest and lowest-roofed room on the ground-floor. There is always a lamp burning, and often one or two pans of charcoal; which sometimes proves of bad consequence even to them, and would certainly suffocate such as have not been accustomed to this bad practice.

The coffee-houses are only frequented by the vulgar. The masters of these houses have often, for the entertainment of their customers, a concert of music, a story-teller, and, in time of *Ramadan* particularly, an obscene, low kind of puppet-show, and sometimes tumblers and jugglers; and these, properly speaking, are all their public diversions.

Their amusements within doors are playing at chess, in which they are very expert, and a sort of backgammon, both borrowed from the *Persians*; draughts, mankala, tabuduk, and the play of the ring, as they call it, which is what the great men often amuse themselves with in the winter-evenings. It consists merely in guessing what coffee-cup, out of a number that are placed on a large salver, the ring is hid under. They have several engaged in the play on each side; and the parties that win have the privilege of blacking the faces of their antagonists, putting fools caps on their heads, and making them stand before them while they sing *extempore* songs in their own praise, and in derision of the losers. But it is only their servants, or ordinary people, that they treat in this manner; and some of these, especially if they have any turn to buffoonry, are always of the party on purpose.

Though some Christians have learned of the *Europeans* to play for money; yet these games are only used by the *Turks* for amusement, and chiefly to pass the long winter-evenings. Sometimes, 'tis true, they will go so far as to play for an entertainment.

Dancing is not, as in *Europe*, reckoned an accomplishment for people of fashion, and is scarce practiced, even among the vulgar, but by such as make a trade of it. Their dexterity does not consist in agility, but chiefly in the motion of the arms and body, putting themselves in different attitudes, many of which (particularly of the women) are none of the most decent. Their manner is not ill described by *Juvenal*.

At their festivals they have also wrestlers as a part of their entertainment. They have still a resemblance to the athletes of the ancients, in anointing their naked bodies, having nothing on but a pair of breeches, and strut and vaunt so much at their entry as seems to promise great matters; but they make but very sorry figures in their performance.

I should not omit among their amusements to mention buffoons, who are the constant attendants at all merry-makings, and without whom their mirth and conversation would soon languish, or conclude.

The music of the country is of two sorts; one for the field, the other for the chamber. The first makes part of the retinue of the *bashaws*, and other great military officers, and is used also in their garrisons. It consists of a sort of hautboy, shorter, but shriller than ours; trumpets, cymbals, large drums, the upper head of which is beat upon with a heavy drumstick, the lower with a small switch. A *vizier-bashaw* has nine of these large drums, while a *bashaw of two tails* has but eight, the distinction by which the music of one may be known from that of the other. Besides these, they have small drums, beat after the manner of our kettle-drums. This music at a distance has a tolerable good effect.

Their chamber-music consists of a dulcimer, guittar, dervises flute, blown in a very particular manner; Arab fiddle, a couple of small drums, and the diff, which serves chiefly to beat time to the voice, the worst of all their music; for they bellow so hideously, that it spoils what without it would be in some degree harmonious. This diff is a hoop, (sometimes with pieces of brass fixed in it to make a jingling) over which a piece of parchment is distended. It is beat with the fingers, and is the true tympanum of the ancients; as appears from its figure in several relievos, representing the orgies of *Bacchus*, and rites of *Cybele*. It is worth observing, that, according to *Juvenal*, the *Romans* had this instrument first from hence. They also have a kind of flute, like the ancient *syrinx*; but it is not much used among them, there being but few that can play upon it.

Besides the above mentioned instruments, they have likewise a sort of bagpipe, which numbers of idle fellows play upon round the skirts of the town, making it a pretence to ask a present of such as pass.

Though they understand the different measures in music, and have names for them; yet they have no method of writing the notes. They learn entirely by the ear; yet it is observable, that when several persons play together they keep time very exactly. They have neither bass, nor other different parts in music, all playing the same.

The print annexed represents a *Turkish* concert, drawn from the life; in which care has been taken also to show, through a window, the inner court-yard of a house, with the little garden, fountain, &c. and through another is seen part of a mosque, with the minaret, from whence the *imaums* call the people to prayers. The dress of the performers also shows the different kinds wore by the ordinary people, according to their sect, &c. The first, who beats the diff, represents that of an ordinary *Turk*; the next a slovenly ordinary Christian; the middle figure is a Dervise; the fourth is a Christian of a middle rank, playing upon the *Arab* fiddle. What is peculiar in his dress, is, that the sash of the turbant is strip'd with blue, and his slippers red. The last is an ordinary fellow, beating the small drums with his fingers, as they often do, instead of drumsticks. His head-dress is such as is worn by many *Janizaries* and commonly by the *Arabgarlees*, a race of *Armenians*, who attend upon the *Europeans*.

Whatever figure the inhabitants of this country made formerly in literature, they are at present very ignorant. Many *bashaws*, and even farmers of the customs, and considerable merchants, cannot either read or write. It must be observed, however, that their youth of late years are better taught than formerly; though, even at this time, their education seldom extends farther than just to read a little of the Koran, and write a common letter, except such as are bred to the law or divinity, which are closely allied in this country. The professors of both usually pretend likewise to some skill in physic. In the time I lived there, only one inhabitant of the place understood enough of astronomy to be able to calculate the time of an eclipse; for which he was looked upon as a very extraordinary person. Numbers there are who imagine they understand judicial astrology, in which the natives have great faith: but it would take up too much time even so much as to mention their various superstitions in this and many other respects.

In the city there are a great number of colleges, but very little taught in them; they being generally built by such as have raised great estates by oppression, and other bad means, and are intended by the founders, partly as an atonement for their wickedness, and partly to secure an estate in the family, their descendents being commonly appointed cura-tors of these endowments, and seldom fail to apply to their own private use what seemed intended for public benefit; and thus the school soon runs to decay. Many of these have a sort of library belonging to them, and a few private men among the learned have some books; but these are very rarely good for much, and are kept more through vanity, than for any use they either make of them themselves, or suffer to be made of them by others.

Though the *Turks* are predestinarians, they are taught however to believe, that tho' God has afflicted mankind with diseases; yet he has sent them also the remedies, and they are therefore to use the proper means for their recovery: so that practitioners in physic are here well esteemed, and very numerous. These are chiefly native Christians, and a few *Jews*. The *Turks* seldom make this their profession. Not one of the natives, however, of any sect, is allowed to practise without a licence from the *Hakeem Bashee*; but a few sequins are sufficient to procure this to the most ignorant; and such most of them are egregiously, for they have no colleges in which any branch of physic is taught: and as the present constitution of their government renders the dissection of human bodies impracticable, and that of brutes is a thing of which they never think, they have a very imperfect idea of the situation of the parts, or their functions.

Of the use of chemistry in medicine they are totally ignorant; but now and then one amongst them just acquires a smattering enough of alchemy to beggar his family by it.

Many of them are brought up under masters who live by the profession of physic; but these are seldom capable of teaching them much; and, to conceal their own ignorance the more effectually, they commonly pretend to a number of secrets not to be disclosed so that such of them as know any thing, must obtain it by their own reading and observation. But to the latter they are seldom much indebted, as they look upon whatever they find in any book as an established fact, and not to be by them contradicted, however opposite it may appear to their own experience.

The books they have amongst them are some of the *Arabian* writers; *Ebensina* in particular, whose authority is indisputable with them. They have likewise some translations of *Hippocrates*, *Galen*, *Dioscorides*, and a few other ancient *Greek* writers. But their copies are in general miserably incorrect. Hence it may easily be seen, that the state of physic among the natives in this country, as well as every other science, is at a very low ebb, and that it is far from being in a way of improvement.

But, ignorant as they are in regard to physic, they are great masters in temporising, and know how to suit a plausible theory to the patient's way of thinking; in doing which they scruple not to quote the authority of *Hippocrates*, *Galen*, and *Ebensina*, in support of opinions the most ridiculous and absurd.

It is from the pulse alone that they pretend, and are expected to discover all diseases, and also pregnancy: from their confidence in which last they are daily the death of numbers of infants, by persuading the women that their complaints are from obstructions, and giving them medicines accordingly; while many others, under real diseases, are amused with the hopes of pregnancy till past recovery.

Their practice is very trifling in most cases, and commonly adapted rather to suit the opinion of the sick, and those about them, than the cure of the disease. While they apprehend the sick to be in no danger, they attend close, and give quantities of medicines; but, as soon as they think they are in danger, they do not go near them unless sent for, and then give no medicines, but advise the relations to use some trifling things; for which indeed they have some reason, for commonly the last medicine taken is held to be the cause of the patient's death.

What has been said with regard to practitioners in physic, relates solely to the natives; for the *Europeans*, of whom there are several, practise in their own way, and are greatly respected by the inhabitants; though, partly to save their money, and partly from a notion of their giving violent medicines, they seldom apply to them, till they have tried their own doctors to no purpose.

Though their bards are the last mentioned, yet they are far from being the least worthy of notice; for at times a poetical genius shows himself among them, and produces some things which they greatly esteem.

A particular description of their dress, as it would be foreign to my purpose, so it would carry me beyond my proposed limits [...] All that I shall finally say, therefore, on this head is, that, notwithstanding their peculiar attachment to ancient customs they are of late become not a little extravagant in this article. And though their fashions do not alter so quick as in *Europe*, yet they do alter, and that not seldom. Such of their singularities, however, in respect to dress and ornament, as seem more immediately to regard their health, it may be proper to mention.

Some of the old men dye their beards, and the old women their hair, of a red colour, with henna, which gives them a very whimsical appearance and many of the men dye their beards black, to conceal their age.

Few of the women paint, except among the *Jews* and such as are common prostitutes; but they generally black their eye-brows, or rather make artificial ones, with a certain composition which they call *hattat*. This practice, however, is daily declining.

[...]

With respect to the people in general, these remarks may be sufficient. But as, in their manner of living, the *Turks* differ from the Christians, and the *Jews* from both, it may not be improper to take a view of each.

To begin with the *Turks*, who are the most numerous, such as can afford, and dare show it, live well, and are far from being the abstemious people that many imagine them to be. As soon as they get up in the morning, they breakfast on fried eggs, cheese, honey, leban, &c. About eleven o'clock in the forenoon in winter, and rather earlier in summer, they dine. Their table is round, and as well as their dishes, is made either of copper tinned, or for *bashaws*, and other persons of high distinction, of silver. It is placed upon a stool about a foot or fourteen inches high. A piece of red cloth, cut in a round form, is spread upon the divan under the table, to prevent that from being soiled, and a long piece of silk-stuff is laid round, to cover the knees of such as sit at the table, which has no covering but the victuals. Pickles, sallads, small basons of leban, bread, and spoons, are disposed in proper order round the edges. The middle is for the dishes, which (among the great people) are brought in one by one; and, after each person has ate a little, they are changed. Their fingers serve them for knives and forks; but for liquids they are obliged to have spoons, which are made of wood, horn, or tortoise-shell, for silver or gold is not permitted them for that purpose by their religion. The first dish is generally a sort of broth, or soup, and the last pilaw. The intermediate dishes, which, generally speaking, are numerous, consist of mutton cut into small pieces, and roasted, or stewed with herbs and cicers; stewed pigeons, fowls, or other birds, which are commonly stuffed with rice and spices. A whole lamb, stuffed with rice, almonds, raisins, pistaches, &c. and stewed, is a favourite dish with them. Rice, and minced meat, wrapped up in vine-leaves, beet, endive, borrage, &c. or stuffed into cucumbers, mad apples (badinjans), gourds, quinces, &c. and stewed, they are very fond of, and call *mahshee*, in *Turkish dolmah*, with the name of the enveloping vegetable added, as *badinjan mahshee* &c. Pastry, both with meat, and of the sweet or fruit kind, they would make very well, if the badness of their butter did not spoil them. A large pilaw, with a dish of sweet starch, which they sometimes eat with it, comes last, excepting the *khushaf;* which is a very thin syrup, with currans, raisins, dried apricots, pistaches, slices of pears, apples, or the like, swimming in it; and of this each person takes a large spoonful, with spoons brought in with it on purpose, and finishes the repast. Water is their liquor at table, and after dinner they drink coffee. Almost all their dishes are either greasy with fat, or butter pretty high-seasoned with salt and spices; many of them made sour with verjuice, pomegranate, or lemon-juice; and onions and garlick often complete the seasoning.

They sup early, that is, about five o'clock in the winter, and six in the summer, in much the same manner that they dine; and in winter, as they often visit one another, and sit up late, they have a collation of *kennafy,* or other sweet dishes.

In the summer their breakfast commonly consists of fruits; and, besides dinner and supper, they often, within the compass of the day, eat water-melons, cucumbers, and other fruits, according to the season.

It is to be observed, that they are not so regular in their times of eating as the *Europeans:* and though it should happen that they are but just rose from table, they cannot withstand the invitation of another company, but sit down and eat again with them.

The common people have no such variety as has been before described. Bread, dibbs, leban, butter, rice, and a very little mutton, make the chief of their food in the winter; as rice, bread, cheese, and fruits, do in the summer. Their principal meal is in the evening, when they return to their families from the exercise of their respective occupations.

Through the whole of the month of Ramadan, they fast from the dawn of day till sunset, and do not either eat or smoke: but, as soon as the sun is down, they eat a hearty meal; and, such as can afford to sleep in the day, keep eating and drinking the greatest part of the night, living more luxuriously than at other times, and generally spending as much money in that one, as in any other two months in the year: but the poor labourers, or those whose business calls them abroad in the day, suffer a great deal during this fast, more especially when it happens in the summer.

Though wine and spirits are only drunk by the irreligious and licentious among the *Turks,* yet the number of these is more than what from appearance one would apprehend: for as these liquors are prohibited by their religion, they chiefly drink in secret at their gardens, or privately in the night; and, if they once begin, they generally drink to great excess whenever they can come at liquor.

By their religion they are obliged to wash before their prayers, which are five times in the twenty-four hours, and also every time they ease nature. As they eat chiefly with their fingers, they are likewise under a necessity to wash after every meal, and the more cleanly do it before meals also. Besides, every time they cohabit with their women, they must go to the bagnio before they can say their prayers; so that they are almost all day long dabbling in water.

Though by law, or rather from an implied toleration, they are allowed four wives, and as many concubines, or more properly female-slaves, as they can or care to maintain; yet as they are obliged to pay money for their wives, few of any rank have more than two; the poorer sort have seldom more than one, and hardly ever a concubine. Those of middling circumstances rarely exceed three or four; though some I have known, of greater opulence, have kept forty, exclusive of those employed in the menial offices of the family. It may appear strange how such a number should agree tolerably well together; and in fact the master of the family hath very frequently enough to do to keep the peace among them. But if we consider, that they are accustomed from their infancy to a servile obedience, that the husband can at pleasure divorce his wife without assigning any cause, and sell such of his slaves as he has had no children by, it will not appear so extraordinary that they live together in a tolerable degree of harmony. On the other hand, the wife has also a check upon him; for if he divorces his wife, it is attended with expence, as he must not only lose all the money she at first cost him, but there is generally a sum equal to that stipulated by the contract to be paid in case he should at any time divorce her.

In this country marriages are commonly brought about by the ladies: and the mothers, in order to find out a proper wife for their sons, take all opportunities of introducing themselves into company where they expect to have a sight of a young woman who may be disengaged; and, when they have met with one they think will be agreeable, they propose to the mother a match between her and the young man. This puts the family upon enquiring into his character and circumstances; and, if matters are likely to be adjusted, she is formally demanded of her parents by the father, the price is fixed that he is to pay for her, and a licence is procured from the *kadè*, for such a person to marry such a woman: each of the young folks then appoint a proxy, who meet with the *imaum*, and several of the male relations; and, after witnesses have been examined to prove those are the proxies regularly appointed, he asks the one, If he is willing to buy the bride for such a sum of money?

and the other, If he is satisfied with the sum? To which having received answers in the affirmative, he joins their hands; and the money being paid, the bargain is concluded with a prayer out of the Koran.

The bridegroom is at liberty after this to take his bride home when-ever he thinks proper; and the day being fixed, he sends a message to her family, acquainting them with it. The money which he paid for her, is laid out in furniture for one chamber, and cloaths and jewels, or gold ornaments for the bride, whose father makes some addition, accord-ing to his circumstances, which are sent with great pomp to the bride-groom's house three days before the wedding. He invites, at the same time, all his friends and acquaintance, and, if a man in power, a great many others, for all who are invited send presents, whether they think proper to go or not. Rejoicings are made, and a sort of open house, is kept for several days preceding the wedding. The women, on the day appointed, go from the bridegroom's to the bride's house, and bring her home to his, accompanied by her mother, and other female relations, where each sex make merry in separate apartments till night. The men then dress the bridegroom, and give notice to the women; upon which he is introduced into the court-yard of the women's apartment, and there met by his own female relations, who dance and sing before him to the stair's foot of the bride's apartment, who is brought half way down stairs to receive him, being veil'd with a piece of red gauze, and often, if young, especially her forehead and cheeks covered – with leaf-gold, cut into various forms. When he has conduced her up stairs, they are left to themselves.

They have a few black slaves, which are commonly brought from Æthiopia by way of *Cairo*; but the greater part of their slaves are white, being mostly furnished from *Georgia* or such as are taken in war; and the beauty of a male-slave enhances the value as much as it does that of a female, occasioned by the frequency among them of a crime not to be named. When I mention their slaves, it will not be amiss to observe, that they are generally very well treated, and, provided they behave as they ought, very often marry their master's daughters, and inherit their whole fortunes.

The *Turks* of *Aleppo* being very jealous, keep their women as much at home as they can; so that it is but seldom they are allowed to visit each other. Necessity however obliges the husband to suffer them to go often to the bagnio, and *Mondays* and *Thursdays* are a sort of licenced days for them to visit the tombs of their deceased relations; which furnishing them, with an opportunity of walking abroad in the gardens or fields, they have so contrived, that almost every *Thursday* in the spring bears the name of some particular *Sheih* whose tomb they must visit on that day. By this means the greatest part of the Turkish women of the city get abroad to breathe the fresh air at such seasons, unless confined (as is not uncommon) to their houses by order of the *bashaw*, and so deprived even of that little freedom which custom had procured them from their husbands. When the women go abroad, they wear white veils, so managed that nothing appears but their eyes, and a small part of the nose. They are usually in large companies, and have always either an old woman or a young lad for a guard.

The *haram*, or women's apartment, among the people of fashion, is guarded by a black eunuch, or young boy. And though necessity obliges many of the inferior people to trust their wives out of doors, yet some are locked up till the husbands return; so that the utmost care in that way is taken among them to prevent a breach of the marriage-vow. But where there are no ties of love or virtue, one may easily conceive that others prove ineffectual; and how far affection has place among them, may be guessed from what has been already mentioned in regard to choice: or at least when to this is added, that it is a kind of reproach among them to be thought fond of their women, or to shew them much tenderness or respect; the best of them being only treated as upper serv-ants, and often abused and drove about by the very eunuchs or boys bought or hired to look after them.

When a *Turk* dies, the women immediately fall a shrieking, (a practice followed by all the natives) and continue so to do till the body is buried; which however is dispatched as soon as possible, for they never keep it longer than is absolutely necessary for acquainting the relations who live in town. The first thing done is to wash the corpse upon a large table, which every *hara* has for this purpose: they next stop all the natural passages with cotton, to prevent any moisture from oozing out, as this would render the body unclean; then wrapping it up in a clean cotton-cloth, they lay it in a kind of coffin, much in the form of ours, only that the lid rises with a ledge in the middle, and at the head there is a wooden battoon, about a foot long, that stands up, on which the proper head-dress of the deceased is placed, if a man; but if a woman, it is not her head-dress, but an old-fashioned one, flat on top like a trencher, and over it is thrown a handkerchief. The middle part of the pall is composed of a small piece of the old covering of the holy house at *Mecca*, the rest of it being of no particular colour or stuff. Over the pall are laid some of the deceased's best cloaths.

When the corpse is carried out, a number of *Sheihs*, with their tat-tered banners, walk first, next come the male-friends, and after them the corpse, carried with the head foremost, upon men's shoulders. The bearers are relieved very often, for every passenger thinks it merito-rious to lend some little help on such solemn occasions. The nearest male-relations immediately follow, and the women close the procession with dreadful shrieks, while the men all the way are singing prayers out of the Koran. Thus they proceed to a mosque; where the bier is set down in the court-yard, and a service said by the *imaum*: after which it is carried on in the same order as before to the burying-place; of which there is but one that is public within the city, the others being all abroad in the fields.

The graves lie east and west, and are lined with stone. The corpse is taken out of the bier, and put in a posture between sitting and lying on the right-side, with the head to the westward, so that the face may be to the south, that is, towards *Mecca*; a small portion of earth being put behind the body to keep it steady, the grave is covered with long stones, which go across, and prevent the earth they put over from falling in upon the corpse. The *imaum* throws on the first handful of earth, say-ing at the same time a prayer for the soul of the deceased, and exhort-ing such as hear him to be mindful of their end. After him every one present throws also a handful of earth, saying, God be merciful unto the deceased person. This done, the grave is filled up. At each end of their graves is set up a stone, upon which are commonly wrote some prayers, and the name of the person there interred. Some have the upper part of the head-stone cut into the form of turbant for a man, or an old-fashioned sort of head-dress if a woman; and as they never open the old graves in less than seven years, or seldom so soon, their cem-etaries occupy a very considerable space round the city.

The nearest relations go to pray at the grave on the third, seventh, and fortieth days, as also that day twelve-month after the person's decease. [...]

The Jews have their synagogue within the city, in *Bahsyta*, near *Garden-Gate*, and they live all in that quarter. Many of their houses are upon the citywall; and the ditch being there turned into gardens, makes their situation agreeable, but not so healthy. The houses of other *Jews* have their court-yards mostly several feet below the level of the street; which, with the natural nastiness of the people, contributes towards ren-dering their dwellings very offensive.

As most of their time during their festivals is employed in the exercise of their religion, on the greatest part of them, they cannot dress victuals; and as it is not lawful for them to eat or drink but of such things as have been managed in a different way from what they find among the Christians or *Turks*, they have no great opportunities of committing excesses; so that they may with justice be pronounced the most abstemious people in *Aleppo*.

It having been agreed, for the benefit of the poor of this religion, that meat shall be sold amongst them at an under-price, and the deficiency made good out of the public stock, the managers take care that their markets shall be very ill supplied, so that sometimes they are for several days without a bit of mutton. This is the reason why they eat more poultry, and the poorer sort chiefly herbs, roots, and pulse, dressed with oil expressed from the sesamum, than most other people.

Six days in the year they fast from about two hours before sunset, till the next evening after the sun is down. All of them attempt once in their lives to fast from *Saturday* night at sunset, till the *Friday* following at the same hour. Some hold out two, some three, others four days, and a few complete it; but there are several who perish in the attempt.

Except the particular ceremonies which their religion obliges them to observe, it would be only repeating a great deal of what has been already said to give an account of their weddings. Amongst the latter, the most remarkable is, that the bride's eye-lids are fastened together with gum; and, if I remember right, the bridegroom is the person that opens them at an appointed time.

Their dead are carried to the grave on a covered bier. They have certain days, wherein they go to the sepulchres; and the women, like those of other sects, often go there to howl and cry over their dead relations.

The *Europeans*, or *Franks* (as they are generally called), residing in *Aleppo*, are chiefly *English* and *French*; of the former at present, besides the consul, chaplain, cancellier, or chancellor, physician, and cheaux, there are ten merchants. The *French* have a consul, and other officers, as mentioned, and their druggomen are likewise of their own nation. The number of those in quality of merchants and clerks is nigh double that of the *English*. Besides which they have many of a lower class, who are married to natives of the country, or others of a mixed race: the number of whom in the *Levant* was become so considerable, and likely to be so troublesome, that the *French* King, not many years ago, issued an edict, ordering all such as were married to return home, and prohibiting any

others from marrying without his licence, which has greatly diminished their number. Under the *French* protection are likewise the *Roman
Catholic* convents, of which there are in the city no less than three and
a college of *Jesuits*. The *Dutch* have a consul residing here, but no other
person of that country. There are also a few *Venetian* merchants, and
some *Italian Jews*.

The major part of the *Europeans* live in *khanes* in the principal quarter of the city. The ground-floor serves for their warehouses, the upper
story is fitted up for their dwellings, by building between the pillars of
the colonade, which forms a long corridore; opening on which are a
number of rooms, so that they much resemble cloisters, and as they are
unmarried, and their communication with the people of the country
is almost solely on account of trade, their way of life also not a little
resembles the monastic. It was formerly customary for all, or most of
them, to wear the *Turkish* habit, retaining only the hat and wig by way
of distinction; but of late years the far greater part have continued in
their proper dress.

The *Italian Jews*, who are mostly married, and such of the *French*
above mentioned as have families, must be excepted, as they have houses
after the manner of the natives, and conform more to their customs than
the other *Europeans*.

As to provisions, it has been already mentioned what the place
affords, and those are dressed after the *European* manner. The evening
being the chief time of entertaining their friends, they eat more animal
food for supper than is customary in *Britain*. In respect to drink they
are exceeding moderate: their common draught at table is a dry white
wine, and *Provence* red wine. In summer, the *English* generally before
dinner and supper drink a draught of weak punch; which is found so
very refreshing, that now the greater part of the other *Europeans*, several
of the Christians (and I might add some *Turks*), follow their example.

All the *English*, and some of the others, keep horses, and ride out
for an hour or two of an afternoon three or four times a-week. On
Saturdays, and often on *Wednesday* likewise, they dine abroad under a
tent in the spring and autumn, and during the good weather in the winter; the month of *April*, and part of *May*, they generally live at the gardens near *Baballah*, and in the heat of summer, in the room of the tent,
they dine at the gardens. Such as love hunting or hawking, usually go
abroad twice a-week, after the second rains, till the weather grows too
warm in the spring; and there is game for such as love shooting at the
same seasons, as also plenty of quails in spring and autumn.

From the above account it would appear that the *English* in particular use a good deal of exercise: but it ought to be considered, that, if we except a little walk in an evening on the house-top, what has been mentioned is the whole they take; the greatest part of their time besides being spent in the compting-house, or in reading; so that they are rather sedentary than active.

Though, from what has been said of the people of this country in general, their character may not appear the most amiable; yet the *Europeans* have no reason to complain of their behaviour. Their capitulations with the *Port* prevents their being any way subject to the oppressions of the government; and the *bashaws*, and the people of distinction, usually treating the consuls with civility and respect, others of course follow their example; so that we live among them in great security in the city, and can travel abroad unmolested by *Arabs* or *Curds*, where the natives dare not venture, though defended by a much greater force. This is owing partly to a small annual present sent to the Prince of the *Arabs* and the civil treatment that the *Curds* sometimes meet with at *Scanderoon* and partly to our travelling with no more money than what is absolutely necessary for our expences; so that they would get but little by us. And besides, an insult of this nature would be made a pretence by the *Turkish* government for chastising them severely: whereas, if they rob a native, they generally, in money and horse-furniture, find a good booty; and, unless he happens to be a person in power, he dare not complain, as he would run the risk of being fleeced of as much more by the very person who should procure him redress.

Chapter Sixteen

A Journal from Calcutta in Bengal, by Sea, to Busserah: from thence across the Great Desart to Aleppo: and from thence to Marseilles, and through France to England. In the Year 1750 (1757)

Bartholomew Plaisted *(?–1767) was a surveyor and sailor who had worked in India in the 1740s. He describes the houses of Aleppo from his visit to the city in July 1750. Having convinced the directors of the East India Company in London*

*that he had been ill-treated in India, he returned in early 1752, and continued to
work for the company until he died in Calcutta on 27 October 1767.*

The houses consist of a ground floor, generally arched, of an upper story
which is flat on the top, and either terraced with hard plaister, or paved
with stone; the apartments are placed on each side of a stone court. The
ceilings are of wood, neatly painted and sometimes gilded, as are also
the window-shutters, of which they have a great number; these taken
together have a very agreeable effect; over the doors and windows on
the inside are written passages out of the Koran or verses of their own
composition. The courtyard is neatly paved, and has generally a bassin
with a jet d'eau in the middle, on one or both sides of which a small spot
of a yard or two square is left unpaved for a garden; the verdure of this,
the flowers in pots, and the play of the fountain produces a very agreeable effect, but they can only be seen by those within, for the passage
into the street is closed with double doors so contrived that there is no
looking in when the doors are opened. Besides there are no windows in
the street except a very few in the upper rooms, which render the streets
very disagreeable to Europeans.

The better sort of houses have an arched alcove in this court open
to the north, and opposite the fountain. The pavement of this alcove is
raised about a foot and a half above the pavement of the court and serves
for a divan. Between this and the fountain the pavement is generally of
mosaic work with marble made of various colours; as is also the floor
of a large hall with a cupola roof, which commonly has a fountain in
the middle, and is a cool room in the summer time. The divan is that
part of a room, in a Turkish house, raised above the floor and is covered
with a carpet in winter, and in summer with fine mats. Along the sides
are thick mattrasses about three feet wide, and commonly covered with
scarlet cloth; there are likewise large bolsters of brocade stuffed with
cotton set against the walls to lean upon. On these they sit cross legged
like taylors, for they have no chairs.

People of fashion have but one or two rooms for themselves in the
outer court, the rest are for the servants and stabling. Above stairs is a
colonnade, if not round the whole court, at least fronting the west, off
from which are their rooms and kiosks. These last are a sort of wooden
divans that project a little way from the other part of the building and
hang over into the street. They are raised about a foot and a half higher
than the floor of the room, to which they are quite open, and by having

windows in the front, and on each side, there is a great draught of air which renders them cool in summer. Beyond this court is another, containing the women's apartments, built in the same manner as other houses. Some few have a garden and a tall cypress tree; there is likewise one of these in the outward yard.

Chapter Seventeen

Voyages and Travels of a Sea Officer (1792)

Francis Vernon, *a naval officer who visited Aleppo in 1785, was one of the growing number of European travellers in the Levant in the late eighteenth and early nineteenth centuries.*

CHAPTER XIV

Remains during the Carnival at Aleppo. The plague breaking out, joins a large caravan.

The principal language used by the ladies is the Italian; and in their company, received an improvement, that by the grammar alone, I could not have attained. Indeed, ladies are generally allowed to be the best instructors, and in consequence, have always paid the highest attention to their example. For tho' the Turkish women immured in the Haram's dare not assert the prerogative of our European females, yet we, by no means, chose to follow the tyrannic conduct of their turbaned Bashaws, but shewed a laudable example, by submitting to the dictates of our fair companions. Nor were we the less happy, being the most jovial set, at that time, within the walls of Aleppo.

The women here are of several classes; 1st, those from Europe, who after some time's residence in Turkey, conform in a great degree to its dress, preserving the language and accomplishments of their respective countries. 2dly, the Christian natives, of the Greek or Armenian church. 3dly, the Jewesess and lastly, the Turkish women; including those brought from Georgia, or Circasia. Every woman in the streets is closely veiled, and if a European attempted to speak to a Turkish woman, it might be attended with fatal consequences, running a risque of being stabbed, of turning Mahometan, or at least of paying a considerable fine; therefore to procure those agreeable interviews, that in spite of philosophy, are so universally sought after, a stranger has only to form an acquaintance at the Jews houses, where the Turkish women frequently visit, and by the master-key of a douceur well applied, the Hebrew lady winks at the innocent recreation of a tete-a-tete.

My respected relation, the Consul, had amply participated of the sweets of Aleppo; and after some visits to Aleppo, from his Consulship at Tripoly, became celebrated for his gallantry; for the Turks once on hearing of his arrival, exclaimed, *Voila! encore Monsieur V____; il a baisé un moitié de notres femmes; et il est retourné pour baiser l'autre.* So much for Harams, or any such confinements where love carries the key, and must gain admittance.

Here are also many veiled coquetts for passing in the street when they supposed no Turk was in sight, I have seen them throw aside the veil, receiving such a broadside from the display of charms, that has frequently kept me in chase the remainder of the day.

The number of inhabitants at Aleppo are computed at about two hundred thousand, consisting in reality, of Turks, Jews, Infidels, and Heretics; the common language is the Arabic, as none but the rich Turks speak the Turkish language; this is accounted for, by the proximity of Aleppo to the desert, and its distance from the interiour part of Turkey.

A considerable trade is carried on by the French and Italians, who supply the Turks with cloth, glass, European toys, and other articles; receiving in return the produce of Turkey, together with East India merchandises that is brought by caravans from Bassora at the head of the Persian Gulf. Our extensive commerce to India round the cape of Good Hope, has gradually caused a decrease of trade at Aleppo, and that of the English is very inconsiderable. The government of the city at this time was under a Bashaw of three tails, he bore a good and peaceable character, whereby the inhabitants enjoyed some degree of repose, after the cruel and turbulent administration of his predecessor; for promoted to commands from the seraglio or palace of the grand Signior at Constantinople, they are frequently obliged to use every extortion, to continue by force of presents, those smiles that promoted them; and the arbitrary and hidden manner that covers the transactions of their government, gives also too great a scope for avarice and self-interest, to gloss over and conceal the abuses it has occasioned. This obliges the Turks in general to live moderate, for if supposed to be rich, they are sure of being fleeced; and by the pretence of a loan, that is never to be repaid, the Aga or Bashaw, with infinite *sang froid* helps to unload their purse.

Different governments have different methods; here the Turk at once knows he is robbed, but is happy to survey the extent of his fate, and divested of patriotic ardour for the good of his country, is not under the necessity of turning his brain by bills, and amendments, that like tricks of legerdemain, are by the artfulness of imposition, too often shewn as false lights to deceive their country, or attempted speciously to oppose the truths and eloquence of a real patriot.

Chapter Eighteen

Travels in Africa, Egypt and Syria from the Year 1792 to 1798 (1799)

William George Browne *(1768–1813). Partly inspired by the great African traveller James Bruce, Browne travelled extensively in Egypt and Africa from 1792, a time when travel in Europe was restricted, owing to the French Revolutionary Wars. In 1797–8 he was in Syria. In 1812 he set out from England on another journey, hoping to explore Central Asia. In late 1813, however, he was murdered, for reasons unknown, on the road from Tabriz to Tehran.*

CHAPTER XXIV
OBSERVATIONS AT ALEPPO

The country adjacent to Aleppo is broken with many inequalities, and even the city stands partly on high and partly on low ground. A small river, called *Coik*, descends from *Aintaby* and, after passing through the city, is lost in a marsh on the West.

So many descriptions of this famous capital having appeared, I shall only offer a few remarks on such objects as struck me during my residence there.

The site is rocky, and the few gardens chiefly produce pistachios. The city is well built, and paved with stone. The tall Cyprus trees, contrasted with the white minarets of numerous mosques, give it a most picturesque appearance. The population and buildings seem to be on the increase; but this affords no proof of public felicity; for, in proportion as the capital swells, the adjacent villages are deserted. The houses are clean, airy, substantial, and commodious. The people in general are distinguished by an air of affected polish, hardly to be observed in the other towns of Syria. Their dialect too has its characteristic marks. The Arabic prevails, though many speak the Turkish language.

A new Pasha had been lately appointed at the time I arrived, but was prevented from entering the city, by the feuds which had prevailed between the Sherîfs and the Janizaries, and induced the latter to suspect that the Pasha had a design of punishing them. This officer was a young man, the son of the Pasha of Adana; his title El Sherîf Mohammed Pasha; of an unblemished character, but unequal, in point of talents and personal weight, to compose the violence of these factions, which, after he had resided a short time in the city, obliged him to retire. The Sherîfs, or descendants of Mohammed, here form a considerable faction; a circumstance also observable at Bagdad, but not in so remarkable a degree. In Aleppo they form a body of near sixty thousand. The Janizaries do not exceed one-fourth of that number. The Sherifs consist of all ranks, from the highest Imâm to the lowest peasant, and are far from excelling in courage: the Janizaries are of superior valour, though little acquainted with the use of arms or aspect of battle. Hence the force of the factions is merely balanced, and continual disputes arise for offices of profit or power, which generally terminate in bloodshed. In the course of this summer, 1797, several of these took place; in one of them it is supposed near three hundred persons perished. This imperfect exercise of authority may be estimated among the symptoms of decline in the Turkish empire.

The manufactures are in a flourishing state, being carried on with great spirit both by Christians and Mohammedans: silk and cotton form

1. Panorama of Aleppo with the citadel in the background, *c*.1940
The skyline of Aleppo had changed little since Ottoman times. The gateway to the citadel dates from Mamluk rule in the late thirteenth century.

2. Andrea Soldi, *Portrait of Henry Lannoy Hunter in Oriental Dress, Resting from Hunting, with a Manservant Holding Game, c.*1733–6
Hunter is shown here with an attendant (recognisable as a local Christian by his cap and dark blue costume). He is depicted wearing Ottoman dress, as foreign merchants in Aleppo often did, although turbans were reserved for Muslims. Soldi visited Aleppo around 1733, on his way to the Holy Land.

3. A souk in Aleppo
Until their destruction in 2012, the souks in Aleppo were among the oldest and largest in the Middle East.

4. Khan al-Wazir
Aleppo had about fifty khans, where merchants could live and trade. Built in 1682, the Khan al-Wazir was one of the largest in the city.

5. The *iwan* of the Beit Jumblatt
The Jumblatt family had long lived in Aleppo, and led a rising against the Ottoman Empire around 1600, in alliance with the Grand Duke of Tuscany and the Shah of Persia.

6. *Iwan* and courtyard of the Beit Ghazaleh
The Beit Ghazaleh was the largest of the houses built in the seventeenth century for Aleppo families. The Ghazaleh were a local Christian family, who left the house in the mid twentieth century, when it was no longer practical to live in. It subsequently became a school. Its present fate is unknown.

7. Salon Marcopoli, *c.*1900
The Marcopoli were among the wealthiest families in Aleppo. They arrived from Chios after the massacres there in 1822, established themselves in commerce and banking, and served until the 1980s as consuls for different European states.

8. A horse and its owner, outside Aleppo, *c*.1940

Aleppo had long been a centre for buying and selling Arabian horses. Most thorough-bred racing horses today descend from horses bought by English merchants in Aleppo before 1750.

9. A camel caravan outside Aleppo, *c*.1940

Camel caravans would soon be replaced by road and rail transport.

10. Greek Catholic priests with members of the Ghazeleh family, *c.*1934
Most Orthodox Christians of Aleppo broke with their hierarchy after 1700, partly because it spoke Greek and they spoke Arabic. While keeping Orthodox rites, they accepted the authority of the Pope. Known as 'Greek Catholics', they made important contributions to the Arab cultural revival, both in Aleppo and elsewhere.

11. Rue Baron, British troops, *c.*1942
British troops, who had already been stationed in Aleppo in 1918-19 after defeating Ottoman forces, again occupied it in 1941-6, after defeating Vichy armies. Their presence helped Syrian nationalists to work for the end of the French mandate.

12. Amina al-Harriri with her son Ghassan in the family house near the Great Mosque, *c.*1939

By 1939, some Muslim women of Aleppo had already begun to wear Western clothes and to uncover their face and hair. Amina al-Harriri was daughter of a leading pistachio merchant. She married Mohammed Zahed Tajeddin, a French teacher, and died in 1996. Most of her descendants now live outside Syria.

13. A costume ball at the Club d'Alep, 1952, formerly a Ghazeleh house
Every year a costume ball was held in the Club d'Alep, founded in 1945 and the main meeting place for the city's merchant elite.

14. Fête-Dieu Procession, 28 May 1964
Girls of the school of the Franciscaines Missionaires de Marie processing through the streets of the Aziziye quarter. Since the nineteenth century, Christian processions had been allowed on the streets of the mainly Muslim city of Aleppo.

the chief articles. Large caravans frequently arrive from Bagdad and Bassora, charged with coffee, which is carried round to the Persian gulf from Moccha, with the tobacco and cherry-tree pipes from Persia, and muslins, shawls, and other produces of India.

Besides the manufactures of Aleppo, and the productions of the surrounding country, which are sent to Europe by sea, three or four caravans, laden with merchandize, proceed annually through Anatolia to Constantinople. Pistachio nuts form no mean article of trade, being the chief produce of the adjacent territory, in the soil of which that tree particularly delights. Aleppo also maintains a commercial intercourse with Damascus, Antioch, Tripoli, Ladakia, and the towns on the East towards the Euphrates.

The last pestilence is supposed to have destroyed sixty thousand of the inhabitants.

The women of Aleppo are rather masculine, of brown complexions, and remarkable for indulging in the Sapphic affection.

The quarries which supplied the stone for the construction on the city, are not far removed from the Antioch gate. They are every way worthy remark. On both sides of a road, cut through the solid rock, are seen the openings of caverns, capable of giving shelter to a vast number of persons. From these again, which are tolerably light, open a number of other passages, in all directions, from the principal apartments. These I had neither time nor instruments to investigate; but the people of the place pretend that one of these passages goes to the castle, another to Antioch, &c. Traditions similar to which abound in every country, which presents any caverns natural or artificial.

The material is a soft stone or tufa, replete with petrified shells. It would appear that the artificers designed those quarries for some useful purpose, as they have not only left rough columns, and cut perpendicular shafts, which admit some portion of light, but the walls are hewn to a much greater degree of smoothness than is usually seen in quarries. It is certain they have afterwards been occupied, as marks of fire, mangers for horses, and even burial places, may be observed. In latter times, disbanded *dellis*, not being admitted into the city, have here fixed their abode, and become dangerous to passengers, whom they have robbed, and sometimes murdered.

There is a large burying-place without the city. Here I observed the tomb of an Englishman, dated 1613.

The dress of the people of Aleppo resembles that of Constantinople more than that of Egypt and southern Syria: both men and women, in rainy weather, wear a kind of wooden patten, which has no agreeable effect either on the eye or the ear.

The hire of a camel from Aleppo to Ladakia or Scanderoon, about sixty miles, was a century ago four piasters, thirty years ago eight piasters, and is at this time nineteen. The price of commodities is much changed in the course of not many years. But since the year 1716 it has increased in a tenfold proportion. I saw an authentic document, that the *ardeb* of rice at that time sold for eleven piasters; it now fetches one hundred and eighteen piasters. They at that time sold 185 rolls of bread, of a particular kind, for a piaster; they now only sell forty of the same kind for that sum. Meat is good and in plenty; it is sold for fifty paras the rotal, 720 drams, or about 4½d. a pound. There are no fish, save a few small eels, found in the *Coik*. Wine is very dear, none being produced in the neighbourhood. On the other articles of provision nothing remarkable occurs.

At Aleppo I first observed the practice of illuminating the mosques on Thursday night, to usher in the Mohammedan Sabbath; this is unknown at Kahira, and other cities of the South.

About this time, the beginning of June 1797, intelligence arrived, that the Pasha of Bagdad had sent a strong detachment of troops, to be joined by the Arabs friendly to the Porte, in repressing the incursions of *Abd-el-aziz ibn Meffoûd el-Wahhâbbé*, a rebel against the government, who by the rapid success of his arms, and his increasing followers, had lately grown formidable. This man, a native of *Nedjed*, respected among the Arabs for his age and wisdom, had two years before first made public his determination to resist the authority of the Porte. He has since collected a considerable body of men, but it is said they are only furnished with spears and swords. He pretends to a divine mission, and gives no quarter to those who oppose him. To invite Christians and Jews to his party, he only requires an annual capitation tax of three piasters and a half. Of the people under his jurisdiction, every owner of a house is obliged to serve in person or find a substitute; and, to encourage them, he divides the spoil into five parts; taking one himself, he gives two to the substitute and two to the principal, or if the latter serve he has four parts. It was supposed his views pointed to Mecca, which he had threatened to attack. His confession of faith is only – 'There is no God but God;' inferring, that a prophet, when dead, deserves no homage, and that of course to mention him in a creed, or in prayers, is absurd. He enjoins the absolute necessity of prayer, under the open canopy of heaven, and destroys all the mosques he can seize. Of the five dogmata of Mohammed, he admits alms, fasting, prayer, and ablution, but rejects pilgrimage. He denies the divine origin of the Korân, but prohibits the use of all liquors but water. Being advanced in age, he had taken care to secure the attachment of his followers to his son, who was generally his substitute in the field.

On the 11th of June set out from Aleppo for Antioch, where I arrived on the 14th. Part of the route is mountainous. We passed the Orontes at a ferry. Country cultivated with Hashîsh, a kind of flax.

Entered Antioch, now called Antáki, by *Bab-Bolûs*, the gate of St. Paul. The walls are extensive, but the houses are chiefly confined to one corner. Numerous towers flank the walls, which are strong and lofty, and run from the river Orontes, the southern boundary of the city, up to the summit of the mountain. There is a substantial bridge over the river, which winds through a fertile vale. A large castle on the mountain, now ruinous, commands an extensive prospect.

Antioch is governed by a *Mohassel*, who derives his appointment from Constantinople. He received me with great politeness, and desired me to make what researches I pleased.

The barley harvest was begun. The length of the plain of Antioch is about three leagues and a half, the width two leagues. The language is here generally Turkish.

It must be remarked with regard to Aleppo and Antioch, that the latter has by far the most convenient situation. The former has no navigable river, the land is little productive, and it is placed at a great distance from the sea. Antioch possesses every opposite advantage, except that of a navigable river, which however far exceeds the diminutive Coik; the air is superior to that of Aleppo, and it is within five hours of the sea. The mountain produces wine, which is sold cheap, and there is plenty of sea-fish. The mouth of the river forms a haven for small vessels, with very deep water.

Between Antioch and the sea, the ridge abounds in mulberry trees, which furnish a copious supply of silk, though not of the best kind.

From Antioch I set out for *Suadéa*, the ancient *Seleucia*, and port of Antioch, and only about four hours removed from it. It presents to the mind the idea of the immense labour used by its former possessors to render it convenient for traffic, which is now rendered useless, by the negligence of its present masters. The road from Antioch is pleasingly diversified by mountain and plain; yet to appearance the country is but thinly inhabited, though filled with all kinds of flowering and odoriferous plants, particularly myrtles, oleanders, and cyclamens. Having crossed four rapid and translucid streams, which descend into the Orontes, I passed the night with a hospitable native, in a garden of mulberries, which afforded support to his numerous family.

A large gate of Seleucia yet remains entire; it approaches to the Doric order. The rock near it has been excavated into various apartments. A part exists of the thick and substantial wall which defended Seleucia toward the sea. The port must have been commodious and secure, though but small, being formed by a mole of very large stones. Though the port be at present dry, the sand in the bottom appears not higher than the surface of the sea. A little to the North is a remarkable passage, cut in the rock, leading by a gentle descent, from the summit of the mountain towards the water. It is above six hundred common paces long, from thirty to fifty feet high, and about twenty broad. In the middle of it is a covered way, arched through the rock, but both the ends are open. A channel for water runs along the side, conveying the pure element down from the mountain to Seleucia. The whole rock above is full of artificial cavities, for what purpose does not appear. There is a Greek inscription on the South side of the cavern comprising, I believe, five lines. Having no glass, and the inscription being lofty, I could only discover the letters TETAP which form a part of the last line but one.

Returning towards the sea, I observed some catacombs. One of the chambers contains thirty niches for the dead, another fourteen. These catacombs are ornamented with pilasters, cornices, and mouldings.

Returned to Antioch, and on the following day set off for Aleppo. The Kûrds occasionally attack the caravans going between these two cities. The Turcomâns form another tribe of rovers; they generally pass the winter in the plains near Antioch, returning in the summer to Anatolia.

Chapter Nineteen

Travels in Syria and the Holy Land (1822)

John Lewis Burckhardt (1784–1817) was a Swiss explorer and scholar, born in Lausanne. In England in 1809 he was commissioned by the African Association to discover the source of the Niger. In order to learn Arabic and Islamic law, and to be able to pass as a Muslim, he lived in Aleppo in 1809–11. He dressed as a Muslim 'in the coarse cotton shirt and woollen abha of the country', took the name of Sheikh Ibrahim Ibn Abdallah, and, although his family denied it, may have converted to Islam. His knowledge of Arabic and the Koran is shown by his later journeys – he rediscovered Petra in the desert east of the Jordan in 1812, and Abu Simbel in Upper Egypt in 1813, and visited Mecca and Medina in 1814–15. While planning further travels, he died of dysentery in Cairo on 15 October 1817. His travel books, based on diaries and notes regularly sent back to England, were published after his death by the African Association.

APPENDIX NO. II

On the political division of Syria, and the recent changes in the Government of Aleppo.

The political division of Syria has not undergone any changes, since the time of de Volney.

The Pashaliks are five in number. To the pashalik of Aleppo belongs the government of Aintab, Badjazze, Alexandretta, and Antakia. Damascus comprehends Hebron, Jerusalem, Nablous, Bostra, Hums, and Hama. The Pashalik of Tripoli extends along the seacoast from Djebail to Latikia; that of Seide or Akka, from Djebail nearly to Jaffa, including the mountains inhabited by the Druses. The Pasha of Gaza governs in Jaffa and Gaza, and in the adjacent plains. The present Pasha of Damascus is at the same time Pasha of Tripoli, and therefore in possession of the greater half of Syria. The Pashalik of Gaza is at present annexed to that of Akka.

Such is the nominal division of Syria. But the power of the Porte in this country has been so much upon the decline, particularly since the time of Djezzar Pasha of Akka, that a number of petty independent chiefs have sprung up, who defy their sovereign. Badjazze, Alexandretta, and Antakia have each an independent Aga. Aintab, to the north of Aleppo, Edlip and Shogre, on the way from Aleppo to Latikia, have their own chiefs, and it was but last year that the Pasha of Damascus succeeded in subduing Berber, a formidable rebel, who had fixed his seat at Tripoli, and had maintained himself there for the last six years. The Pashas themselves follow the same practice; it is true that neither the Pasha of Damascus nor that of Akka has yet dared openly to erect the standard of rebellion; they enjoy all the benefits of the protection of the supreme government, but depend much more upon their own strength, than on the caprice of the Sultan, or on their intrigues in the seraglio for the continuance of their power. The policy of the Porte is to flatter and load with honours those whom she cannot ruin, and to wait for some lucky accident by which she may regain her power; but, above all, to avoid a formal rupture, which would only serve to expose her own weakness and to familiarize the Pashas and their subjects with the ideas of rebellion. The Pashas of Damascus and of Akka continue to be dutiful subjects of the Grand Signior in appearance; and they even send considerable sums of money to Constantinople, to ensure the yearly renewal of their offices. (The Pashaliks all over the Turkish dominions are given for the term of one year only, and at the beginning of the Mohammedan year, the Pashas receive their confirmation or dismissal.) The Agas of Aintab, Antakia, Alexandretta, Edlip, and Shogre, pay also for the renewal of their offices. There are a few chiefs who have completely thrown off the mask of subjection; Kutshuk Ali, the Lord of Badjazze openly declares his contempt of all orders from the Porte, plunders and insults the Sultan's officers, as well as all strangers passing through his mountains, and with a force of less than two hundred men, and a territory confined to the half ruined town of Badjazze, in the gulf of Alexandretta, and a few miles of the surrounding mountains, his father and himself have for the last thirty years defied all the attempts of the neighbouring Pashas to subdue them.

The inhabitants of Aleppo have been for several years past divided into two parties; the Sherifs (the real or pretended descendants of the Prophet), and the Janissaries. The former distinguish themselves by twisting a green turban round a small red cap, the latter wear high Barbary caps, with a turban of shawl, or white muslin, and a Khandjar, or long crooked knife in their girdles. There are few Turks in the city who have been able to keep aloof from both parties.

The Sherifs first showed their strength about forty years ago, during a tumult excited by their chiefs in consequence of a supposed insult received by Mr. Clarke, the then British Consul. Aleppo was governed by them in a disorderly manner for several years without a Pasha, until the Bey of Alexandretta, being appointed to the Pashalik, surprised the town and ordered all the chief Sherifs to be strangled. The Pasha, however, found his authority greatly limited by the influence which Tshelebi Effendi, an independent Aleppine grandee, had gained over his countrymen. The immense property of Tshelebi's family, added to his personal qualities, rendered his influence and power so great that during twenty years he obliged several Pashas who would not yield to his counsels and designs to quit the town. He never would accept of the repeated offers made by the Porte to raise him to the Pashalik. His interests were in some measure supported by the corps of Janissaries; who in Aleppo, as in other Turkish towns, constitute the regular military force of the Porte; but until that period their chiefs had been without the smallest weight in the management of public affairs. One of Tshelebi's household officers, Ibrahim Beg, had meanwhile been promoted, through the friends of his patron at Constantinople, to the first dignities in the town. He was made Mutsellim (vice governor), and Mohassel (chief custom house officer), and after the death of Tshelebi, his power devolved upon Ibrahim. This was in 1786.

Kussa Pasha, a man of probity and talents, was sent at that time as Pasha to Aleppo. Being naturally jealous of Ibrahim Beg's influence, he endeavoured to get possession of his person, by ordering him to be detained during a visit, made by Ibrahim to compliment the Pasha upon his arrival, for a debt which Ibrahim owed to a foreign merchant, who had preferred his complaints to the Pasha's tribunal. Ibrahim paid the debt, and was no sooner out of the Pasha's immediate reach, than he engaged Ahmed Aga (one of the present Janissary chiefs), to enter with him into a formal league against Kussa. The Janissaries, together with Ibrahim's party, attacked the Pasha's troops; who after several days' fighting, were driven out of the town, and Ibrahim was soon afterwards named Pasha of three tails, and for the first time Pasha of Aleppo. From that period (1788–89) may be dated the power of the Janissaries. Ibrahim had been the cause of their rising into consideration, but he soon found that their party was acquiring too much strength; he therefore deemed it necessary to countenance the Sherifs, and being a man of great talents, he governed and plundered the town, by artfully opposing the two parties to each other. In the year 1789, Ibrahim was nominated to the Pashalik of Damascus. Sherif Pasha, a man of ordinary capacity, being sent to Aleppo, the Janissaries soon usurped the powers of government.

At the time of the French invasion of Egypt, the intrigues of Djezzar Pasha of Akka drove Ibrahim from his post at Damascus, and he was obliged to follow the Grand Vizir's army into Egypt. When after the campaign of Egypt the Grand Vizir with the remains of his army, was approaching Aleppo upon his return to Constantinople, Ibrahim conceived hopes of regaining his lost seat at Aleppo. Through the means of his son Mohammed Beg, then Mohassel, the Janissaries were persuaded that the Vizir had evil intentions against them, forged letters were produced to that effect, and the whole body of Janissaries left the town before the Vizir's arrival in its neighbourhood. Their flight gave Ibrahim the sought for opportunity to represent the fugitives to the Vizir as rebels afraid to meet their master's presence; they were shortly afterwards, by a Firman from the Porte, formally proscribed as rebels, and the killing of any of them who should enter the territory of Aleppo was declared lawful. They had retired to Damascus, Latikia, Tripoli, and the mountains of the Druses, and they spared no money to get the edict of their exile rescinded. After a tedious bargain for the price of their pardon, they succeeded at last in obtaining it, on condition of paying one hundred thousand piastres into the Sultan's treasury. Ibrahim Pasha, who had in the meanwhile regained the Pashalik of Aleppo, was to receive that sum from them, and he had so well played his game, that the Janissaries still thought him their secret friend. The principal chiefs, trusting to Ibrahim's assurances, came to the town for the purpose of paying down the money; they were a few days afterwards arrested, and it was generally believed that Ibrahim would order them the same night to be strangled. In Turkey, however, there are always hopes as long as the purse is not exhausted. The prisoners engaged Mohammed, Ibrahim's beloved son, to intercede in their favour; they paid him for that service one thousand zequins in advance, and promised as much more: and he effectually extorted from his father a promise not to kill any of them. It is said that Ibrahim foretold his son that the time would come when he would repent of his intercession. A short time afterwards Ibrahim was nominated a second time to the Pashalik of Damascus, which became vacant by Djezzar's death, in 1804. His prisoners were obliged to follow him to Damascus; from whence they found means to open a correspondence with the Emir Beshir, the chief of the Druses, and to prevail upon him to use all his interest with Ibrahim to effect their deliverance. Ibrahim stood at that time in need of the Emir's friendship; he had received orders from the Porte to seize upon Djezzar's treasures at Akka, and to effect this the co-operation of the Druse chief was absolutely necessary. Upon the Emir's reiterated applications, the prisoners were at last liberated.

When Ibrahim Pasha removed to Damascus, he procured the Pashalik of Aleppo for his son Mohammed Pasha, a man who possesses in a high degree the qualification so necessary in a delegate of the Porte, of understanding how to plunder his subjects. The chief of a Sherif family, Ibn Hassan Aga Khalas (who has since entered into the corps of the Janissaries, and is now one of their principal men), was the first who resolved to oppose open force to his measures; he engaged at first only seven or eight other families to join him, and it was with this feeble force that the rebellion broke out which put an end to the Pasha's government. The confederates began by knocking down the Pasha's men in the streets wherever they met them, Janissaries soon assembled from all quarters to join Hassan's party; and between two or three hundred Deli Bashi or regular troops of the Pasha were massacred in the night in their own habitations, to which the rebels found access from the neighbouring terraces or flat roofs. Still the Pasha's troops would have subdued the insurgents had it not been for the desperate bravery of Hassan Aga.

After several months daily fighting in the streets, in which the Pasha's troops had thrown up entrenchments, want of food began to be sensibly felt in the part of the city which his adherents occupied near the Serai, a very spacious building now in ruins. He came therefore to the resolution of abandoning the city. At Mohammed's request a Tartar was sent, from Constantinople, with orders enjoining him to march against Berber, governor of Tripoli, who had been declared a rebel. Having thus covered the disgrace of his defeat, he marched out of Aleppo in the end of 1804, but instead of proceeding to Tripoli, he established his head quarters at Sheikh Abou Beker, a monastery of Derwishes situated upon an elevation only at one mile's distance from Aleppo, where he recruited his troops and prepared himself to besiege the town. His affairs, however, took a more favourable turn upon the arrival of a Kapidgi Bashi or officer of the Porte from Constantinople, who carried with him the most positive orders that Mohammed Pasha should remain governor of Aleppo, and be acknowledged as such by the inhabitants, The Kapidgi's persuasions, as well as the Sultan's commands, which the Janissaries did not dare openly to disobey, brought on a compromise, in consequence of which the Pasha re-entered the city. So far he had gained his point, but he soon found himself in his palace without friends or influence; the Janissaries were heard to declare that every body who should visit him would be looked upon as a spy; on Fridays alone, the great people paid him their visit in a body. The place meanwhile was governed by the chiefs of the Janissaries and the Sherifs. At length the Pasha succeeded, by a secret nightly correspondence, to detach the latter from the Janissaries, who were gaining the ascendancy. The Sherifs are the natural supporters of government in this country; most of the villages round Aleppo were then in their possession, they command the landed interests, all the Aleppo grandees of ancient families, and all the Ulemas and Effendis belong to their body, and the generality of them have received some education, while out of one hundred Janissaries, there are scarcely five who know how to read or to write their own names. The civil war now broke out afresh, and Mohammed had again the worst of it. After remaining three months in the town, he returned to his former encampment at Sheikh Abou Beker, from whence he assisted his party in the town who had taken possession of the castle and several mosques. This warfare lasted nearly two years without any considerable losses on either side. The Sherifs were driven out of the mosques, but defended themselves in the castle.

Generally, the people of Aleppo, Janissaries as well as Sherifs, are a cowardly race. The former never ventured to meet the Pasha's troops on the outside of their walls, the latter did not once sally forth from the castle, but contented themselves with firing into the town, and principally against Bankousa, a quarter exclusively inhabited by Janissaries. The Pasha on his side would have ordered his Arnaouts to take the town by assault, had not his own party been jealous of his military power, and apprehensive of the fury of an assaulting army, for which reason they constantly endeavoured to prevent any vigorous attack, promising that they would alone bring the enemy to terms. After nearly two years' fighting, during which time a considerable part of the town was laid in ruins, the Pasha with the Sherifs were on the point of succeeding, and compelling the Janissaries to surrender. The chiefs of the Janissaries had applied to the European Consuls for their mediation between them and the Pasha, the conditions of their surrender were already drawn up, and in a few days more their power in Aleppo would probably have been for ever annihilated by a treacherous infraction of the capitulation, when, by a fortunate mistake, a Tartar, sent from Constantinople to Mohammed, entered the town, instead of taking his packet to Sheikh Abou Beker; the Janissaries opened the dispatches, and found them to contain a Firman, by which Mohammed Pasha was recalled from his Pashalik of Aleppo. This put an end to the war; Mohammed dismissed the greater part of his troops and retired: the Janissaries came to a compromise with the Sherifs in the castle, and have since that time been absolute masters of the city.

I cannot omit mentioning that during the whole of the civil war, the persons and property of the Franks were rigidly respected. It sometimes happened that parties of Sherifs and Janissaries skirmishing in the Bazars, left off firing by common consent, when a Frank was seen passing, and that the firing from the Minarets ceased, when Franks passed over their flat roofs from one house to another. The Janissaries have this virtue in the eyes of the Franks, that they are not in the smallest degree fanatical; the character of a Sherif is quite the contrary, and whenever religious disputes happen, they are always excited and supported by some greenhead.

Since the removal of Mohammed Pasha the Porte has continued to nominate his successors; but the name of Pasha of Aleppo is now nothing more than a vain title. His first successor was Alla eddin Pasha, a near relation of Sultan Selim: then Waledin Pasha, Othman Pasha

Darukly, Ibrahim Pasha, a third time, and the present governor Seruri Mohammed Pasha. Except the last, who is now in the Grand Vizir's camp near Constantinople, they have all resided at Aleppo, but they occupied the Serai more like state prisoners than governors. They never were able to carry the most trifling orders into effect, without feeing in some way or other the chiefs of the Ja[n]issaries to grant their consent.

The corps of Janissaries, or the Odjak of Aleppo, was formerly divided, as in other Turkish towns, into companies or Ortas, but since the time of their getting into power, they have ceased to submit to any regular discipline: they form a disorderly body of from three to four thousand men, and daily increase their strength and number by recruits from the Sherifs. Those who possess the greatest riches, and whose family and friends are the most numerous, are looked upon as their chiefs, though they are unable to exercise any kind of discipline. Of these chiefs there are at present six principal ones, who have succeeded in sharing the most lucrative branches of the revenue, and what seems almost incredible, they have for the last six years preserved harmony amongst themselves; Hadji Ibrahim Ibn Herbely is at this moment the richest and most potent of them all.

The legal forms of Government have not been changed, and the Janissaries outwardly profess to be the dutiful subjects of the Porte. The civil administration is nominally in the hands of the Mutsellim, who is named by the Pasha and confirmed by the Porte: the Kadi presides in the court of justice, and the Mohassel or chief custom house officer is allowed to perform his functions in the name of his master, but the Mutsellim dares not enforce any orders from the Porte nor the Kadi decide any law suit of importance, without being previously sure of the consent of some of the chief Janissaries. The revenue which the grand Signior receives at this moment from Aleppo is limited to the Miri, or general landtax, which the Janissaries themselves pay, the Kharatsh or tribute of the Christians and Jews, and the income of the custom house, which is now rented at the yearly rate of eighty thousand piastres. Besides these there are several civil appointments in the town, which are sold every year at Constantinople to the highest bidder: the Janissaries are in the possession of the most lucrative of them, and remit regularly to the Porte the purchase money. The outward decorum which the Janissaries have never ceased to observe towards the Porte is owing to their fear of offending public opinion, so as to endanger their own security. The Porte, on the other hand, has not the means of subduing these rebels, established as their power now is, without calling forth all her resources and ordering an army to march against them, from Constantinople. The expense of such an enterprize would hardly be counterbalanced by the profits of its success; for the Janissaries, pushed to extremities, would leave the town and find a secure retreat for themselves and their treasures in the mountains of the Druses: both parties therefore endeavour to avoid an open rupture; it is well known that the chief Janissaries send considerable presents to Constantinople to appease their master's anger, and provided the latter draws supplies for his pressing wants, no matter how or from whence, the insults offered to his supreme authority are easily overlooked.

The Janissaries chiefly exercise their power with a view to the filling of their purses. Every inhabitant of Aleppo, whether Turk or Christian, provided he be not himself a Janissary, is obliged to have a protector among them to whom he applies in case of need, to arrange his litigations, to enforce payment from his creditors, and to protect him from the vexations and exactions of other Janissaries. Each protector receives from his client a sum proportionate to the circumstances of the client's affairs. It varies from twenty to two thousand piastres a year, besides which, whenever the protector terminates an important business to the client's wishes, he expects some extraordinary reward. If two protectors happen to be opposed to each other on account of their clients, the more powerful of the two sometimes carries the point, or if they are equal in influence, they endeavour to settle the business by compromise, in such a way as to give to justice only half its due. Those Janissaries, who have the greatest number of clients are of course the richest, and command the greatest influence. But these are not the only means which the Janissaries employ to extort money. They monopolize the trade of most of the articles of consumption (which have risen in consequence, to nearly double the price which they bore six years ago), as well as of several of the manufactures of Aleppo; upon others they levy heavy taxes; in short their power is despotic and oppressive; yet they have hitherto abstained from making, like the Pashas, avanies upon individuals by open force, and it is for that reason that the greater part of the Aleppines do not wish for the return of a Pasha. Though the Janissaries extort from the public, by direct and indirect means, more than the Pashas ever did by their avanies, each individual discharges the burthen imposed upon him more readily, because he is confident that it insures the remainder of his fortune; in the Pasha's time, living was cheaper, and regular taxes not oppressive; but the Pasha would upon the most frivolous pretexts order a man of property to be thrown into prison and demand the sacrifice of one fourth of his fortune to grant him his deliverance. Notwithstanding the immense income of the chief Janissaries, they live poorly, without indulging themselves in the usual luxuries of Turks – women and horses. Their gains are hoarded in gold coin, and it is easy to calculate, such is the publicity with which all sort of business is conducted, that the yearly income of several of them cannot amount to less than thirty or forty thousand pounds sterling.

It is necessary to have lived for some time among the Turks, and to have experienced the mildness and peacefulness of their character, and the sobriety and regularity of their habits, to conceive it possible that the inhabitants of a town like Aleppo, should continue to live for years without any legal master, or administration of justice, protected only by a miserable guard of police, and yet that the town should be a safe and quiet residence. No disorders, or nightly tumults occur; and instances of murder and robbery are extremely rare. If serious quarrels sometimes happen, it is chiefly among the young Janissaries heated with brandy and amorous passion, who after sunset fight their rivals at the door of some prostitute. This precarious security is however enjoyed only within the walls of the city; the whole neighbourhood of Aleppo is infested by obscure tribes of Arab and Kurdine robbers, who through the negligence of the Janissaries, acquire every day more insolence and more confidence in the success of their enterprises. Caravans of forty or fifty camels have in the course of last winter been several times attacked and plundered at five hundred yards from the city gate, not a week passes without somebody being ill-treated and stripped in the gardens near the town; and the robbers have even sometimes taken their night's rest in one of the suburbs of the city, and there sold their cheaply acquired booty. In the time of Ibrahim Pasha, the neighbourhood of Aleppo to the distance of four or five hours, was kept in perfect security from all hostile inroads of the Arabs, by the Pasha's cavalry guard of Deli Bashi. But the Janissaries are very averse from exposing themselves to danger; there is moreover no head among them to command, no common purse to pay the necessary expences, nor any individual to whose hands the public money might be trusted.

Chapter Twenty

Travels among the Arab Tribes inhabiting the Countries East of Syria and Palestine (1825)

*James Silk Buckingham (1786–1855) was a traveller, sailor and radical jour-
nalist. He spent much of 1815–16 travelling in the Ottoman Empire and Persia.
In Syria he lived among Arab tribes, explored the ruined towns and cities of the
Hauran south of Damascus, visited Lady Hester Stanhope and in May 1816
stayed with John Barker in Aleppo. He then moved on to India, but in 1823
his criticisms of the East India Company led to his expulsion. He subsequently
became a reforming MP and President of the London Temperance League.*

CHAPTER XXVIII
STAY AT ALEPPO, AND RECORD OF
TRANSACTIONS THERE

On entering Aleppo we proceeded through many streets, until we
reached the house of Mr. Barker, the British consul here, where we
alighted; and going up into the ante-room I desired the janissary to

announce my arrival. There was a delay, and enquiries, and messages, for at least half an hour, which I did not at all understand, until I was at length desired to walk into the hall of audience. Here I was received with a very marked coldness, which I could not but notice; my questions were replied to with studied brevity, my observations often scrutinized, and, in short, the treatment such as could leave me no longer in doubt of there being some cause for it, of which I was entirely ignorant. A younger brother of Mr. Barker, whom I had known at Smyrna, in the service of Mr. Wilkinson, was in the house at the time, but purposely absent, and all was too plain to be misunderstood. After a cup of coffee had been taken, the explanation came. Mr. Barker observed, that having no personal knowledge of me or of my family, and my not having been mentioned to him in any way by any of his correspondents or friends, he had refused acceptance to a bill which I had drawn on him for 1000 piastres from Damascus.

The circumstances under which that transaction took place were these: – I had left Alexandria with fifty sequins in gold, and a letter of credit furnished me by Mr. Lee, for any sum which might be necessary for my journey to India, addressed to Mr. Barker here. In my attempt to get across the Desert direct to Bagdad, that money brought with me was all expended, and on my arrival at Damascus I had even a debt to discharge to Georgis, the man who was my guide from Nazareth to Assalt, and from thence up through the Hauran. Having no duplicate of my letter of credit, and conceiving there would be always greater risk of its loss while in other hands than while in my own, as well as that, if so lost, my distress would be irretrievable, I forwarded to Mr. Barker a copy of that letter, at the same time advising him of my having drawn the sum in question, not doubting but that he would accept it. I had supplied my wants therefrom, and had now come safe to Aleppo on the remainder, where, for the first time, I heard of the bill being refused payment, and protested.

The motives assigned by Mr. Barker for such a step were these: – He said, upon the face of the thing itself, it appeared highly improbable, that a merchant from his cradle, as Mr. Lee was, would give an unlimited letter of credit to any man; that it was also usual in such transactions for a letter of advice to be forwarded at the same time by some other hand, limiting the sum, or making such other observations as might be thought necessary; but that, in the present case, no letter of any sort had reached him (Mr. Barker) from Alexandria, since the date of this supposed, or pretended, letter of credit, of which I had sent a copy; that in all the correspondence of Mr. Lee, of Colonel Misset, of

contained, from one of whose very name I was before ignorant, afforded me some faint consolation, inasmuch as it reminded me, that though thus treated as a villain of the darkest cast, and denied the common rites of hospitality, from one of whom I had a right to claim assistance and protection, I had not myself been entirely insensible to the common duties of charity towards the poor and friendless stranger.

My afternoon was passed in the dark hovel to which I had been driven, yet here I was not suffered to be at rest, nor enjoy even the retirement which I courted. The khan below was filled with Arabs, and Turkish soldiers, as passengers through the town; and in the gallery above, in one corner of which my room was, were shoemakers, silkthread spinners, and other mechanics, who, not yet being wealthy enough to rent a better station, pursued their respective labours here in chambers similar to my own, for which the highest pay was three piastres per month, or about sixpence sterling per week.

All these having learnt, from the Consul's servants who conducted me here, that I was an Englishman, and judging from my horses and servant that I was a stranger and a traveller on my journey, naturally expressed their surprise at my being turned away from his house, where all other Englishmen that they had before seen were always kindly and honourably received. Many of these forced themselves into my room, and sitting beside me asked a thousand questions; a staring crowd was gathered round the door, and every one pointed their finger at me as a suspected character; by far the greater part, however, openly pronounced me an impostor, saying either that I was not an Englishman, as pretended, or that if so, I must be some criminal escaped from my country, and arrested by the Consul, since they considered my being conducted here by his people, as a consignment to a sort of prison; more particularly as one or other of these attendants came frequently to the khan, with a view, perhaps, to watch my motions, and prevent my making an escape. My refusal to enter into the explanations demanded of me, my having the appearance and manners of a Mussulman, with a full beard, and speaking the Arabic language, were all so many received confirmations of my guilt; and the ultimate general impression was, either that I had been exiled from my country for crime, or had forcibly escaped from condemnation there, and sought refuge and protection in becoming a renegado, abandoning my faith, and giving myself up to the Sultan as a convert to Islam.

My situation was more full of misery than can be described; and even the consolations of innocence and integrity, sweet as they may be, and as they are, under most circumstances of persecution, were scarcely sufficient to outweigh all the complicated evils of contempt, disdain, and public scorn, to which I was condemned.

Wednesday, May 15. 1816. – My night was almost as void of repose as the preceding one, and from the same causes, a foul and suffocating air, and crawling myriads of vermin, evils in themselves of but a temporary and even trivial kind when encountered in the common course of one's way; but here augmented more than a hundred fold, by the consideration that I was suffering them as a punishment for supposed crime: – so true is it that the lightest chains of iron, which fasten the captive to his cell, hang more weightily upon his neck than far heavier ones of gold would do, if worn like those of Daniel, as an emblem and a pledge of honour.

I remained within, during the whole of the day, and closed my door for greater privacy, preferring all the inconveniencies of darkness and a stagnant atmosphere, to the gazing stare of those who came to regard me as a beast of prey, secured to his den, after escaping and preying on his species. My appetite had now entirely failed; my health was beginning to be affected by languor, and I was alternately tormented by impatience for the arrival of my baggage, and by a longing desire to breathe again the free and hospitable air of the Desert.

As I was perfectly alone, and without occupation, I beguiled the time by committing to writing, in these preceding pages, the circumstances of my reception, my treatment, &c. They form no part, properly speaking, of such notes as are devoted to the collection of new information regarding the countries through which my route lay; but, since they show to what mortifications one may be subject in the way, and that, too, when least of all expected, the record of them may not, perhaps, be without their use, either to myself or to others, whom it may be my lot and duty to advise.

Aleppo, May 16 to 26. – During the ten days included within these dates, my stay having been prolonged for that period at Aleppo, from the difficulty of finding a safe and fit opportunity for proceeding, I was as much overwhelmed with the kindness and hospitality of Mr. Barker, as I had been before subjected to undeserved indignity and mortification by his unnecessary harshness and severity. To render his character ample justice, it is necessary to place the acts alluded to on record, in doing which I shall observe the strictest possible impartiality.

[…]

To repair, as soon as possible, the evil of any impressions that might have gone abroad respecting me among the Consuls of other European nations at Aleppo, Mr. Barker proposed that we should without delay commence a round of ceremonious visits to them all; which, as they did not live far apart from each other, and these visits never occupied more than half an hour each, might be easily accomplished. I readily consented to this proposal, and Mr. Bankes accompanying us, we paid our personal respects to all the principal Consuls in the course of the day, and the secondary ones on the following.

I was now removed to Mr. Barker's country-house, at the distance of a few miles only from Aleppo, where Mr. Bankes and myself were admitted as members of the family, each having also a separate apartment in the Consular-house in town, and each being treated with all the respect, kindness, and honour that we could wish; Mr. Barker, and all his family, appearing to do every thing in their power to obliterate the painful impressions of the past, and to make the present as agreeable as possible, without neglecting the exertion of their efforts to procure for me a safe and easy journey, through the rest of my way.

Mr. Bankes having heard of the death of some rich relative, by whose will he had been bequeathed a large property, in addition to his already ample fortune, had determined on hastening home; and accordingly made arrangements for visiting Palmyra from hence, and returning direct to Aleppo, from whence he proposed going with all speed to England, while my journey had to be still extended farther eastward, even to India. Mr. Bankes was very desirous that I should accompany him in his journey to Palmyra, as we had always contemplated the probability of our going there together; in the belief that Arab guides might be found at Aleppo, who would take any person bent on the journey from thence to Baghdad, across the Desert, in eight or ten days at the utmost. Our enquiries were very assiduously directed after such a guide; but the troubled state of the whole Desert, south and east of Palmyra, then in commotion from the wars of the Wahabees, was such, that no one could be found who would venture to go beyond Palmyra, and not many, indeed, who felt disposed to go even so far. At length, however, a party or escort was got together for this purpose. Mr. Bankes again urged me to accompany him in the excursion; but, although it would not have taken more than ten days at the farthest to go and return to Aleppo, I resisted this highly tempting opportunity of visiting the most attractive ruins in the world, without the shadow of a hope of my ever having it in my power to repair this loss at any future period, merely from a sense of duty, which induced me to think that as my journey to India had been already so much delayed by circumstances altogether beyond my power to obviate or controul, I should not willingly add to that delay by any interruptions beyond the many that were still likely to occur without my agency or consent, in the future progress of my way. I accordingly yielded to this conviction, and thereby lost an opportunity of seeing Palmyra, which was never likely again to be enjoyed.

[...]

After parting with Mr. Bankes, all my attention was directed to securing a safe journey from Aleppo to Baghdad, in which Mr. Barker rendered me every assistance that I could desire. Through his influence, principally, a respectable merchant of Moosul, who had halted at Aleppo on his return from a pilgrimage to Mecca to purchase goods, and was about to return to his native city with a large caravan, consented, for a moderate sum, to take me under his protection as one of his party; enjoining only a certain condition on my part, that I should conceal the fact of my being an Englishman or Christian from all but himself and his immediate dependants; and that I should conform in every respect to whatever rules he might think proper to lay down for the guidance of all the individuals of his party during the journey. To this I readily consented. I was to provide my own horse and baggage for the way; but as I could now speak the Arabic language pretty fluently, neither servant nor interpreter were needed; and I had the prospect before me of as safe and pleasant a journey as can well be expected in a caravan made up of all sorts of characters, and passing through so unsettled and uncivilized a country.

The day of our departure was fixed for the 26th, and I employed the short time that remained before this should arrive in writing letters to my friends in Europe, and in completing all the preparations that I thought necessary for the journey. The circumstances of my stay at Aleppo had been extremely unfavourable to the indulgence of my usual habit of visiting every place of interest, and preserving daily notes of what I saw and heard; from which alone faithful pictures of persons, places, or things, can be afterwards drawn. My confinement in the khan had so depressed my spirits as to render me absolutely incompetent to do more than preserve a narrative of that confinement itself. And after my removal to Mr. Barker's house, every successive day, from morning to night, was one entire round of entertainment and pleasure, excursions to gardens, visits of ceremony, evening parties, &c. which rendered it impossible either to read, write, or reflect with advantage, so that these duties were necessarily abandoned. In consequence of these obstacles, I preserved fewer recollections of Aleppo than of any other place in which I had passed so many days; but, as this city has been much more frequently described than any other in Syria, and has had even a separate history of it written by Doctor Russell, who resided there as an English physician for many years, it is of the less importance. I can only say that it appeared to me one of the best built of all the cities of the East that I had yet seen; and though a considerable distance from the sea, it has a greater number of European residents, and these all enjoying greater freedom, than any of the larger cities subject to Turkish government, excepting only Constantinople, Smyrna, and Alexandria. The native population appeared also more actively happy, and in better condition, than the subjects of irresponsible despots usually are.

The character of the present governor was sufficient to account for all this. Though possessing unlimited power, like all his predecessors, it had been retained in the family of his immediate ancestors for several years back, and he wished to transmit it to his children. He silently acknowledged, therefore, the influence of public opinion, and thought it not derogatory to his dignity to consult the welfare of his subjects in most of the measures that he pursued. The result was increased happiness to them, and increased popularity and security to himself; and, though far short of the freedom which men ought to enjoy, the condition of the people at Aleppo appeared to me to be more favourable than in any other part of Syria, because their industry was less taxed, and their governor was more liberal and more enlightened than Turkish rulers in general.

The continuation of this comparative state of happiness depended, however, entirely on the continued life or continued disposition of the individual then at the head of affairs. Securities for good government there were absolutely none. The laws were uncertain and unknown; the people had no share whatever in the administration of their own concerns; and if the present pasha, from caprice, or evil disposition, should determine on taking off the heads of the most innocent individuals in the city, there was no power that could prevent the indulgence of his cruelty. Such are the blessings of absolute and irresponsible despotism!

Chapter Twenty One

Narrative of a Tour through Some Parts of the Turkish Empire (1829)

*John **Fuller** travelled from Apulia to Greece, Constantinople, Egypt and Syria in 1818. Little is known about him. He admitted in his preface that 'The countries of the East have been of late years so much visited and so often described, that they are, or may be sufficiently known; and a new publication on the subject may well be thought superfluous.' Nevertheless this privately printed book, with no mention of the author's name, is 560 pages long. He concludes with the reflection that 'A fertile soil, a genial climate and a bright sunshine may produce much individual happiness even in those countries where Trial by Jury is unknown and the writ of Habeas Corpus runneth not.' He was in Aleppo in 1820.*

CHAPTER XVI
ANTIOCH.–ALEPPO.–LATAKIA

About the middle of the next day we reached Aleppo. The approach to that city is striking, from the wildness and solitude which reign around it. It stands in a slight hollow among wide open downs, and scarcely a tree is to be seen except in the gardens, which skirt several little streams at no great distance from the walls. It is, or rather was (for since I was there it has been almost entirely destroyed by an earthquake), more substantially built than any city which I saw in the Turkish empire, the houses being mostly of stone. They had terraced roofs, and arches here and there thrown across the streets, communicating from the terrace of one house to that of another. The Franks occupied several large khans in the neighbourhood of the bazar, consisting of a number of houses built round a spacious quadrangle. When they were more numerous at Aleppo, each nation had its respective khan, which still retained the name of the English, the French, the Dutch khan, and so on, though no longer exclusively occupied by the subjects of those countries. The European commerce of Aleppo declined with the progress of navigation, as the voyage round the Cape of Good Hope became more easy and expeditious. Its internal trade had also of late years much diminished, from the general impoverishment of the surrounding country; and the inhabitants, dispirited by the late rebellion and siege, were full of gloomy forebodings, and predicted that the city would soon fall into utter decay, and become, like Palmyra, a heap of ruins in the Desert, – a prediction which has been accomplished by the hand of Nature more speedily than they anticipated.

As yet, however, Aleppo was by far the most cheerful place in Syria; the Franks were numerous, lived very sociably among themselves, and were very polite to strangers. They retained much of the ceremony of the old school; and at first receiving or returning their visits, it was necessary to be tutored by some experienced practitioner as to the precise form and number of bows and congés which were due to the degree of the person or the importance of the occasion. Mr. Barker, the English consul, was at this time absent; but his younger brother, who acted as his agent, was exceedingly assiduous in what was now, I believe, the most important duty of the office – attention to his wandering fellow-countrymen. I resided with Mr. Masyck the Dutch consul, a very agreeable and intelligent man. He was a native of Aleppo, and had scarcely ever quitted the place of his birth: but he had a knowledge of life seldom to be found even among those who have had a more extensive field of observation; spoke fluently five or six languages, and had an inexhaustible fund of entertaining anecdotes with regard to Oriental affairs. In early life he had mixed more with the higher classes of the Mahometan inhabitants, than Franks in general are in the habit of doing; he wore their dress, and had acquired much of their tranquil philosophy and their dignity of appearance and manners.

The Jews at this time enjoyed great consideration at Aleppo, and were exempted from many of those injuries and indignities which the belief that they are under the displeasure of Heaven has afforded men a convenient pretence for inflicting on them. This security they chiefly owed to the powerful family of Picciotto, who were strong in foreign protection, and whose wealth enabled them to hold under pecuniary obligations many of the great Turks of Aleppo, a notoriously prodigal race. The head of the family I have before mentioned as living in a sort of monastic retirement at Tabaria: the elder son Don Ezra was Austrian consul, and the Russian and Prussian consulships were held by two younger brothers. From all these gentlemen I received very great civility and attention during my stay, and frequently went to their houses, especially on the day of their sabbath, when they received visits of ceremony. On these occasions the ladies of the family, some of whom were very pretty, made their appearance in their best dresses, which, with a few occasional variations, may be given as a specimen of the general costume of the wealthier classes throughout the empire. On their heads they wear a shawl turban studded with pearls and precious stones, with festoons of pearls hanging down on each side the face. On the bosom the under garment only appears, over which is worn a sort of gown called an *antari* or *compaz*, made straight to the shape, so as just to meet in front, and when accidentally parted, to show a thin gauze tunic and loose rose-coloured trowsers underneath. It has long hanging sleeves, and the edges are sometimes curiously embroidered in different colours. Over the *compaz* is a vest of rich stuff or silk coming down a little below the knees, and with sleeves cut off at the elbows, which is sometimes lined with fur, and forms a pelisse, A shawl is tied negligently round the figure below the waist, with a bow and ends depending on the left side. From the waist, which is very short, hangs a double row of gold coins, sometimes reaching nearly to the ground. The bracelets are of gold chains. The hair is cut off quite square on the forehead, with a long tress hanging down on each side, and is wove behind into numerous plaits, which cover the whole of the back, and are tipped at the end with gold coins. Thus attired, these fair Jewesses sat on their divan to receive their guests, each with a Persian *nargillay* in her hand. Smoking is almost universally practised by the Aleppine ladies, and the greatest compliment that they can pay you is to transfer the pipe from their own lips to yours.

Chapter Twenty Two

The Ansaryii (or Assassins), with Travels in the Further East in 1850–51 (1851)

Lt. the Hon. Frederick Walpole R.N. *(1822–76), later MP for North Norfolk, was third son of the third Earl of Orford and of Mary Fawkener, whose grandfather Sir Everard Fawkener had been a merchant in Aleppo in 1716–25. He visited Aleppo in 1850–1 when he was exploring the coast of Syria, home to members of the Alawi and Ismaili sects, on the grounds that it was the only 'wild part [...] never before visited by Europeans'.*

CHAPTER XIII

I passed several khans, the first halt without the walls of the traveller who wishes to start ere the sun rises the following day. Passed the Koeyk in a deep gulley, the river of Aleppo, and reached the outside of the city. I was directed to skirt along the walls, which, though shaken and ruined, are a beautiful specimen of their style. Entering, the streets struck me as cleaner, and the houses which are built of stone, finer than those of any Eastern city I have seen; and finding my way to the convent, I was kindly received by some friends whose acquaintance I had made before. My companion arrived some hours afterwards; but our baggage not till late the following morning.

We were unable to procure lodgings in the convent, but at last were put up at the house of the consul's dragoman's sister. Her husband was a Constantinople Italian, dressed in the native dress, and more Arab than any thing else. I can speak warmly of the kindness we met; every attention was paid us during our stay; but I would advise any future traveller to make an arrangement before hand, as we paid rather dearer than we should have done at the Clarendon, and our table, rooms, &c., were execrable – a bad ad-mixture of Anglo-Franko, Italian, Arabic.

At Aleppo the mode of life, the habits of the people, – all induces a perfect idleness. Days were dozed, smoked, lounged away imperceptibly, and we could not muster resolution enough to prepare for the road, to exchange the soft divan and softer company, the perfect kief and undisturbed repose, for the saddle, the sun, the glare, the toil, and the fatigues of the road.

It, indeed, is a listless day made; where, sooth to say,
No living wight could work, nor cared to play.

We idled away the long morning, for all rose early; paid visits till eve, then made kief till late at night. At this time my Arabic was very scanty, so I was unable fairly to judge of the truth of the Arabic saying, 'Wit was born in Egypt, pointed at Damascus, died at Aleppo.' But the romantic dress, the Eastern manners, all were enough to enchant one already in love with every thing Oriental. I took a walk to the outside of the town to the castle: it is built on a lofty mound, the front of which is faced with stones, well built. The whole has a fine and noble appearance.

The bazaars are finer than those of most Eastern towns; many have arcades over the buildings, which are lofty and well built. The streets struck me as finer and the exterior of the houses better built, as I have before said, than any I have seen in the East. Here and there are the picturesque fountains so peculiarly Eastern, with their pious inscriptions. To the natives who constantly drink water, this must be a great boon.

The present Pasha has placed the cleansing of the street department under the Frank military officer, and he energetically puts his power in force. Yesterday as I passed, he was, much to their disgust, compelling each person to cleanse the street before his door.

The day following my arrival being Sunday, I proceeded to the house of the American missionary to attend the service. It was Presbyterian; and though fondly wedded to the forms and creed of my own loved mother Church, there was much comfort in thus meeting with sincere Christians, and lifting up together humble prayers in a heathen land. The not kneeling seems a cold form of adoration, and in extempore prayers the preacher, unless singularly gifted, must grow vague and wandering, using repetitions. The mission here bides its time, and perhaps I may say nothing has yet been done by them. It is invidious to speak of individuals, but those in Aleppo seemed well-meaning and earnest in their calling; quiet, gentlemanly, and well informed – in fact, much what missionaries ought to be.

We also made the acquaintance of several Hungarians: there were, I think, above ninety resident at Aleppo. They seemed very discontented, and censured each other's conduct in no measured terms. Two of them whom we knew, had, at all events, the negative merit of not having changed their religion. General Bem, since dead, and whose funeral was conducted with every high Mussulman ceremony, was also a resident. I regret much I had not the opportunity of seeing this man, whose singularly eventful career has thus ignobly closed.

Walked out to the Bab el Faradge, or Gate of Fair Prospect. Here is one of the favourite lounges of the Halebeen ladies; all who are, or fancy they are sick, come here at an early hour to drink milk. The animals are brought and milked on the spot. On my way passed three stones, two erect and one placed across, thus affording a passage beneath. This, which either is the tomb, or near the tomb, or in some way sacred to a famous sheik, all the women not blessed with families pass under. Its efficacy I heard nobody doubt. About one hundred veiled figures were there; many bore a cup in their hands; some were sitting, others sauntering about. This meeting of solid ghosts, with their fluttering garments, was very pretty.

It being still early morning, I prolonged my walk on amidst the Mussulman tombs. It was pleasing to see the pious Moslem thus bowing down before his God – bowing down on his father's grave – to the same God in the same way his father bowed before. With flowing robes and abstracted mien, each chooses some small eminence, and there worships. Probably they use much the same attitudes and wear the same dress as Abraham did of old. Their shoes are always removed, for the ground they tread on is accounted holy.

We visited the best Christian house here; probably finer might be found amidst the Mussulmans. Beit Sada is situated in Judaida, which, as its name imports, was formerly the Jewish quarter. Proceeding up a narrow street, bounded on either side by dead walls, we passed through a low door, and crossing a small narrow passage, entered a magnificent court, planted with oranges, lemons, and jessamines. Round this are built the rooms. The floor and front of the lewan are of marble, the whole walls stone. Within there were two or three noble rooms, the walls wainscot, and richly gilt, covered with curious scrolls and figures, the whole very rich and handsome. There is one upstairs room, a perfect bijou. The date on it is two hundred and odd years, yet the gilding is as fresh as if done yesterday; also the other colours. Underground are three stories of vaults, built on arches, one beneath the other, and passages also, which communicate with other houses. Thus, in times of danger or persecution, communication could be kept up throughout the quarter, for I am assured all the houses have the same. The three stories of vaults were to secrete, I suppose, their riches. The entrances to these also were well concealed.

The family of Sada is of antiquity, but fines, avernizing, misrule, and persecution, have dilapidated its once noble fortune. We were most hospitably entertained by the family; and the noise the pretty maids made with their cabcabs as they hastened about to prepare coffee, sweets and sherbets, haunted me as I slept that night. And thus rolled on the day. If one had not much leisure allowed one, the society was of a nice sleepy sort, where each said what he liked, or held his tongue if he thought fit. This palls after a time; but I had just come from the west, and the bent bow, the strained intellect, revelled in the repose. Body, heart – all reposed, and felt inexpressibly happy at the rest.

> Pleasant now without a check,
> To lay the rein on fancy's neck,
> And let her gay caprices vary,
> Through many a frolicsome vagary.
> Nonsense, thou delicious thing,

Thought and feeling's effervescence,
Like the bubbles of a spring,
In their sparkling evanescence.

The natives themselves are peculiarly impregnated with what dear
Warburton would style this self-indulgent life; no wonder, therefore,
they grow fat and sleek when the first blush of youth is over. Those in
trade take it coolly, happy if business comes, but resigned if it does not.
Ask a man, 'Fee shay jedeid eliom?' (Any news today?) 'Thank God,
no,' he will reply. The women, who do all the domestic duties of their
household, and do them well too, do them in a quiet full-dress sort
of way; the servants, who get through their work well also, do it in a
lazy, indolent, slipshod way, and appear always as if they had nothing
to do but sit in the sun or sleep. There is no 'My horse at three,' and
he is there; 'My dinner so and so.' They require to be told everything,
and possess another quality we English do not much appreciate. If,
for instance, I say 'Bring me a glass of water,' he answers, 'What for?'
'Do this;' 'Why?' 'Bring so and so;' 'What for?' nor will a few lessons
unteach this habit.

I must, however, from my own experience, now confirmed by a
year's acquaintance, say they are honest and attached, quick and faithful; but the Englishman must submit to the dawdle, procrastination,
and loiter, which attend all Eastern motions, or he will be endlessly hot,
uncomfortable, and complaining. I was dreadfully so at first, but have
now philosophised, till even no dinner and wet ground to sleep on have
ceased to excite me. But to return to my journal, with a pardon sought
for my long digression.

I observe no note on the day in question, except being vaccinated for
preventing the Aleppo button. The operation was performed much in
the same manner as for the small-pox. A fat child was brought with an
atrocious-looking button, and my arm received in various punctures the
matter. It was as well to avoid a nasty sore if it could be done at so cheap
a rate; and though the vaccination never took, yet, as I also escaped the
button, there was no great harm done. The Aleppo button, which forms
a formidable objection with many to visiting Aleppo, is an endemical
disorder, called the *habeb el seneh* or ulcer of the year. It is a large pimple
which is, at first, inflammatory, but, at length, becomes a large ulcer;
remaining one year, and leaving a very disagreeable discoloured scar
behind it. It does not attack people twice: it sometimes appears in several places at once, and the children of Aleppo may be seen with two or

three at once, apparently not caring. It is so common that none seemed ashamed of it.

It sadly disfigures all the people, and you may know an Aleppene any where by his scarred face. Nor is it confined, as is commonly believed, to Aleppo: it occurs in certain localities at Damascus, and through all the country from Aleppo to Diarbeker. No care is thought necessary, as nothing can apparently remove it before the year is out; patience and resignation, *kismet*, are the best remedies.

A curious cure occurred here; the fact was related to me by the patient, and several others bore testimony to the fact. The poor fellow suffered long and severely with the fever, which at last terminated in a complete lock-jaw. The Frank doctors were called in, pronounced the case hopeless, and withdrew: the native sages came, saw, and departed, saying they could do nothing. The poor man folded his robes, and turned to the wall, resigned to his fate. Resolved, however, to make one more effort, he told a Frank doctor, who was young and enter-prising, to do something. The practitioner immediately proceeded to operate, trying to force open his jaws with a knife. This proving inef-fectual, the poor man again settled to death, and thus lay three days. His friends came to pay their last sad farewell, and, among the rest, a Koord, from Mosul, a fine liberal-minded man, whom I knew very well. On entering the room, he looked closely at Mr. K. and, approaching him, gave his ear a peculiar twitch, repeating some words, and then ordered a plaster of dates to be applied to his jaw. Three days afterwards he was convalescent, and soon quite recovered. The Koord refused to tell me the cure; he said it was a secret handed down, in his family, from many generations.

A slave was much pressed on me as an eligible purchase: 2000 pias-tres, or about 18*l.*, was the lowest price. He belonged to a curious fellow who, after wandering everywhere, lost to his friends, &c., turned up after many years, a zealous Turk. He had accompanied Mr. Banks dur-ing part of his Eastern travels, and the reason assigned by him for parting with the lad was the same as so frequently appears in our newspapers with regard to a carriage, &c., the owner having no further use for him.

CHAPTER XIV

While passing the Mussulman burial-ground I saw one of their cere-monies. The body had been laid in the ground; it being that of a man of some consequence, a rich pall covered the monument. The men stood round it, and with their hands raised and open on either side of the head, bowed simultaneously. It is difficult to say exactly the prayer they repeated: the women sat at a distance looking on. I visited the old serai without the town: it covers the crest of a hill about half a mile from the town, but is now in ruins. In it is a tomb of Abou Beker – not the famous one – he did not move from his capital.

In the next page of my journal I find an excessively ugly fellow wished to marry a young and very pretty girl. The parents, being poor, readily consented to the match, for he was very rich, which all ugly men are not. By force of presents, jewels, gold and promises, they obtained her consent. Unfortunately, a few days before the marriage, she happened to see him, and immediately told her married sister it was impossible – she could not marry him. However, she was answered that it was far too late to retreat, and the preparations were completed. During the ceremony, she twice withdrew her hand from his, and when asked, 'Will you take this man?' her sister forced her head down, the only sign of assent they could make her to give. After nine days, however, she returned to her father's house, a virgin. Supplications, prayers, entreaties, were in vain – she would not go back to her husband. The bishop has just dissolved the marriage, at the same time stating, that this is no precedent.

Our next door neighbour has two daughters affianced, pretty little girls of from seven to nine years of age. They told the elder, 'Your betrothed is ugly;' he, however, was shown to her one day, and she said, 'He is not so bad.' And this is marriage; this is the way to choose a help meet for one. Better the old proverb:

> I would advise a man to pause
> Before he takes a wife;
> In fact, dear sir, I see no cause
> He should not pause for life.

However, my opinion is rapidly changing – not as regards marrying, but as respects the way it is done here in the East, in comparison with our way. Of one thing I am sure, that wives in the East are fully as true and faithful, and more economical, domestic, and useful than even in England. In these engagements the man certainly has the worst of it; he can rarely, if ever, see his betrothed. If she walks, she is shrouded up, while she can see him freely, and watch him, while perhaps he little deems those eyes are upon him.

Sunday: attended divine service. These three Sundays, viz., Friday with the Mussulmans (not that that shuts their trade for above three hours) – then Saturday with the Jew traders; then Sunday with the Christians – it is a sad invasion on the week, as far as business is concerned. In fact what with the different sects of Christians, fêtes, &c., it is rare to see all the shops open at once.

[…]

Among the fairer part of the population it is the Paris, the emporium of fashion, and they dress from it. Do not think the change of mode is, however, as monthly as among our own gayer, more versatile neighbours (that any change is made at all, is a wonderful improvement); no, it takes a few years among them to alter the cut of a petticoat or the ornaments of a tarboush. The last change is, that a petticoat is now worn over the voluminous graceful trousers of the women. Formerly, the skirts of the shirts, slit to the breast, descended to the ankles; and many, even now, retain this, to me infinitely more graceful, costume. The petticoat is ill adapted for their mode of sitting, and, being single, sits badly at all times.

I may mention, while speaking of dress, the difference between the trousers of the men and those of the women – and it might have been instanced, in 'The spirit of the East,' as another striking difference between the inhabitants of the East and the West – we divide the legs of the men; they do so with the trousers of the women. Those of the men consist of a long doubled affair, the upper parts not sewn together, but a ridge made, through which a silk, thin, plaited sash is passed; more frequently, however, a long strip of rag or stout tape. Thus gathered together, and the plaits carefully adjusted, it is tied round the middle. At either extremity is a small hole worked, through which the leg is passed.

In the women's garment, the upper part is the same; but the whole bottom is unsewn, the centre cut, and two legs formed, which are drawn together by tape loops, through which passes a string, which gathers them up round the ankle. Those of the women are longer than the men's, reaching to, or even below, the ankle, over which they fall gracefully, while the men's seldom descend below the half of the calf. In parts of Asia Minor, they wear things like very ill-made western trousers, loose above, and gradually tightening below the knee. The labourers wear far less voluminous affairs (some put fifteen or twenty yards of stuff in their trousers), as they cannot work in them; all, when they wish to run, catch up the folds from between their legs, so inconvenient do they find them.

On my return, we set out for a picnic, which E— and myself were told it would be right to give. We provided carpets, nargillehs, horse-loads of sundries, cushions, a cargo of lettuces; and thus equipped, we sallied out, a very numerous party. The first thing to select was a garden, a point on which our own choice, and not the owner's will, seemed alone to be consulted. Let not the reader fancy an Eastern garden is what a warm Western fancy would paint it; wild with luxuriant but weedless verdure, heavy with the scent of roses and jessamine, thrilling with the songs of the bulbul and the nightingale, where fair women with plaited tresses touch the soulful lute in graceful attitudes – no; it is a piece of ground enclosed by high walls, varying in size. A wretched gate, invariably badly made, probably ruined, admits you to the interior. Some enclose a house with two or three rooms – windowless, white-washed places. Before this is a reservoir of dirty, stagnant water, turned up from a neighbouring well by an apparatus as rude as it is ungainly and laborious: this is used to irrigate the ground, which therefore is alternately mud and dust. Fruit trees or mulberries are planted in rows, and the ground beneath, being ploughed up, is productive of vegetables or corn. One or two trees, for ornament, may be planted in the first row, but nothing more; and weeds, uncut, undestroyed, spring up in every direction. Such, without exaggeration, is the *Bistan zareff! quiess*, the Lovely Garden.

We selected one, that belonged to the Mollah. Oh, true believer! in thy pot we boiled a ham; on thy divan we ate the forbidden beast; thy gardener, for base reward, assisting to cook – who knows, but also to eat the same? We chose a spot shaded by a noble walnut tree, and spread carpets and cushions. Fire was lighted, nargillehs bubbled, and kief began. The principal occupation of the ladies was picking the lettuces – huge, coarse, overgrown things. From every leaf they strip the green, leaving only the spine of the leaf. Taper fingers then, with winning smile, soft, pleasant words, and graceful arm, present you a vegetable reduced to the appearance of a worn, useless birch-broom.

The spot selected had one advantage which the owner probably never contemplated. A huge ruin in the wall let in a view of the river, which, making a sharp turn, ran before us away to the town, and, on our left, rushed from its bed in pretty petulance. Dyers, blue with their work, passed by, smoking; idlers in the shade filled in the picture: while gardens, rendered pretty by their distance, wall, tower, and housetop, formed the background. It was proper that the walnut-tree should lend us its thickest shade; for, by a suspicious red mark upon its trunk, I found it owed its present existence to British protection.

Ibrahim Pasha used to have these trees cut, and then bought them at a small price, to make military carts and other engines. This had been marked to fall, but the English came, and it still lived to throw its protecting arms over the humblest of her sons. It is incalculable how much damage Ibrahim did, though all of it was more or less forced on him by his precarious tenure of the country. His conscription, in six years more, would have depopulated the country, but the force was necessary to maintain his position; and could his own talents have become hereditary, there seems no doubt the rule was every way preferable to that of the Sultan.

To him the Christians owe the dawn of liberty they now possess; his government was just and prompt, and far less venal than that of any the Sultan can form for years to come; and from my own experience I perfectly agree in the truth of his own expression: 'Were it not for the conscription I should be adored.' The troops he levied in Syria were generally hurried to Egypt, while, vice versa, the Egyptians garrisoned Syria. The Christians under him were first rendered eligible for all public offices, and though relieved, as now, from all military service, they were levied as rigidly for other works. It is related of Ibrahim, that the plain (near Aleppo, I think,) being infested by locusts, constant complaints were made of their devastations: hearing this, Ibrahim sallied forth with his whole army, armed with sticks, and their morning's work was probably more productive of good than some of their victories.

When the sun had nearly run his course, we entered the house and drank water and sherbets. The raisin is mostly used for sherbets in Aleppo; and the grapes once so famous for their excellence, have now so degenerated as not to be worth the trouble of making into wine. Two dishes of Arabic sweets figured advantageously – bucktoua, made of honey, walnuts, butter, and flour; the other, knaffee, made of a grain so called, mixed with butter, cream (or cheese), sugar, and honey. Each occupied an enormous flat brass tinned dish. The economy of using cheap substitutes, such as honey, grease, &c., spoils most Arabic sweets, and they make mixtures which we, who are unaccustomed to them, can hardly find palatable. Four musicians had sounded noisily all the day, nor must they now be forgotten; they formed the best company of musicians at Aleppo. No fantasia could be good where they were not.

No. 1 played on a small instrument of wood hollowed out, rounded towards the bottom, the top covered by a tight drawn skin; these he beat with two sticks, called Na Areat. No. 2 played the tambourine, called dira. In addition to the noise produced by shaking it, he struck the skin and played on the cymbals set in the edges. No. 3 played the violin; this is now in common use all over the East, having probably superseded some less sonorous instrument of their own of a similar description: it is called kamangee, and they stoutly maintain it to be their own invention. The next plays a flute without covers to the notes, called nare, and tones of singular sweetness are produced by it. The last, a lively fellow, played the kannoon, a species of harp: it has seventy-two strings. Each sang a verse, the whole then joining in chorus; and this they kept up untiringly; being refreshed (though they were Mussulmans) by frequent draughts of ardent spirits. Some of the gay ones of the party danced, and so the evening wore on. The frogs outcroaked the music; the dark came on; and then we sauntered home, to other divans, to continue the same lazy sort of amusement, till we felt inclined to go to bed.

It seemed quite impossible to quit Aleppo, and any attempt at it was met by so many difficulties that we half thought our journey was finished. At last, however, we slipped off, having dismissed our dragoman for most frequent robberies. Fresh servants were hired, and, our own horses being insufficient, some baggage animals were added to the train.

Chapter Twenty Three

The Lands of the Saracen; or, Pictures of Palestine, Asia Minor, Sicily and Spain (1854)

*Bayard Taylor (1825–78) was a popular American poet, translator and jour-
nalist. He travelled the world, writing books about Africa, India, China and
'Europe seen with Knapsack and Staff'. In* The Lands of the Saracen *he
describes a journey through the Ottoman Empire in 1851 – it also contains
chapters called 'Visions of Hasheesh' and 'Bathing and Bodies', in which he
refers to 'thrills of the purest physical pleasure', although he found local bodies
'apt to be lank and with imperfect muscular development'. Of his hammam
attendant, he wrote: 'Give yourself with a blind submission into the arms of the
brown Fate and he will lead you to new chambers of Delight.' He was in Aleppo
in June 1852.*

CHAPTER XV
LIFE IN ALEPPO

The citadel is now a mass of ruins, having been deserted since the earth-quake. Grass is growing on the ramparts, and the caper plant, with its white-and-purple blossoms, flourishes among the piles of rubbish. Since the late rebellion, however, a small military barrack has been built, and two companies of soldiers are stationed there. We walked around the walls, which command a magnificent view of the city and the wide plains to the south and east. It well deserves to rank with the panorama of Cairo from the citadel, and that of Damascus from the Anti-Lebanon, in extent, pictur-esqueness and rich oriental character. Out of the gray ring of the city, which incloses the mound, rise the great white domes and the whiter minarets of its numerous mosques, many of which are grand and imposing structures. The course of the river through the centre of the picture is marked by a belt of the greenest verdure, beyond which, to the west, rises a chain of naked red hills, and still further, fading on the horizon, the blue summit of Mt. St. Simon, and the coast range of Akma Dagh. Eastward, over vast orchards of pistachio trees, the barren plain of the Euphrates fades away to a glimmering, hot horizon. Looking downwards on the heart of the city, I was surprised to see a number of open, grassy tracts, out of which, here and there, small trees were growing. But, perceiving what appeared to be subterranean entrances at various points, I found that these tracts were upon the roofs of the houses and bazaars, verifying what I had frequently heard, that in Aleppo the inhab-itants visit their friends in different parts of the city, by passing over the roofs of the houses. Previous to the earthquake of 1822, these vast roof-plains were cultivated as gardens, and presented an extent of airy bowers as large, if not as magnificent, as the renowned Hanging Gardens of ancient Babylon.

Accompanied by Signor di Picciotto, we spent two or three days in visiting the houses of the principal Jewish and Christian families in Aleppo. We found, it is true, no such splendor as in Damascus, but more solid and durable architecture, and a more chastened elegance of taste. The buildings are all of hewn stone, the court-yards paved with marble, and the walls rich with gilding and carved wood. Some of the larger dwellings have small but beautiful gardens attached to them. We were everywhere received with the greatest hospitality, and the visits were considered as a favor rather than an intrusion. Indeed, I was frequently obliged to run the risk of giving offence, by declining the refreshments which were offered us. Each round of visits was a feat of strength, and we were obliged to desist from sheer inability to support more coffee, rose-water, pipes, and aromatic sweetmeats. The character of society in Aleppo is singular; its very life and essence is etiquette. The laws which govern it are more inviolable than those of the Medes and Persians. The question of precedence among the different families is adjusted by the most delicate scale, and rigorously adhered to in the most trifling matters. Even we, humble voyagers as we are, have been obliged to regulate our conduct according to it. After our having visited certain families, certain others would have been deeply mortified had we neglected to call upon them. Formerly, when a traveller arrived here, he was expected to call upon the different Consuls, in the order of their established precedence: the Austrian first, English second, French third, &c. After this, he was obliged to stay at home several days, to give the Consuls an opportunity of returning the visits, which they made in the same order. There was a diplomatic importance about all his movements, and the least violation of etiquette, through ignorance or neglect, was the town talk for days.

This peculiarity in society is evidently a relic of the formal times, when Aleppo was a semi-Venetian city, and the opulent seat of Eastern commerce. Many of the inhabitants are descended from the traders of those times, and they all speak the *lingua franca*, or Levantine Italian. The women wear a costume partly Turkish and partly European, combining the graces of both; it is, in my eyes, the most beautiful dress in the world. They wear a rich scarf of some dark color on the head, which, on festive occasions, is almost concealed by their jewels, and the heavy scarlet pomegranate blossoms which adorn their dark hair. A Turkish vest and sleeves of embroidered silk, open in front, and a skirt of white or some light color, completes the costume. The Jewesses wear in addition a short Turkish *caftan*, and full trousers gathered at the ankles. At a ball given by Mr. Very, the English Consul, which we attended, all the Christian beauties of Aleppo were present. There was a fine display of diamonds, many of the ladies wearing several thousand dollars' worth on their heads. The peculiar etiquette of the place was again illustrated on this occasion. The custom is, that the music must be heard for at least one hour before the guests come. The hour appointed was eight, but when we went there, at nine, nobody had arrived. As it was generally supposed that the ball was given on our account, several of the families had servants in the neighborhood to watch our arrival; and, accordingly, we had not been there five minutes before the guests crowded through the door in large numbers. When the first dance (an Arab dance, performed by two ladies at a time) was proposed, the wives of the French and Spanish Consuls were first led, or rather dragged, out. When a lady is asked to dance, she invariably refuses. She is asked a second and a third time; and if the gentleman does not solicit most earnestly, and use some gentle force in getting her upon the floor, she never forgives him.

At one of the Jewish houses which we visited, the wedding festivities of one of the daughters were being celebrated. We were welcomed with great cordiality, and immediately ushered into the room of state, an elegant apartment, overlooking the gardens below the city wall. Half the room was occupied by a raised platform, with a divan of blue silk cushions. Here the ladies reclined, in superb dresses of blue, pink, and gold, while the gentlemen were ranged on the floor below. They all rose at our entrance, and we were conducted to seats among the ladies. Pipes and perfumed drinks were served, and the bridal cake, made of twenty-six different fruits, was presented on a golden salver. Our fair neighbors, some of whom literally blazed with jewels, were strikingly beautiful. Presently the bride appeared at the door, and we all rose and remained standing, as she advanced, supported on each side by the two *shebeeniyeh*, or bridesmaids. She was about sixteen, slight and graceful in appearance, though not decidedly beautiful, and was attired with the utmost elegance. Her dress was a pale blue silk, heavy with gold embroidery; and over her long dark hair, her neck, bosom, and wrists, played a thousand rainbow gleams from the jewels which covered them. The Jewish musicians, seated at the bottom of the hall, struck up a loud, rejoicing harmony on their violins, guitars, and dulcimers, and the women servants, grouped at the door, uttered in chorus that wild, shrill cry, which accompanies all such festivals in the East. The bride was careful to preserve the decorum expected of her, by speaking no word, nor losing the sad, resigned expression of her countenance. She ascended to the divan, bowed to each of us with a low, reverential inclination, and seated herself on the cushions. The music and dances lasted some time, accompanied by the *zughàreet*, or cry of the women, which was repeated with double force when we rose to take leave. The whole company waited on us to the street door, and one of the servants, stationed in the court, shouted some long, sing-song phrases after us as we passed out. I could not learn the words, but was told that it was an invocation of prosperity upon us, in return for the honor which our visit had conferred.

In the evening I went to view a Christian marriage procession, which, about midnight, conveyed the bride to the house of the bridegroom. The house, it appeared, was too small to receive all the friends of the family, and I joined a large number of them, who repaired to the terrace of the English Consulate, to greet the procession as it passed. The first persons who appeared were a company of buffoons; after them four janissaries, carrying silver maces; then the male friends, bearing colored lanterns and perfumed torches, raised on gilded poles; then the females, among whom I saw some beautiful Madonna faces in the torchlight; and finally the bride herself, covered from head to foot with a veil of cloth of gold, and urged along by two maidens: for it is the etiquette of such occasions that the bride should resist being taken, and must be forced every step of the way, so that she is frequently three hours in going the distance of a mile. We watched the procession a long time, winding away through the streets – a line of torches, and songs, and incense, and noisy jubilee – under the sweet starlit heaven.

The other evening, Signor di Picciotto mounted us from his fine Arabian stud, and we rode around the city, outside of the suburbs. The sun was low, and a pale yellow lustre touched the clusters of minarets that rose out of the stately masses of buildings, and the bare, chalky hills to the north. After leaving the gardens on the banks of the Koweik, we came upon a dreary waste of ruins, among which the antiquarian finds traces of the ancient Aleppo of the Greeks, the Mongolian conquerors of the Middle Ages, and the Saracens who succeeded them. There are many mosques and tombs, which were once imposing specimens of Saracenic art; but now, split and shivered by wars and earthquakes, are slowly tumbling into utter decay. On the south-eastern side of the city, its chalk foundations have been hollowed into vast, arched caverns, which extend deep into the earth. Pillars have been left at regular intervals, to support the masses above, and their huge, dim labyrinths resemble the crypts of some great cathedral. They are now used as rope-walks, and filled with cheerful workmen.

Our last excursion was to a country-house of Signor di Picciotto, in the Gardens of Babala, about four miles from Aleppo. We set out in the afternoon on our Arabians, with our host's son on a large white donkey of the Baghdad breed. Passing the Turkish cemetery, where we stopped to view the tomb of General Bem, we loosened rein and sped away at full gallop over the hot, white hills. In dashing down a stony rise, the ambitious donkey, who was doing his best to keep up with the horses, fell, hurling Master Picciotto over his head. The boy was bruised a little, but set his teeth together and showed no sign of pain, mounted again, and followed us. The Gardens of Babala are a wilderness of fruit-trees, like those of Damascus. Signor P.'s country-house is buried in a wild grove of apricot, fig, orange, and pomegranate-trees.

A large marble tank, in front of the open, arched *liwan*, supplies it with water. We mounted to the flat roof, and watched the sunset fade from the beautiful landscape. Beyond the bowers of dazzling greenness which surrounded us, stretched the wide, gray hills; the minarets of Aleppo, and the walls of its castled mount shone rosily in the last rays of the sun; an old palace of the Pashas, with the long, low barracks of the soldiery, crowned the top of a hill to the north; dark, spiry cypresses betrayed the place of tombs; and, to the west, beyond the bare red peak of Mount St. Simon, rose the faint blue outline of Giaour Dagh, whose mural chain divides Syria from the plains of Cilicia. As the twilight deepened over the scene, there came a long, melodious cry of passion and of sorrow from the heart of a starry-flowered pomegranate tree in the garden. Other voices answered it from the gardens around, until not one, but fifty nightingales charmed the repose of the hour. They vied with each other in their bursts of passionate music. Each strain soared over the last, or united with others, near and far, in a chorus of the divinest pathos – an expression of sweet, unutterable, unquenchable longing. It was an ecstasy, yet a pain, to listen. 'Away!' said Jean Paul to Music: 'thou tellest me of that which I have not, and never can have – which I forever seek, and never find!'

But space fails me to describe half the incidents of our stay in Aleppo. There are two things peculiar to the city, however, which I must not omit mentioning. One is the Aleppo Button, a singular ulcer, which attacks every person born in the city, and every stranger who spends more than a month there. It can neither be prevented nor cured, and always lasts for a year. The inhabitants almost invariably have it on the face – either on the cheek, forehead, or tip of the nose – where it often leaves an indelible and disfiguring scar. Strangers, on the contrary, have it on one of the joints; either the elbow, wrist, knee, or ankle. So strictly is its visitation confined to the city proper, that in none of the neighboring villages, nor even in a distant suburb, is it known. Physicians have vainly attempted to prevent it by inoculation, and are at a loss to what cause to ascribe it. We are liable to have it, even after five days' stay; but I hope it will postpone its appearance until after I reach home.

The other remarkable thing here is the Hospital for Cats. This was founded long ago by a rich, cat-loving Mussulman, and is one of the best endowed institutions in the city. An old mosque is appropriated to the purpose, under the charge of several directors; and here sick cats are nursed, homeless cats find shelter, and decrepit cats gratefully purr away their declining years. The whole category embraces several hundreds, and it is quite a sight to behold the court, the corridors, and terraces of the mosque swarming with them. Here, one with a bruised limb is receiving a cataplasm; there, a cataleptic patient is tenderly cared for; and so on, through the long concatenation of feline diseases. Aleppo, moreover, rejoices in a greater number of cats than even Jerusalem. At a rough guess, I should thus state the population of the city: Turks and Arabs, 70,000; Christians of all denominations, 15,000; Jews, 10,000; dogs, 12,000; and cats, 8,000.

Among other persons whom I have met here, is Ferhat Pasha, formerly General Stein, Hungarian Minister of War, and Governor of Transylvania. He accepted Moslemism with Bem and others, and now rejoices in his circumcision and 7,000 piastres a month. He is a fat, companionable sort of man, who, by his own confession, never labored very zealously for the independence of Hungary, being an Austrian by birth. He conversed with me for several hours on the scenes in which he had participated, and attributed the failure of the Hungarians to the want of material means. General Bem, who died here, is spoken of with the utmost respect, both by Turks and Christians. The former have honored him with a large tomb, or mausoleum, covered with a dome.

But I must close, leaving half unsaid. Suffice it to say that no Oriental city has interested me so profoundly as Aleppo, and in none have I received such universal and cordial hospitality. We leave tomorrow for Asia Minor, having engaged men and horses for the whole route to Constantinople.

Chapter Twenty Four

Personal Narrative in Letters; Principally from Turkey, in the Years 1830–33 (1856)

Like Burckhardt twenty years earlier, in 1831–2 **Francis William Newman** *(1805–1897), a younger brother of the future cardinal, came to Aleppo to learn Arabic. In contrast to Burckhardt, his motive was to pursue a calling as a Christian missionary. He stayed with a local Levantine family, but was dismayed by the 'want of mind', 'painful sense of emptiness' and 'general signs of a break-up'. 'In such an imbroglio of people, there seems to be no nation, no union, no strength.' In 1832 he joined missionaries in Baghdad, but soon returned to England and became a prominent teacher, and biblical scholar, whose books included a* Dictionary of Modern Arabic *(2 vols, 1871). He became a theist, rumoured to have 'unsound views' on eternal punishment.*

LETTER XI

Aleppo, Feb. 1831

You will be glad to know we are safe here; you will not care about any travelling details. I fear a war with Bagdad impends – a frightful calamity to the country and a vexation to us. If we were to travel on now (though I believe it will be not only inexpedient, but impossible), it might severely try our principle of *going unarmed*. All I have seen and heard confirms my first conviction, that this is a thing which cannot be done by halves. We must be wholly unarmed, or ready to fight in very earnest. I suppose there is a petty pilfering, which is controlled by the mere sight of a pistol; but its obvious resource is to steal the weapon first: and really if a party is small, like ours, and driven into forced marches by muleteers, it has no strength to keep sentinel all night, and its weapons fall into the enemy's hand.

At one place, in our road from Ladakia hither, we were crossed by a sham brigand, who fired his musket and demanded payments. Nobody took the least notice of him, and he did not dare to stop the beasts and try to plunder; the muleteers knew it was a trick to practise on our fears. In any case, to defend oneself by murderous weapons against petty demands, would be a most doubtful prudence. It might rouse the cry for vengeance, where you are vastly outnumbered. Of all martyrdoms, I should least covet to lose my life in a fray for some paltry sum with these hungry villagers. You will see from this, that even should religious patience fail me, still I am not likely to be too brave in the future. If the whole country were disorganized, and if (through the exasperation of a horrible guerilla) murder and not pilfering were the object – we surely ought not to go into the mell of confusion at all, while we can keep away.

We never thought of tarrying here. I am in the house of a native Frank – a Levantine, I believe, is the English word. The children's gossip is pleasant and useful to me. It is awful to hear a child of three years say 'Mlíhh,' the word here for Good. I did not think infantine organs could manufacture consonants on such a scale. After the long vowel, one hears distinctly what the French would call an *e mute* interposed; it is the 'Furtive Patahh' of the Hebrew grammars. Now I must confess to you, slight as is my knowledge of Arabic, I have already gone deep enough to see the falsehood and the mischief of Parkhurst's system of learning Hebrew *without points*. I used to argue, that, as it is conceded that our vowel points are a late system, superadded to the old text, we ought to discard them, in order to go back to the pure and alone divine originals.

I now see that this is an invalid inference. One might as well propose to read the Greek Testament with all the words written in a heap without divisions, if we so find them in the earliest M.S. The divisions of words and the stops are not conceived of as authoritative, and we alter them at pleasure by mere criticism: yet they add much ease to reading and more to learning. But this does not tell the worst of Parkhurst. He elaborately gives false explanations, in order to make an unpointed text less defective; as in his exploding of the verbal forms Pihhel and Puhhal. In short, it is just as if some foreigner were to insist on expounding *hot* and *heat* into the same English word, because he found them both written *ht* in a system of short hand, and because he chose to lay down that Englishmen are not to be trusted as expositors of their hereditary pronunciation. I now believe, nothing but the utter prostration of Hebrew study at our universities will account for the currency which Parkhurst's works have had in England.

The Jews are great persons here – great in the mercantile world: I do not find that they have any learned men. Inconvenient as is the system of domestic service here to the richer part of the community, I think it more natural and reasonable than ours. There are isolated men-servants to be had, namely Armenians, who come hither for wages, leaving their families afar: I do not admire *that*. But our consul (for instance) has whole families in his domestic service; for all the women marry; and this is the only sure way of getting female domestics at all. My friends had great difficulty in getting one. This system must be very expensive to the rich, but when an expense is a fixed condition counted on beforehand, it is not felt as a burden; and the rich man gets more love and honour, and it is a permanent attachment of family to family – a sort of liberal clientship, without any other compulsion but such as public opinion exerts. This is not feudality: there is no power of the sword, nor exclusive right of land, given to the few. These are mere merchants, in an open market: – except, I should add, that consuls pay no port dues to the Sultan, which is a bonus to their traffic.

The importance of the Jews here, their dignity and influence, I suspect, is, even religiously, a benefit to the place. The Romish clergy would else have their own way among the Franks too much. I do not understand half the politics of the place; but I see intrigue to be very eager; and indeed there is so little else to engage men or women of active mind, that perhaps they cannot help intriguing. It is something like a little country-town in England, in which everybody knows where everybody bought everything. In fact, their inquisitiveness is above Yankee-pitch. Strangers feel the material of my cloak, and ask how much it cost, not imagining offence. To know the actual prices of everything, where market-prices are uncertain in the extreme, seems to be a universal necessary of life. F. W. N.

LETTER XII

Aleppo, Feb. 10, 1831

How soon this letter will go, I do not know. I hope, from my letter of Jan. 14th to my dear mother, you will have learnt our safe arrival here. How long we must stay, seems quite uncertain. The news of these parts are probably known to you through the newspapers more completely than to us, who pick up fragments: I presume therefore you are aware that David Pasha of Bagdad has rebelled against the Sultan. I believe the war which ended so calamitously by the treaty of Adrianople, made the distant Pashas despise the Sultan as too weak to control them. Probably the imagination of the people is also affected. The Arab and Syrian Moslems are impressed by the Russian triumph with the idea that the days of Ottoman supremacy are numbered. David Pasha has withheld his tribute two years, and has employed it in material of war, preparing to resist the vengeance which he foresees. He is said to be formidable in artillery as well as cavalry. However; the Sultan, understanding what the refusal of tribute means, has taken the course of ceding the whole Pashalik of Bagdad to be incorporated with that of Aleppo, on condition that the Aleppine Pasha will reduce the other to submission. Fifty thousand men (it is said) are to come from Constantinople to his aid. Meanwhile our Pasha is making every exertion to raise an army, and has engaged all the mules and camels for his service. The merchants would in no case send any caravan before peace is re-established with Bagdad: but in truth, all departures for that place have been publicly forbidden; so that our way thither is quite blocked up.

We have been here a month. We were at first accommodated in the European khan (caravanserai) with clean and dry rooms, where an old servant, who goes to market for one, also sweeps the pavement of the rooms, and keeps up fires – wretched laughable fires, to warm such cold flags. (Please to tell my mother, that I have now got a raised bed, and thick cotton quilt; yet I suffer even in my present room much from cold, and have chilblains on my feet). We were dissatisfied that the rooms, though lofty, were too dark to study; for the windows are pigeon-holes: also household-cares occupied too much time. The women here do not easily become domestic servants. But besides, we find that the Roman Catholic priests try to keep Christian servants away from us. The Bishop even endeavoured to expel us from the khan: the man of whom we hired the rooms told us of the spiritual threats held out against him. There is only one Protestant beside ourselves in the city: he is a Swiss watchmaker, and talks French. He tells me, he is hindered from marrying, unless he turns Catholic; the priestly influence has put an insuperable bar in his way. But I was going to say: after finding the inconveniences of the khan, we tried to get other accommodation; in vain. In fact, Aleppo is not fully rebuilt since the earthquake of 1822, and no one will fit up their empty houses (which are always ruinous), unless we engage them for at least a year. I myself managed to induce a native Frank merchant to take me in. He had a rude large room beyond his court, with a grated door and no window. I have had glass put in, and have now more tranquillity and leisure: in fact I am a student again. I converse in French, and get daily lessons in Arabic from my host. He has no theoretic nor grammatical knowledge. For modern Arabic our only really good book is Caussin de Perceval's Dictionary Français-Arabe, which I got at Dulau's, Soho Square. Everybody here is envying me that book. I find Herbin's grammar, given me by Pusey, to be highly useful, though often too polished in his vocabulary. Caussin de Perceval's grammar is also very serviceable: Dr. Macbride gave it me. I should like him and Pusey to know how useful we find these books.

My friends will shortly be able to join me in this house; we have masons at work to make certain rooms habitable for them.

The other day, I received a piece of information for which I was not at all prepared. The Pasha's engineer, a Frenchman by descent and a Roman Catholic, a serious sort of man and devoted to surveying and geography, assures me that the majority of the Roman Catholics and of the Turks (that is, of the Mohammedans), are *philosophers*; by which he means, unbelievers in their ostensible creed; but he adds, *those who are most 'philosophe' at heart are generally most bigoted outwardly, to conceal it.* Does not Blanco White say something similar about Spain? If we are to believe the Franks, the native Christians are sad villains: but many of the Turks (say they) are 'braves gens.' Many of these (Syrian Moslems) have called on us upon various excuses, and are very familiar and easy, but not obtrusive or rude. People here say *Osmánli* for Ottoman; Turk with the Franks, means a Mohammedan; most of whom here talk Arabic. Aleppo and Constantinople, we are told, are the only Turkish cities where French prevails over Italian. I talk more French than is good for my Arabic, but cannot hope to improve in French by it. Most of the

consuls here are Jews, and, except the French consul, are believed to
have bought their places of the ambassadors. Consuls pay no customs,
hence merchants covet the consulate. In all the world, Judaism seems to
culminate at Aleppo. F. W. N.

LETTER XVI

Aleppo, April 1831

I am absorbed in Arabic: too much perhaps: but it is inevitable. It is no
use to write about that, nor about graver cares. I shall tell you whatever comes uppermost. We are lodged with a Frank family (Levantine,
I should say); with a weak husband, amiable wife, pleasant children
very young. The frankness of language here startles one a little: it is
like the Bible: mere children speak of natural mysteries in such plain
terms. A child, five years old, wishing to know whether I was an
Englishman or a Frenchman, put to me the question: 'Where did you
come out of your mother's belly?' I cannot tell what to think, whether
the state of mind which goes along with such phraseology in a nation,
is *more* or *less* conducive to mental purity than our state. In acting as
French interpreter to Mr. C. when he is called on as physician, I have
on more than one occasion been struck at the unconscious simplicity
with which Levantine ladies say, not only before me but to me, what
is embarrassing to me. I incline to think this is a more wholesome
state of mind than ours, though I cannot get myself into it. With
much that is frank, even to the point of coarseness, in expression,
some of the ladies here have a natural refinement, which I admire the
more when, as in our hostess, it is joined with much domestic drudg-
ery. I suppose, none of them have any scholastic education; few can
even read: yet they have an education of sensibility and graciousness.
I fear they are and must be gossips and intriguers, when they have too
few domestic cares; for there is nothing to spend mental energies on.
What is called education in *men*, is the attainment of fine penman-
ship. A young man was introduced to me, and by way of setting off his
high accomplishment, was called 'the most beautiful pen in Aleppo.'

On the whole, both sexes give me a painful sense of *emptiness*. They
have often active minds, but there seems a want of food. At Larnica
in Cyprus the kind consul introduced us to his numerous daughters,
who sat ranged close against the wall of a spacious room wholly empty
of chairs except along the sides. (This is the usual mode). They were
evidently much excited by curiosity, but something in the manner of
them all impressed me as very puerile. The daughters of our consul here

(a Jew) are very goodnatured and frank, and I ingratiated myself with them by walking in their pattens. They are women in age, but children in mind. I must explain about the pattens. Our streets, being generally unpaved, and barely broad enough for two horses (or strictly, two loaded camels), to pass between foot passengers, are beaten into mud by the feet of beasts stepping always along the same lines: hence ladies, except when they ride on asses, are very apt to need pattens. In fact, all women have them, and the rich wear them ornamental. Their material is mere wood, and some have them so high, as to be incipient stilts. In the wood and upper strap, is fine inlaid work, which I cannot describe, but which marks the rich lady. The Jewesses made me walk about their father's pavement (how Homeric the phrase sounds!) in these stilts, in which they stroll up and down with a strange gait. A fall from them on to the pavement would be no joke, and I had to be very cautious. I suppose it is in cold weather that they get a habit so strange as that of walking on high pattens indoors. The pavement is cold though dry, and the ladies content themselves with the inner boot, which has no proper sole.

I spoke of the asses. They are really delightful animals for ladies' riding. If I were an English lord, I would certainly have one for my lady: I cannot think why we so neglect the breed. I do not believe our *climate* spoils them. There is here a good share of rain and mud, and in England it would always be possible to keep the feet of asses dry in the stable. Of course a close carriage is pleasanter for town-visits; but all our young ladies like to ride – until they are married; and then their husbands, or their physicians, are too prudent to allow it; and with good reason, on spirited and susceptible horses; especially since on a side-saddle a shying horse is an unmanageable peril. The ass is so steady, he never shies; his pace is a fast walk or little amble of five miles an hour, from which he never wants to deviate. They are willing, and most untiring, and the pace is as smooth as a sofa; I mean, of a good ass. They are not cheap, as things go here. They are not shod; the hoof is very hard, and they skip along like goats over pavement and rock. To ride on a rocky road with an iron-shod horse I found very disagreeable, especially as they here use plate-shoes, which are soon rubbed into slipperiness. In the country, I mean in England, for ladies' riding, along rough lanes and up hills where carriages cannot go, I feel convinced that good asses would be a delight that ladies do not now imagine. Perhaps, however, an essential pre-requisite is, that they should lay aside their prejudices against Turkish trowsers. I do not say that sidesaddles cannot be used with these asses: I suppose they could: but they would not be so convenient, nor nearly so safe. The mules here are not so large as we saw at Beziers: those, I suppose, were Spanish – as large as horses. The mules walked with their loads *on good ground* a full four miles an hour, as we came to Aleppo, but the caravan average pace can barely reach three miles. F. W. N.

LETTER XVII

Aleppo, April 1831

There is something fearful in the general signs of a break-up all round one here. I do not think this is an illusion of my own religious theories: the facts are very powerful, and I will tell you a few. I need not speak of the late Russian war, and its disorganising action on the mind of Pashas. I will not press the war against Bagdad. These are calamities which may pass, and would pass, if the empire were sound within. But the internal signs of decay are what one cannot mistake. It is true, Aleppo has not recovered from the earthquake of 1822: I must not impute the ruined aspect of things wholly to Turkish misgovernment: but if there were any spring of vitality, one would see the effort to heal follow the pang of a wound. Perhaps you know how many days it took in Paris to obliterate all signs of damage done by the convulsion which ejected Charles X. I do not know exactly; but I know it was a very rapid process. Here, it is not that the curative action has not yet overtaken the mischief, but it does not make the slightest attempt to grapple with it. For instance: a gate of Aleppo falls in; the huge vault fills up the road: – what would seem more vital to the commerce of a large city, than to clear away the obstruction? Twenty labourers could do it in a couple of days, if walls and gates are useless. But nothing is done. The laden mules and camels change their course, as they do on the mountains, and find their way out over the ruins of the wall fifty yards on one side. If a camel falls with its load and dies on the spot (their favourite way of dying, I suspect, when they get old), the body is just pushed a few yards away – if it were not actually in the bazaar – and left for dogs to devour. When the flesh is gone, there still lie the bones. I have asked – Are there no city revenues, no local taxation, no townships, no parishes, bound to attend to the streets and walls? The Franks of whom I have inquired appear to me to despise the Turkish government too much to have made minute inquiries into the relations of its theory and practice; but putting together all that I can learn, my inference is as follows. The Ottoman system being that of perpetually delegated despotism, it is the undoubted duty of the Pasha to tax the town for the benefit of the town. In theory, here, as in all the

world, every town owes a moderate tax to uphold the empire, and a larger tax for its own establishments; but in practice, no division is possible,
because both go through the hands of the same irresponsible Pasha. He
owes a certain tribute to the Sultan, year by year; but he probably has
also paid far larger sums in bribes to gain his place: he has to repay these,
it may be, to an Armenian banker: and he wants to fill his own private
purse beside. Even if he could be sure of the permanence of his own
position, he is too uneducated to compute the loss he brings on himself
by destroying the tax-bearing powers of the community: so he will not
spend the taxes on the town itself, but only on his own palace and his
military establishment. I do not think I can be wrong in this outline.
I am made less severe against the Turks, by what I have read of our own
infatuation in India; where, from the central despotism grasping all local
funds, local prosperity is awfully undermined. A centralized military
despotism, when native, and standing on the good will of the people,
is sometimes the *best* or almost the *only* sort of government possible: but
when it is foreign, and imposed on an unwilling people, history seems
to pass a stern vote against it.

The native Christians here seem to have no fierceness. They are
partly cowed; partly (like townspeople everywhere) too full of their
trade to think of public affairs, they accept state-imposts as a law of
fate. But they are humiliated by seeing the Moslems wear arms, which
they may not; and undoubtedly feel themselves to be conquered and
kept down. They feel no allegiance to the Sultan. They not only
are inadmissible to his armies (so that he has but a fraction of the
military strength proportioned to his territory), but they are made
disaffected by the miserable poll-tax. I am told (and my informant
seemed to have accurate knowledge), that though in the large cities
Moslems and Christians live together, yet this is too dangerous in
villages. Every village is of a pure population – one is Mussulman –
one is Christian. To mix them would produce frays, insurrections,
massacre. What kind of strength can the Sultan possibly have, until
he has new principles pervading alike the organization of the empire
and the hearts of the population? He wishes well: he tries to introduce Europeanism: but he does not conciliate the Christians, and he
disgusts the old-fashioned Turks. Two generations must pass, and this
state of things be forgotten (even if peace and obedience and wisdom
conspired so long) before any cohesion could commence. We know
what Ireland is. There are ten Irelands here.

Do not think I write thus as a partizan of these Christians – the Franks would teach me to despise them *as individuals* far more than the Moslems. After all, I do not see that the resident Franks are *much* different from the native Levantines, or these from the Sultan's Christian subjects. I have been thinking that I like the old men and the children here better than the middle-aged men. The men are without anything that enriches or elevates life. They have no enthusiasm in their religion, though I believe they perform its exterior diligently; I mean, even the Christians. They have no poetry, no science, no patriotism, for in fact no country; no other care of politics than a vibration from distant France; and as the French here complain, no theatre, no public amusements. Of course I do not say how much any of these things would improve them: I am merely saying, that the men have nothing in which heart and soul can go out, but family interests. Well: there is plenty of money-getting in England: still, we have many elevating impulses there, which leave men as unreligious as ever, yet certainly make life less despicable. The elder men here have something *patriarchal about them*. Paternal affection and paternal pride seem to grow with the child's growth, instead of turning into antagonism, as so often in England. (In ludicrous illustration, here, instead of patronymics to sons, there are *hyionymics* to fathers. A man has a son George: when the son reaches man's estate, the father drops his own name, and is called 'father of George,' Abu Georgi. I am telling you a *fact* of the old man who waits at the khan; and people say it is common). I speculate: – 'Perhaps, where there is so shallow an education of books, the education of life is, as in savage tribes, of greater proportionate importance, and the old man has a larger monopoly of wisdom.' Anyhow, affection seems to overpower money-getting principles in the old men, and has a sort of hallowing effect. I admire the Spanish consul here for manliness, dignity, and a sweet frankness. Though he has never done us any kindness, I feel as if I could ask it, were it needed. There are various other nice old men. F.W.N.

P.S. Does not the supersession of a father by his adult son appertain to savage or half savage life? Old Peleus and old Laertes vanish early before their sons' rising splendour; and Ulysses himself began in very early days to call himself 'Father of Telemachus.' This seems to be a very antique Abu Georgi. Do not think, I mean that the desire to amass *large fortunes* is very vehement here in the middleaged. Perhaps there is no facility sufficient to call out the passion. But *all* passions here may seem to be weak, even money-getting. *Why*: – is a long story.

Chapter Twenty Five

Through Turkish Arabia: A Journey from the Mediterranean to Bombay by the Euphrates and Tigris Valleys and the Persian Gulf (1894)

Henry Swainson Cowper (1865–1941) was an antiquarian who normally wrote about Lancashire. In 1890, however, after wintering in Cairo, he visited the area between Iskenderun and the Gulf, including Aleppo and Baghdad. In 1894, he published Through Turkish Arabia, *illustrated with his sketches and photographs.*

CHAPTER III
IN ALEPPO

Owing to all sorts of unseen delays, it was eleven days before I left Aleppo, and during that time I was able to ramble about the town. I therefore postpone such descriptive notes of the place as I was enabled to make, to a later chapter, and devote a page or two to my own proceedings during my stay, as it will afford intending travellers in the East some idea of the difficulties that beset one's path when once off the tourist track in Syria.

The so-called Azizia Hotel, at which I took up my quarters, is situated in a new suburb of that name on the west of the town. It was kept by an Armenian, and, although it hardly merited the European name of hotel, was very comfortable. From the street one entered straight into a little courtyard, in which was a well, and having to the right and left a building of two stories. The upper stories, which had only just been added, were occupied by about four bedrooms each, all of which opened straight on to a balcony which ran in front of them, and to which access was gained by a staircase from the courtyard. Beneath were the offices of the house, and the only public room, the dining apartment. When I arrived the rooms were all occupied but one, very clean and nice, but which had not yet been furnished; and on my arrival the landlord at once sent to the town and obtained a neat iron bedstead and other requisites to make me comfortable. The bed was erected while I was busy in the town, and I retired early, tired with my long journey, and anticipating a good night in the comfortable-looking little bed and clean bedding. Unfortunately, Carabet, the Armenian handy-man of the house, had in his haste or in his ignorance, omitted to secure at their ends the iron laths which sustain both the bedding and the sleeper; so that I awoke some time in the night feeling very uncomfortable, and curled up like a prawn, with my feet and my head at their proper elevation, but with the rest of my body deposited on the floor; the centre of the bed, owing to the giving way of the laths, and to the force known as the attraction of gravity, having softly and silently subsided. When I ascertained the real cause, pleased at finding that I had not just arrived in time for a repetition of the 1822 Aleppo earthquake, I strengthened my situation to the best of my ability, and passed a fairly comfortable night. The other occupants of the Azizia were mostly Turks; there were two army doctors (one a Greek), and several tarbushed Effendis, one or two of whom were in business in Aleppo. Lunch and dinner I took with these gentlemen downstairs. Breakfast was a moveable feast, partaken in the bedroom. When Carabet asked me what I would have for breakfast, I replied, 'Coffee, bread, butter and eggs.' Now boiled eggs are a dish unknown in the Armenian 'cuisine,' so that the five eggs which were brought, I discovered, when I scalped them, were still in their interiors in that liquid form in which they had first seen the light of day. I remonstrated afterwards with the worthy Carabet, but he had never before boiled an egg, and my remonstrances were ineffective. The Arabs have a peculiar term for smoking; they talk of drinking their pipe (shrub narjileh), or tobacco: so, although I object strongly to cold liquid eggs, I drank my five eggs to breakfast every morning in Aleppo. I could not possibly have altered Carabet's cooking, unless I had stood over him and his brazier in the courtyard, with a watch in one hand and a drawn sword in the other.

Although I had picked up odds and ends of Arabic two years previously in Egypt, and had taken lessons in colloquial Arabic from a Syrian in London, I found the Aleppo dialect so different, that my slight knowledge of the language was even of less use than I expected. The people in the hotel also talked almost entirely Turkish and Armenian, so that I was glad when little Jaleel turned up, wishing to engage himself to me as servant to Bagdad. Of course it was out of the question to take a little delicate boy like him for an eight or nine hundred mile journey overland, but I found him very useful during my stay in the town. He was an amusing, bright little chap, full of larkiness and fun, but troublesome on account of his insatiable curiosity and avarice. He would carefully examine my Norfolk jacket and knickerbockers – a garb, perhaps, never seen before in Aleppo, and then ask, 'How much did these cost, Mr. Cowper?' a question which would be immediately followed by, 'Will you give me *something to remember you by*, when you go to Bagdad, Mr. Cowper?' The idea of Jaleel, with his great black eyes and shrewd Eastern face, in knickerbockers and Norfolk jacket and red tarbush was so screamingly funny that, had there been an English tailor in the town, I should almost have been inclined to have fitted him out.

Jaleel could also lie – lie with the grace and facility which can only be found in ingenuous Eastern boyhood. Once I asked him if he could read an inscription in ancient Arabic on an old Saracenic well. Without a moment's hesitation he scrutinised the writing with an earnest gaze; writing which was about four hundred years old; and then gravely informed me that it contained the name of Sultan Abdul Hamid Khan, the reigning monarch.

Lunch and dinner at the Azizia were respectively at six and twelve o'clock, Turkish time – a muddling arrangement for a European, as Turkish time starts from sunset, and therefore the meals were a little earlier every day. The cookery was Turkish, and very good of its kind, the chief dishes being pilaf, kubabs, and yoghurt. Wine was, of course, not drunk at the table, except by myself and the Greek doctor, but the Effendis often had a little arak party together just before dinner, at which meal they would then appear strangely jovial and elated. It is a question whether their custom of coming 'jolly' to table is not preferable to ours of getting up 'jolly' from it. One young Turk asked me if I drank arak. I replied, 'No; is it not a sort of wine?' At this he was piously horrified, and solemnly informed me that it was a bitter, or rather what we call in England a digestive or stomachic. The house, being used by Turks of the new school, boasted table, chairs, knives, forks, and spoons, though these latter were somewhat scarce. The table-cloth was the worst feature in the entertainment, as each guest reached across and helped himself indiscriminately from the dish, in doing which a portion of the help-ing generally fell on the cloth, which, as far as I could ascertain, had never been washed since the opening of the house. I found the Beys and Effendis courtesy itself, always pressing me to help myself to each dish first. One or two of them could speak French.

I made no arrangement as to charges when I went to the Azizia, and my bill was eight francs a day, board and lodging. No doubt if I had made an arrangement it would have been less.

One of the first things I did on arrival was to call on our Consul, Mr. Jago, and to the hospitality and kindness of him and Mrs. Jago I owe much. Mr. Jago, indeed, put me in the way of making my arrangements, and during several pleasant walks we had together, in and about the town, gave me much interesting information concerning the district. The Consulate is a pleasant bungalow-built house close to the Azizia quarter, and standing in a pleasant garden of its own, and there were few days of the eleven I remained in Aleppo when I did not spend a pleasant hour at the Consulate.

I was pleased to find on my arrival that the cholera, which had been bad at Aleppo, was now at an end. The previous year there had been nine hundred deaths from this cause, and the year before about fourteen hundred. The influenza, which was devastating England when I left, was still lingering in a milder form at Aleppo, and was funnily termed by natives, 'Abu Rakab,' *i.e.*, the father of the knees, because after an attack the patient feels so weak in those members. Mr. Jago told me that I was the first European traveller who had arrived in Aleppo for about six months, which shows how completely off the track the town is.
[...]

CHAPTER IV
SOMETHING ABOUT ALEPPO

The Aleppines have a tradition of their own about the origin of the name of their town. The story runs that Abraham on his way to Canaan remained some time at the hill, which is now their citadel. Within its walls still stand the fragments of a mosque sacred to his memory. It is said that at certain hours of the day the patriarch distributed milk to the assembled villagers of the neighbouring country. These people collected at the foot of the hill, and the word was passed about 'Ibrahim halab,' 'Abraham has milked;' or 'Ibrahim halab as shahba,' 'Abraham has milked his dappled cow.' Hence came, they say, the name Haleb, which we have long Anglicised into Aleppo.
[...]

The general aspect of the interior of the town is extremely substantial for an Oriental city. The streets are built of excellent freestone, well fashioned, and the masonry fairly well put together. They are, however, with the exception of some of the bazaars, crooked, and of course narrow, although there are one or two by which a carriage can enter the bazaar.

The roads are mostly fairly well paved, and on the whole moderately clean. The private houses, of course, present, except in some of the non-Muslim quarters, a plain and uninteresting expanse of wall to the road. A great proportion of them are only one-storied buildings, experience having taught the inhabitants the danger of tall edifices in a town where earthquakes seem to be 'laid on.' Some of them, however, have two stories. As a rule they surround a somewhat pretty little courtyard, into which the windows of the establishment look. In the case of some of the older houses, pretty little panels of arabesque are to be seen over these windows, and over the entrance-door. Sometimes windows themselves are cut into geometrical or other tracery in stone, which has a good effect. In the courtyard there is almost invariably a well.

The roofs are, of course, flat, and upon them the inhabitants pass a great deal of their time. It is said that a great part of the town can be passed over without entering the street, by passing over the roofs.

To the stranger making a call at a native house, Muslim or Christian, the mode of procedure is somewhat embarrassing. The door is generally furnished with a knocker, in many cases now a French importation in the shape of a lady's hand in iron or bronze. Upon this being applied no one opens the door, as Europeans would expect, but instead a squeaky voice is heard somewhere in the distance saying 'Min' (Who) – a somewhat awkward query to the traveller.

There is no European quarter in Aleppo, and consequently there are no European shops. There is, however, one street which is particularly occupied by shops selling Frankish wares, and these are mostly kept by Levantines. There is among them one shop where a good many useful things for a journey, such as tinned provisions, biscuits, and similar things can be obtained.

The bazaars themselves are extensive, and though, compared with Cairo, in every way inferior, yet they are superior to those seen at the present day at the more famous Bagdad. They are as a rule fairly wide, arched or covered over, and the shops (square niches in the wall, in which sits the merchant among his merchandise) are often larger, though less characteristic, than those of Cairo. Manchester cotton and prints are seen everywhere, which ugly, but cheap and serviceable, manufactures are cutting out the beautiful old silks of native make. Of course the silk manufacture is still carried on in Syria, at Aleppo and elsewhere, and beautiful things can be bought; but the industry is sadly on the wane. Separate bazaars or markets are devoted to separate wares; and the curious traveller can inspect markets teeming with wool, cotton, or hides, or tramp through long alleys hung with festoons of red slippers or silk kaffiehs. Under the friendly guidance of Mr. Jago, I had many rambles through these picturesque scenes. The size of the bazaars is shown by the fact that I was as much at sea as to my whereabouts in them at my last ramble as at my first; but whether Van Egmont's seventy-seven bazaars exist now, or ever did, I have no means of knowing.

A barber's shop in Aleppo is very characteristic. A square room is surrounded by a wooden bench, which is divided by arms into separate seats. This bench is very high, so that the individual to be operated on has his feet about twelve inches above the floor. His face is thus brought out the correct level for operations. In the centre of the apartment is a tank, from which the water is taken, which after use is thrown on to the stone floor. The attendants of the barber are boys, who are fitted with tall pattens varying according to their own stature. A small boy has pattens a foot high, so as to bring him on to the right level.

Of the mosques of Aleppo I saw nothing but the exteriors, as it is not customary to allow Europeans to enter. The great mosque, situated in the west part of the town, is called the Jamah Zakari, or Amawi, and is supposed to contain the tomb of Zacharias, and to replace a Christian church. Its chief feature is a handsome square minaret, divided externally into five stages by string courses; the upper two being enriched with cusped arcades. The remainder of the building is a square court surrounded by colonnades. The mosque is said to have been twice burned down and rebuilt, so that between this and earthquakes it is improbable that much early work remains. The tower, however, which is said to bear the date of 1290, is in fair preservation. Some travellers assert that it is the belfry of St. Zacharias' church itself, which has been incorporated with the Muslim mosque. The church is said to have been built by the Empress Helena.

There is rather a pretty, though small, mosque on the south side of the citadel opposite the great gateway. It is called Sultanieh, or sometimes by Levantines and Franks, the Cruch or Crouche Mosque. It is now unused, and the doors are blocked up, so that I could not get inside. The front has a very tall pointed arch, in the recess of which is the doorway. To the spectator's left of the door are three tall square recesses, with stalactite work at the top. They are almost as tall as the great arch, which is in fact the height of the building as it is at present. These recesses each contain a square opening near the ground, and a small pointed window above. On the right of the door are three other similar recesses, which are not, however, close together, like those to the left. An octagonal minaret and two small domes rise above the building.

Both upon the doorway described, and upon one on the north side of the building are coats of arms, which may be blazoned – On a fess a goblet, another in base.

The citadel is by far the most interesting and remarkable place in the town. It is placed rather towards the east of the centre of the walled city, upon the highest ground within the walls. The great mound upon which the ancient fortifications stand is roughly circular, and surrounded by a wide and deep ditch. The circumference, taken at the edge of the ditch, must be close on three-quarters of a mile. The hill or mound itself is about two hundred feet in height, and although continually stated to be artificial, is in all probability only partly so, as Russell states that live rock has been found near the summit. It is not improbable that the citadel occupies part, possibly the whole, of the site of ancient Beroea, and it may be compared to some of the large mounds which stud the great plains of Northern Syria and Mesopotamia. The old Arab authors record a tradition that the hill is supported by two thousand columns, which may be but Oriental romance, or possibly have its origin from the discovery of ancient columns and buildings at the time when it was fortified by the Mohammedan conquerors. Indeed, Dr. Pococke states that he was informed that marble columns were frequently found deep in the earth to the north-east of the citadel. Mr. Jago kindly obtained an order for me to view the place, and accompanied me himself on the occasion of my visit. We made our way to the great entrance on the south, which is by far the finest feature of the whole structure. I noticed that the slope of the mound was strongly faced with masonry, which proves that even if the hill is partly natural, it has been much improved and fashioned by art, as this masonry is no doubt meant to keep loose made earth from slipping down. The arrangement of the entrance is this: A massive square gate-house of great size has been built on the summit and slope of the hill, from which a stone bridge of six pointed arches crosses the moat to a smaller gate-house, or barbican, placed within, but near the outer edge of the ditch. From this, again, a half-arch is thrown into the counterscarp, completing the connexion across.

The barbican is a handsome construction, square in plan, with the angles rounded. The doorway is plain, with a flat segmental arch, and on either side is a small window. Straight above is a triple machico-lation for the purposes of defence. The summit is battlemented. The great gate-house is a noble structure thrown out nearly a square from the *enceinte* wall of the citadel. The entrance is through a lofty pointed arch, above which, rising to the present summit of the building, is a tall, right-angled recess, ornate with variegated masonry, and finished at the top with pendant or stalactite work. On either side of the entrance, at the spring of the arch, which is about half the total height of the building, are three sets of machicolations, those at the angles being sextuple and the others triple. Below these is a long inscription in the Kufy character, which is said to bear the name of Malik ad Dahir, A.H. 605. On either side of the tall square recess are small windows, and on the face of the building are various circular medallions, some of which are inscribed. The citadel is at present unoccupied, except by a few soldiers, as the interior is quite ruinous. The Pasha of Aleppo, however, is a man who is particularly anxious to present a smart and soldier-like appearance in things military to any Europeans, and especially Englishmen, who visit the town, and whose curiosity leads them to examine or inquire in any way into such matters. The consequence of this was, that on our arrival at the great gate we were received by a guard of four men under the command of a junior officer, or captain over ten, who all came smartly to the 'present' as we approached. The consular dragoman was in attendance, and the officer first drew our attention to a great number of holes in the outer wall, which he informed us were made by arrows and bolts, the heads of many of which, he stated, were still imbedded in the stone. The holes are certainly there, but it is difficult to believe that an arrow launched from an ordinary hand-bow would have sufficient strength and penetration to force its way two inches or more into hard freestone. They are more probably formed by bullets, but if, as is stated, the arrow-heads are still within the holes, some very powerful engine must have been used to launch them at the walls. Passing under the great arch we found ourselves within a lofty recess, all three sides of which were defended by machicolations, which were carried on at the same level, and were, in fact, the continuation of the line of machicolations observed outside.

The approach to the interior of the castle from here is by a long winding staircase of great breadth, and vaulted above at a great height. This stair turns first to the right, out of the arched recess, and afterwards makes several turns in either direction, before the level of the *enceinte* is reached. It is defended at intervals by strong iron doors. I believe, though here I speak from memory, that these are three in number. The outer one is plain, but the inner ones are decorated in a somewhat curious fashion, the surface of the metal being divided into small squares, each of which has in the centre a horse-shoe of wrought iron. On one of the gates there is also an inscription in the same metal. At the last turn before the *enceinte* is reached there are on the right the tombs of two holy men, whose names I was not able to ascertain. These are decorated with tattered flags.

Just inside the gate, a grating close to the ground, and giving light apparently to an underground chamber, was pointed out to us as a window of the old castle prison; and close by, our attention was gravely drawn to a large tank of water, which tradition said was the identical vessel in which Abraham kept the milk of the self-same dappled cow who had the honour to giving a name to Aleppo. From here we were conducted through desolate ruins to the north side of the hill, where there still stands a square minaret, the solitary remnant of the citadel mosque. Here chairs were brought for us to sit, and another officer, of superior grade, appeared to point out the beauties of the scene, while coffee and glasses of the citadel water were brought us. The latter was drawn from a well, said to be one hundred and fifty yards deep, at the bottom of which is a roaring torrent, an assertion which we received with the utmost gravity, and tried to look as if we swallowed it with the same facility with which we swallowed the water. The view from the summit of the minaret is extremely fine. At one's feet lies the town, which in itself, however, is somewhat uninteresting, as little besides the courts of the mosques and the roof-tops is to be seen. One notices but half-a-dozen minarets and a few domes. How different from the gorgeous spectacle that unrolls itself at the feet when one gazes from the citadel of Cairo. At the same time one realises for the first time the great size of Aleppo, and the buzz rising from the city apprises one of the great population thronging it. To the north-west lay in the distance the mountains about Beilan, which I had but a few days before crossed; due north at a great distance another low blue mountain, which must be somewhere close to Aintab; in the same direction at our feet was the Serai, while just outside the city the domes of Skeikhu Bekr, a monastery of durwishes, formed a striking object; and close to it an ugly range of barracks. East, lay miles of moory desert, stretching away towards the Euphrates; south-east could be discerned the depression in which lies the great salt lake of Jibul; while on the west and south-west we saw the blue plain through which the river winds in its orchards of fruit trees. Due west rose against the sky the snow peaks about Antioch.

Leaving the minaret, we were conducted to the castle well, where the water is raised by means of a horse and windlass. From the sound caused by dropping a stone into it, it appears to be of very great depth. All the while we were moving about, soldiers rushed hither and thither with chairs, to stick them down before us whenever we paused. Having now seen the sights, a third officer, still more mighty than his predecessors, appeared, having apparently been kept hidden to the last as a special treat and mark of honour. With him we proceeded to a small room in the walls, which was furnished with divans and was apparently used for the reception of superior officers when they visited the citadel. We

were no sooner seated than coffee was again served, followed immediately by enormous glasses of orange sherbet. Etiquette demanded that
we should drink them, which we did, all swelling visibly under the
operation. Some desultory conversation followed, and we then departed
with much bowing, salaming, hat removing, and bakhshishing; the latter, of course, being conveyed to the guard of honour of four men,
commanded by the captain of ten, who in their exuberance came to the
'present' with redoubled violence as we left the building.

Mr. Jago informed me that such a display of fantasia was quite unusual
on the occasion of the citadel being visited by Europeans. As a rule a
solitary soldier conducts the stranger over the place.

The wall enclosing the citadel is strengthened at frequent intervals,
but the whole is now in a state of utter ruin. There are also one or two
outworks in the shape of towers, built out into the ditch, and connected
with the main fortification by walls.

The citadel, of course, played an important part in the various vicis-
situdes which Aleppo passed through, and of which mention has already
been made. In 1630 the Sultan Amurath IV. stripped it of such artillery
as it then possessed, to make use of in besieging Bagdad. Van Egmont
informs us that in his time the castle contained about two hundred and
fifty houses; its inhabitants were usually twelve thousand, and its garrison three hundred and fifty; that the janissaries in garrison never took
the field in any emergency, but when once in the castle lived and died
in that service, and that it did 'not seem to be answerably provided with
cannon and other military stores.' Some of the vaults are now said to
contain a quantity of ancient bows, arrows, and other weapons.

Being now upon things military, I may mention that the only troops
I had an opportunity of seeing at Aleppo on parade were live batter-
ies of artillery that passed one morning through the Azizia quarter,
on their way to the plain outside the town, where they were going to
exercise. The guns were Krupps in good order, and some of the horses
excellent. But the men were dirty, and the harness and trappings very
rotten-looking and not clean. The latter was, as I learnt afterwards, a job
lot, bought cheap after the American Civil War.

There are many khans in Aleppo, in which, indeed, even at this day,
much of the trade of Oriental towns is transacted, and the great court-
yards of which are generally stored with vast piles of merchandise. Some
among them are handsome structures, vividly recalling the romances of
the 'Thousand and One Nights.' One, probably the finest in Aleppo, is

called the Khan al-Wazir, and is situated in the west of the town. It is entered by a fine gateway, the masonry of which on the side facing the street is in courses of black and white laid alternately. On the front are carved panels and bosses sculptured with lions. The inner side of the entrance has a pointed arch supported on columns, with stalactite caps. Passing through this gate I found myself in a large square, in the centre of which was a fountain, so that the whole building had very much the appearance of an early mosque. The quadrangle buildings were of two stories, the lower plain, with doorways entering from the court, while the front of the upper was an open arcade on all sides, except that on which was the entrance. This colonnade was mostly of plain character, being simple arches supported on square columns; but in two places – namely, at the left end of the side to the left on entering, and a section at the same end of the side opposite the entrance – there was arcade work of more ornate character, having slightly ogee arches supported by Saracenic columns with stalactite, or otherwise ornamented capitals. At first I was inclined to think that this indicated a difference of date, but as, where the two styles joined, there was a bastard column consisting of a square support, with a demi-column built to its side, it is possible the whole building is of one date, and may, perhaps, have been built a hundred and fifty years ago. Many of the windows looking into the court had very pretty arabesques over them. The fountain was also supported by columns of the same character as the ornate part of the arcade. [...]

Although so much of the bazaars and streets in the town is covered over, this mode of building has now been made illegal. Close to the hotel was a new street, all of which belonged to one owner. He, wishing to vault it over in the old style, bakhshished the authorities handsomely, and having got everything in readiness, ran up the scaffolding in a night, and when morning broke two hundred men were just getting to work to set the arches. Unfortunately for the enterprise, it came to the ears of some superior authority, I think the Waly, who dropped on the proceedings in a trice, and put an end to them. The walls all stand unfinished, with the corbels fixed, on which the arches were to rest.

Aleppo, as I have said, is completely surrounded by cemeteries. The majority are of course Moslem, but on the north are to be found the European, Armenian, and Jewish burying-grounds. The former is close to the Azizia quarter, and contains many inscriptions in remembrance of English and other European merchants, who were members of the factories during the last two hundred years. I should have liked, if I had had time, to have transcribed the English ones. They are mostly very simple as,

Charles Robert Thompson, Esq., of Whitehaven in England. Died in Aleppo on the 20th of December, 1865.

Some, probably foreign, are embellished with florid coats of arms and nearly all are unfortunately in a sad state of repair.

Chapter Twenty Six

Syria: The Desert and the Sown (1907) and *Amurath to Amurath* (1911)

Gertrude Bell *(1868–1926), the celebrated traveller, writer, archaeologist and British agent was in Aleppo in 1905, 1909, 1911 and 1919. Sultan Abdulhamid II assumed she had 'bad intentions for the caliphate' and had her followed. After the First World War, she helped establish the Kingdom of Iraq and died in Baghdad in 1926. In* Syria: The Desert and the Sown *Bell describes Aleppo in 1905. In* Amurath to Amurath *she describes her visit to Aleppo in 1909, after the Young Turk Revolution of 1908 had transformed the Ottoman Empire.*

Syria: The Desert and the Sown

CHAPTER XI

About half an hour to the north of Kefr 'Abid there is a little beehive village which contains a very perfect mosaic of geometrical patterns. The fragments of other mosaics are to be found scattered through the village, some in the houses, and some in the courtyards, and the whole district needs careful exploration while the new settlers are turning up the ground and before they destroy what they may find. We reached Aleppo at midday, approaching it by an open drain. Whether it were because of the evil smell or because of the heavy sky and dust-laden wind I do not know, but the first impression of Aleppo was disappointing. The name, in its charming Europeanised form, should belong to a more attractive city, and attractive Aleppo certainly is not, for it is set in a barren, tree-less, featureless world, the beginning of the great Mesopotamian flats. The site of the town is like a cup and saucer, the houses lie in the saucer and the castle stands on the up-turned cup, its minaret visible several hours away while no vestige of the city appears until the last mile of the road. I stayed two days, during which time it rained almost cease-lessly, therefore I do not know Aleppo – an Oriental city will not admit you into the circle of its intimates unless you spend months within its walls, and not even then if you will not take pains to please – but I did not leave without having perceived dimly that there was something to be known. It has been a splendid Arab city; as you walk down the nar-row streets you pass minarets and gateways of the finest period of Arab architecture; some of the mosques and baths and khans (especially those half ruined and closed) are in the same style, and the castle is the best example of twelfth-century Arab workmanship in all Syria, with iron doors of the same period – they are dated – and beautiful bits of decor-ation. There must be some native vitality still that corresponds to these signs of past greatness, but the town has fallen on evil days. It has been caught between the jealousies of European concession hunters, and it suffers more than most Syrian towns from the strangling grasp of the Ottoman Government. It is slowly dying for want of an outlet to the sea, and neither the French nor the German railway will supply its need. Hitherto the two companies have been busily engaged in thwarting one another. The original concession to the Rayak-Hamah railway extended to Aleppo and north to Birijik – I was told that the tickets to Birijik were printed off when the first rails were laid at Rayak. Then came

Germany, with her great scheme of a railway to Baghdad. She secured a concession for a branch line from Killiz to Aleppo, and did what she could to prevent the French from advancing beyond Hamah, on the plea that the French railway would detract from the value of the German concession – my information, it may be well imagined, is not from the Imperial Chancery, but from native sources in Aleppo itself. Since I left, the French have taken up their interrupted work on the Rayak-Hamah line, though it is to be carried forward, I believe, not to Birijik, but only as far as Aleppo. It will be of no benefit to the town. Aleppo merchants do not wish to send their goods a three days' journey to Beyrout; they want a handy seaport of their own, which will enable them to pocket all the profits of the trade, and that port should be Alexandretta. Neither does the Baghdad railway, if it be continued, offer any prospect of advantage. By a branch line already existing (it was built by English and French capitalists, but has recently passed under German control) the railway will touch the sea at Mersina, but Mersina is as far from Aleppo as is Beyrout. That a line should be laid direct from Aleppo to Alexandretta is extremely improbable, since the Sultan fears above all things to connect the inland caravan routes with the coast, lest the troops of the foreigner, and particularly of England, should find it perilously easy to land from their warships and march up country. Aleppo should be still, as it was in times past, the great distributing centre for the merchandise of the interior, but traffic is throttled by the fatal frequency with which the Government commandeers the baggage camels. Last year, with the Yemen war on hand and the consequent necessity of transporting men and military stores to the coast that they might be shipped to the Red Sea, this grievance had become acute. For over a month trade had been stagnant and goods bound for the coast had lain piled in the bazaar – a little more and they would cease to come at all, the camel owners from the East not daring to enter the zone of danger to their beasts. Here, as in all other Turkish towns, I heard the cry of official bankruptcy. The Government had no funds wherewith to undertake the most necessary works, the treasuries were completely empty.

Though my stay was short I was not without acquaintances, among whom the most important was the Vāli. Kiāzim Pasha is a man of very different stamp from the Vāli of Damascus. To the extent that the latter is, according to his lights, a real statesman, in so far is Kiāzim nothing but a *farceur*. He received me in his harem, for which I was grateful when I saw his wife, who is one of the most beautiful women that it is possible to behold. She is tall and stately, with a small dark head, set on magnificent shoulders, a small straight nose, a pointed chin and brows arching over eyes that are like dark pools – I could not take mine from her face while she sat with us. Both she and her husband are Circassians, a fact that had put me on my guard before the Vāli opened his lips. They both spoke French, and he spoke it very well. He received me in an offhand manner, and his first remark was:

'Je suis le jeune pasha qui a fait la paix entre les églises.'

I knew enough of his history to realise that he had been Muteserrif of Jerusalem at a time when the rivalries between the Christian sects had ended in more murders than are customary, and that some kind of uneasy compromise had been reached, whether through his ingenuity or the necessities of the case I had not heard.

'How old do you think I am?' said the pasha.

I replied tactfully that I should give him thirty-five years.

'Thirty-six!' he said triumphantly. 'But the consuls listened to me. Mon Dieu! that was a better post than this, though I am Vāli now. Here I have no occasion to hold conferences with the consuls, and a man like me needs the society of educated Europeans.'

(Mistrust the second: an Oriental official, who declares that he prefers the company of Europeans.)

'I am very Anglophil,' said he.

I expressed the gratitude of my country in suitable terms.

'But what are you doing in Yemen?' he added quickly.

'Excellency,' said I, 'we English are a maritime people, and there are but two places that concern us in all Arabia.'

'I know,' he interpolated. 'Mecca and Medina.'

'No,' said I. 'Aden and Kweit.'

'And you hold them both,' he returned angrily – yes, I am bound to confess that the tones of his voice were not those of an Anglo-maniac.

Presently he began to tell me that he alone among pashas had grasped modern necessities. He meant to build a fine metalled road to Alexandria – not that it will be of much use, thought I, if there are no camels to walk in it like the road he had built from Samaria to Jerusalem. That was a road like none other in Turkey – did I know it? I had but lately travelled over it, and seized the opportunity of congratulating the maker of it; but I did not think it necessary to mention that it breaks off at the bottom of the only serious ascent and does not begin again till the summit of the Judaean plateau is reached.

This is all that need be said of Kiāzim Pasha's methods.

A far more sympathetic acquaintance was the Greek Catholic archbishop, a Damascene educated in Paris and for some time curé of the Greek Catholic congregation in that city, though he is still comparatively young. I had been given a letter to him, on the presentation of which he received me with great affability in his own house. We sat in a room filled with books, the windows opening on to the silent courtyard of his palace, and talked of the paths into which thought had wandered in Europe; but I found to my pleasure that for all his learning and his long sojourn in the West, the archbishop had remained an Oriental at heart.

'I rejoiced,' said he, 'when I was ordered to return from Paris to my own land. There is much knowledge, but little faith in France; while in Syria, though there is much ignorance, religion rests upon a sure foundation of belief.'

The conclusion that may be drawn from this statement is not flattering to the Church, but I refrained from comment.

He appeared in the afternoon to return my call – from the Vāli downwards all must conform to this social obligation – wearing his gold cross and carrying his archiepiscopal staff in his hand. From his tall brimless hat a black veil fell down his back, his black robes were edged with purple, and an obsequious chaplain walked behind him. He found another visitor sitting with me in the inn parlour, Nicola Homsi, a rich banker of his own congregation. Homsi belongs to an important Christian family settled in Aleppo, and his banking house has representatives in Marseilles and in London. He and the Archbishop between them were fairly representative of the most enterprising and the best educated classes in Syria. It is they who suffer at the hands of the Turk, the ecclesiastic, because of a blind and meaningless official opposition that meets the Christian at every turn; the banker, because his interests call aloud for progress, and progress is what the Turk will never understand. I therefore asked them what they thought would be the future of the country. They looked at one another, and the Archbishop answered:

'I do not know. I have thought deeply on the subject, and I can see no future for Syria, whichever way I turn.'

That is the only credible answer I have heard to any part of the Turkish question.

The air of Aleppo is judged by the Sultan to be particularly suitable for pashas who have fallen under his displeasure at Constantinople. The town is so full of exiles that even the most casual visitor can scarcely help making acquaintance with a few of them. One was lodged in my hotel, a mild-mannered dyspeptic, whom no one would have suspected of revolutionary sympathies. Probably he was indeed without them, and owed his banishment merely to some chance word, reported and magnified by an enemy or a spy. I was to see many of these exiles scattered up and down Asia Minor, and none that I encountered could tell me for what cause they had suffered banishment. Some, no doubt, must have had a suspicion, and some were perfectly well aware of their offence, but most of them were as innocently ignorant as they professed to be. Now this has a wider bearing on the subject of Turkish patriotic feeling than may at first appear; for the truth is that these exiled pashas are very rarely patriots paying the price of devotion to a national ideal, but rather men whom an unlucky turn of events has alienated from the existing order. If there is any chance that they may be taken back into favour you will find them nervously anxious, even in exile, to refrain from action that would tend to increase official suspicion; and it is only when they have determined that there is no hope for them as long as the present Sultan lives, that they are willing to associate freely with Europeans or to speak openly of their grievances. There is, so far as I can see, no organised body of liberal opinion in Turkey, but merely individual discontents, founded on personal misfortune. It seems improbable that when the exiles return to Constantinople on the death of the Sultan they will provide any scheme of re-form or show any desire to alter a system under which, by the natural revolution of affairs, they will again find themselves persons of consideration.

There is another form of exile to be met with in Turkey, the honourable banishment of a distant appointment. To this class, I fancy, belongs Nāzim Pasha himself, and so does my friend Muḥammad 'Ali Pasha of Aleppo. The latter is an agreeable man of about thirty, married to an English wife. He accompanied me to the Vali's house, obtained permission that I should see the citadel, and in many ways contrived to make himself useful. His wife was a pleasant little lady from Brixton; he had met her in Constantinople and there married her, which may, for ought I know, have been partly the reason of his fall from favour, the English nation not being a *gens grata* at Yildiz Kiosk. Muḥammad 'Ali Pasha is a gentleman in the full sense of the word, and he seems to have made his wife happy; but it must be clearly understood that I could not as a general rule recommend Turkish pashas as husbands to the maidens of Brixton. Though she played tennis at the Tennis

Club, and went to the sewing parties of the European colony, she was obliged to conform to some extent to the habits of Moslem women. She never went into the streets without being veiled; 'because people would talk if a pasha's wife were to show her face,' said she.

We reached the citadel in the one hour of sunlight that shone on Aleppo during my stay, and were taken round by polite officers, splendid in uniforms and clanking swords and spurs, who were particularly anxious that I should not miss the small mosque in the middle of the fortress, erected on the very spot where Abraham milked his cow. The very name of Aleppo, said they, is due to this historic occurrence, and there can be no doubt that its Arabic form, Haleb, is composed of the same root letters as those that form the verb to milk. In spite of the deep significance of the mosque, I was more interested in the view from the top of the minaret. The Mesopotamian plain lay outspread before us, as flat as a board – Euphrates stream is visible from that tower on a clear day, and indeed you might see Baghdad but for the tiresome way in which the round earth curves, for there is no barrier to the eye in all that great level. Below us, were the clustered roofs of bazaar and khan, with here and there a bird's-eye glimpse of marble courtyards, and here and there the fine spire of a minaret. Trees and water were lacking in the landscape, and water is the main difficulty in Aleppo itself. The sluggish stream that flows out of the Matkh dries up in the summer, and the wells are brackish all the year round. Good drinking water must be brought from a great distance and costs every household at least a piastre a day, a serious addition to the cost of living. But the climate is good, sharply cold in winter and not over hot for more than a month or two in the summer. Such is Aleppo, the great city with the high-sounding name and the traces of a splendid past.

Amurath to Amurath

CHAPTER I
ALEPPO TO TELL AHMAR
Feb. 3–Feb. 21

If there be a better gate to Asia than Aleppo, I do not know it. A virile population, a splendid architecture, the quickening sense of a fine Arab tradition have combined to give the town an individuality sharply cut, and more than any other Syrian city she seems instinct with an inherent vitality. The princes who drew the line of massive masonry about her flanks and led her armies against the emperors of the West, the merchants who gathered the wealth of inner Asia into her bazaars and bartered it against the riches of the Levant Company have handed down the spirit of enterprise to the latest of her sons. They drive her caravans south to Baghdad, and east to Vân, and north to Konia, and in the remotest cities of the Turkish empire I have seldom failed to find a native of Aleppo eager to provide me with a local delicacy and to gossip over local politics.

[...]

It was at Aleppo that I made acquaintance with the Turkey which had come into being on July 24, 1908. Even among those whose sympathies were deeply engaged on behalf of the new order, there were not many Europeans who, in January 1909, had any clue to public opinion outside Constantinople and Salonica. The events of the six stirring months that had just elapsed had yet to be heard and apprehended, and no sooner had I landed in Beyrout than I began to shed European formulas and to look for the Asiatic value of the great catchwords of revolution. In Aleppo, sitting at the feet of many masters, who ranged down all the social grades from the high official to the humblest labourer for hire, I learnt something of the hopes and fears, the satisfaction, the bewilderment, and the indifference of Asia. The populace had shared in the outburst of enthusiasm which had greeted the granting of the constitution – a moment of unbridled expectation when, in the brief transport of universal benevolence, it seemed as if the age-long problems of the Turkish empire had been solved with a stroke of the pen; they had journeyed back from that Utopia to find that human nature remained much as it had been before. The public mind was unhinged; men were obsessed with a sense of change, perplexed because change was slow to come, and alarmed lest it should spring upon them unawares. The relaxation of the rule of fear had worked in certain directions with immediate effect, but not invariably to the increase of security. True, there was a definite gain of personal liberty. The spies had disappeared from official quarters, and with them the exiles, who had been condemned by 'Abdu'l Hamîd, on known or unknown pretexts, to languish helplessly in the provincial capitals. Everywhere a daily press had sprung into existence and foreign books and papers passed unhindered through the post. The childish and exasperating restrictions with which the Sultan had fettered his Christian subjects had fallen away. The Armenians were no longer tied to the spot whereon they dwelt; they could, and did, travel where they pleased. The nâmûsîyeh, the identification certificate, had received the annual government stamp without delay, and without need of bribes. In every company, Christian and Moslem, tongues were unloosed in outspoken criticism of official dealings, but it was extremely rare to find in these freely vented opinions anything of a constructive nature. The government was still, to the bulk of the population, a higher power, disconnected from those upon whom it exercised its will. You might complain of its lack of understanding just as you cursed the hailstorm that destroyed your crops, but you were in no way answerable for it, nor would you attempt to control or advise it, any more than you would offer advice to the hail cloud. Many a time have I searched for some trace of the Anglo-Saxon acceptance of a common responsibility in the problems that beset the State, a sense the germs of which exist in the Turkish village community and in the tribal system of the Arab and the Kurd; it never went beyond an embryonic application to small local matters, and the answers I received resembled, *mutatis mutandis*, that of Fattûh when I questioned him as to the part he had played in the recent general election. 'Your Excellency knows that I am a carriage-driver, what have I to do with government? But I can tell you that the new government is no better than the old. Look now at Aleppo; have we a juster law? wallah, no!'

In some respects they had indeed a yet more laggard justice than in 'the days of tyranny' – so we spoke of the years that were past – or perhaps it would be truer to say a yet more laggard administration. The dislocation of the old order was a fact considerably more salient than the substitution for it of another system. The officials shared to the full the general sense of impermanence that is inevitable to revolution, however soberly it may be conducted; they were uncertain of the limits of their own authority, and as far as possible each one would shuffle out of definite action lest it might prove that he had overstepped the mark. In the old days a person of influence would occasionally rectify by processes superlegal a miscarriage of the law; the miscarriages continued, but intervention was curtailed by doubts and misgivings. The spies had been in part replaced by the agents of the Committee, who wielded a varying but practically irresponsible power. How far the supremacy of the local committees extended it was difficult to judge, nor would a conclusion based upon evidence from one province have been applicable to another; but my impression is that nowhere were they of much account, and that the further the district was removed from the coast, that is, from contact with the European centres of the new movement, the less influential did they become. Possibly in the remoter provinces the local committee was itself reactionary, as I have heard it affirmed, or at best an object of ridicule, but in Syria, at any rate, the committees existed in more than the name. Their inner organization was at that time secret, as was the organization of the parent society. They had taken form at the moment when the constitution was proclaimed, and had undergone a subsequent reconstruction at the hands of delegates from Salonica, who were sent to instruct them in their duties. I came across one case where these delegates, having been unwisely selected, left the committee less well qualified to cope with local conditions than they found it, but usually they discharged their functions with discretion. The committees opened clubs of Union and Progress, the members of which numbered in the bigger towns several hundreds. The club of Aleppo was a flourishing institution lodged in a large bare room in the centre of the town. It offered no luxuries to the members, military and civilian, who gathered round its tables of an evening, but it supplied them with a good stock of newspapers, which they read gravely under the shadow of a life-sized portrait of Midhat Pasha, the hero and the victim of the first constitution. The night of my visit the newly formed sub-committee for commerce was holding its first deliberations on a subject which is of the utmost importance to the prosperity of Aleppo: the railway connection with the port of Alexandretta. To this discussion I was admitted, but the proceedings after I had taken my seat at the board were of an emotional rather than of a practical character, and I left with cries of 'Yasha Inghilterra!' ('Long live England!') in my ears. I carried away with me the impression that whatever might be the future scope of its activities, the committee could not fail, in these early days, to be of some educational value. It brought men together to debate on matters that touched the common good and invited them to bear a part in their promotion. The controlling authority of the executive body was of much more questionable advantage. Its members, whose names were kept profoundly secret, were supposed to keep watch over the conduct of affairs and to forward reports to the central committee: I say *supposed*, because I have no means of knowing whether they actually carried out what they stated to be their duties. They justified their position by declaring that it was a temporary expedient which would lapse as soon as the leaders of the new movement were assured of official loyalty to the constitution, and arbitrary as their functions may appear it would have been impossible to assert that Asiatic Turkey was fit to run without leading-strings. But I do not believe that the enterprise of the committees was sufficient to hamper a strong governor; and so far as my observation went, the welfare of each province depended, and must depend for many a year to come, upon the rectitude and the determination of the man who is placed in authority over it.

Underlying all Turkish politics are the closely interwoven problems of race and religion, which had been stirred to fresh activity by exuberant promises. Fraternity and equality are dangerous words to scatter broadcast across an empire composed of many nationalities and controlled by a dominant race. Under conditions such as these equality in its most rigid sense can scarcely be said to exist, while fraternity is complicated by the fact that the ruling race professes Islam, whereas many of the subordinate elements are Christian. The Christian population of Aleppo was bitterly disheartened at having failed to return one of their own creed out of the six deputies who represent the vilayet. I met, in the house of a common friend, a distinguished member of the Christian community who threw a great deal of light on this subject. He began by observing that even in the vilayet of Beyrout, though so large a proportion of the inhabitants are Christian, the appointment of a non-Moslem governor would be impossible; so much, he said, for the boast of equality. This is, of course, undeniable, though in the central government, where they are not brought into direct contact with a Moslem population, Christians are admitted to the highest office. He complained that when the Christians of Aleppo had urged that they should be permitted to return a representative to the chamber, the Moslems had given them no assistance. 'They replied,' interposed our host, 'that it was all one, since Christians and Moslems are merged in Ottoman.' I turned to my original interlocutor and inquired whether the various communions had agreed upon a common candidate.

'No,' he answered with some heat. 'They brought forward as many candidates as there are sects. Thus it is in our unhappy country; even the Christians are not brothers, and one church will not trust the other.'

I said that this regrettable want of confidence was not confined to Turkey, and asked whether, if they could have commanded a united vote, they would have carried their candidate. He admitted with reluctance that he thought it would have been possible, and this view was confirmed by an independent witness who said that a Christian candidate, carefully chosen and well supported, would have received in addition the Jewish vote, since that community was too small to return a separate representative.

As for administrative reform, it hangs upon the urgent problem of finance. From men who are overworked and underpaid neither efficiency nor honesty can be expected, but to increase their number or their salary is an expensive business, and money is not to be had. How small are the local resources may be judged from the fact that Aleppo, a town of at least 120,000 inhabitants, possesses a municipal income of from £3,000 to £4,000 a year. Judges who enjoy an annual salary of from £60 to £90 are not likely to prove incorruptible, and it is difficult to see how a mounted policeman can support existence on less than £12 a year, though one of my zaptiehs assured me that the pay was sufficient if it had been regular. In the vilayet of Aleppo and the mutesarriflik of Deir all the zaptiehs who accompanied me had received the arrears due to them as well as their weekly wage, but this fortunate condition did not extend to other parts of the empire.

The plain man of Aleppo did not trouble his head with fiscal problems; he judged the new government by immediate results and found it wanting. I rode one sunny afternoon with the boy, Fattûh's brother-in-law, who was to accompany us on our journey, to the spring of 'Ain Tell, a mile or two north of the town. Jûsef – his name, as Fattûḥ was careful to point out, is French: 'I thought your Excellency knew French,' he said severely, in answer to my tactless inquiry – Jûsef conducted me across wet meadows, where in spring the citizens of Aleppo take the air, and past a small mound, no doubt artificial, a relic perhaps of the constructions of Seif ed Dauleh, whose palace once occupied these fields. Close to the spring stands a mill with a pair of stone lions carved on the slab above the door, the heraldic supporters of some prince of Aleppo. They had been dug out of the mound together with a fine basalt door, like those which are found among the fourth and fifth century ruins in the neighbouring hills; the miller dusted it with his sleeve and observed that it was an antîca. A party of dyers, who were engaged in spreading their striped cotton cloths upon the sward, did me the honours of their drying-ground – merry fellows they were, the typical sturdy Christians of Aleppo, who hold their own with their Moslem brothers and reckon little of distinctions of creed.

'Christian and Moslem,' said one, 'see how we labour! If the constitution were worth anything, the poor would not work for such small rewards.'

'At any rate,' said I, 'you got your nâmûsîyeh cheaper this year.'

'Eh true!' he replied, 'but who can tell how long that will last?'

'Please God, it will endure,' said I.

'Please God,' he answered. 'But we should have been better satisfied to see the soldiers govern. A strong hand we need here in Aleppo, that the poor may enjoy the fruits of their toil.'

'Eh wah!' said another, 'and a government that we know.'

Between them they had summed up popular opinion, which is ever blind to the difficulties of reform and impatient because progress is necessarily slow footed.

We passed on our return the tekîyeh of Abu Bekr, a beautiful Mamlûk shrine with cypresses in its courtyard, which lift their black spires proudly over that treeless land. The brother of the hereditary sheikh showed me the mosque; it contains an exquisite miḥrāb of laced stone work, and windows that are protected by carved wooden shutters and filled with old coloured glass. Near the mosque is the square hall of a bath, now fallen into disrepair. Four pendentives convert the square into an octagon, and eight more hold the circle of the dome – as fine a piece of massive construction as you would wish to see. The sheikh and his family occupied some small adjoining rooms, and the young wife of my guide made me welcome with smiles and lemon sherbet. From the deep embrasure of her window I looked out upon Aleppo citadel and congratulated her upon her secluded house set in the thickness of ancient walls.

'Yes,' she replied, eagerly detailing the benefits of providence, 'and we have a carpet for winter time, and there is no mother-in-law.'

[...]

The sombre splendour of the architecture of Aleppo is displayed nowhere better than in the Bîmâristân of El Malik eẓ Ẓâhir, which was built as a place of confinement for criminal lunatics and is still used for that purpose. The central court terminates at the southern end in the lîwân of a mosque covered with an oval dome; before it lies the ceremonial water-tank, if any one should have the heart to wash or pray in that house of despair. A door from the court leads into a stone corridor, out of which open rectangular stone chambers with massive walls rising to a great height, and carrying round and oval domes. Through narrow window slits, feeble shafts of light fall into the dank well beneath and shiver through the iron bars that close the cells of the lunatics. They sit more like beasts than men, loaded with chains in their dark cages, and glower at each other through the bars; and one was sick and moaned upon his wisp of straw, and one rattled his chains and clawed at the bars as though he would cry for mercy, but had forgotten human speech. 'They do not often recover,' said the gaoler, gazing indifferently into the sick man's cell, and I wondered in my heart whether there were any terms in which to reckon up the misery that had accumulated for generations under El Malik eẓ Ẓâhir's domes.

Like the numismatic emblem of a city goddess, Aleppo wears a towered crown. The citadel lies immediately to the east of the bazaars. A masonry bridge resting on tall narrow arches spans the moat between a crenelated outpost and the great square block of the inner gatehouse. Through a worked iron door, dated in the reign of El Malik eẓ Ẓâhir, you pass into a vaulted corridor which turns at right angles under an arch decorated with interlaced dragons [...] and ends at another arched doorway on which stand the leopards of Sultan Baybars, who rebuilt the castle in the thirteenth century. Above the entrance is a columned hall, grass-grown and ruined; passages lead down from it into vaulted chambers which would seem to have been repaired after Timûr had sacked Aleppo. Some of the blocks used in the walls here are Jewish tombstones dated by Hebrew inscriptions in the thirteenth century, and since it is scarcely possible that Baybars should have desecrated a cemetery of his own day, they must indicate a later period of reconstruction. The garrison was supplied with water from a well eighty metres deep which lies near the northern edge of the castle mound. Besides the well-hole, a stair goes down to the water level, near which point vaulted passages branch out to right and left. Tradition says that the whole mound is raised upon a substructure of masonry, but tradition is always ready with such tales, and the only inscription in the passages near the well is Cufic. At the northern limit of the enclosure stands a high square tower, up which, if you would know Aleppo, you must climb. From the muedhdhin's gallery the town lies revealed, a wide expanse of flat roof covering the bazaars, broken by dome and minaret, by the narrow clefts of streets and the courts of mosque and khan. The cypresses of Abu Bekr stand sentinel to the north; from that direction Timûr entered through the Bâb el Ḥadîd. In the low ground beyond the Antioch Gate, the armies of the Crusaders lay encamped; the railway, an invader more powerful than Baldwin, holds it now. Turn to the east, and as far as the eye can see, stretch rolling uplands, the granary of North Syria, and across them wind the caravan tracks that lead into inner Asia. There through the waste flows the Euphrates – you might almost from the tower catch the glint of its waters, so near to the western sea does its channel approach here.

I have never come to know an Oriental city without finding that it possesses a distinctive personality much more strongly accentuated than is usually the case in Europe, and this is essentially true of the Syrian towns. To compare Damascus, for example, with Aleppo, would be to set side by side two different conceptions of civilization. Damascus is the capital of the desert, Aleppo of the fertile plain. Damascus is the city of the Arab tribes who conquered her and set their stamp upon her; Aleppo, standing astride the trade routes of northern Mesopotamia, is a city of merchants quick to defend the wealth that they had gathered afar. So I read the history that is written upon her walls and impressed deep into the character of her adventurous sons.

At Aleppo the current of the imagination is tributary to the Euphrates. With Xenophon, with Julian, with all the armies captained by a dream of empire that dashed and broke against the Ancient East, the thoughts go marching down to the river which was the most famous of all frontier lines.

Chapter Twenty Seven

Dead Towns and
Living Men (1920)

*Leonard Woolley (1880–1960) was an assistant in the Ashmolean Museum
in Oxford, who later led the excavation of Ur in Iraq and became one of the
most admired British archaeologists of his day. From 1912 to 1914 (and again
in 1920) he excavated the Hittite city of Carchemish on the Euphrates, sixty
miles from Aleppo, near the railway line to Baghdad then being constructed under
German supervision; T. E. Lawrence was one of his assistants.*

ALEPPO

Aleppo is one of the oldest, the largest, and the most picturesque cities
of Turkey. Coming in by the French railway from Rayak, you climb a
low rise that had bounded your horizon and see the town lying in a shallow, saucer-like hollow whose rim of rounded hills is broken to north
and south by the valley of the Kuwaik River. High above its close-built
houses of white or grey-weathered stone rises the Mound capped with

the rust-red castle ruins, and clear of its outskirts on the nearest hillside a great Dervish 'teke' or monastery with graceful minarets and dark secular pines stands out boldly against the grey-green slopes of stony pasture; northwards a broad band of fruit orchards and gardens winds along the stream and fills all the valley bottom, where green shade, the murmur of running streams, and the droning music of the water-wheels give welcome refuge from the sweltering streets.

The railway skirts the saucer-rim to a station built outside the town against the hill's foot, and hence you will be driven past the ugly new suburb, across the Kuwaik, here a dwindled and a dirty stream, to the only hotel professing Western comforts, or up a long straight and hideous street to the Konak by the castle moat. The town which from the railway carriage window looked so splendid seems in this first drive to have lost all its glamour, but in truth these bastard European houses and half-built shops, the pride of the Aleppine, are but the modern blot on a still lovely Oriental city; pay off your ramshackle cab and plunge on foot into the native quarter and you will forget the monstrous 'improvements' of the West End in wonder and in delight.

The bazaars of Aleppo are an unending joy. If from the airy ramparts of the castle you look down upon the city spread map-like at your feet you will be surprised to see, hemmed in by crowded roofs, a wide stretch of meadow where goats and cattle pasture, a meadow broken here and there by square sunken wells and dome-like mounds, and by slender minarets which spring like builded poplars from the grass. This seeming meadow is the roof of the bazaar. Go down through the streets and pass under a massive archway with iron-studded doors and ponderous bars, and you will find yourself in a maze of cobbled lanes bordered with booths and roofed with vaults of stone. Here is coolness and a subdued light which at your first entering seems well-nigh darkness, but to the accustomed eye resolves itself into a very riot of colour. At every so many paces a small hole in the vaulting lets through a slant ray of intense sunshine to the narrow ways: the shops, open recesses with a low counter whereon the merchant sits, are brightly lit in front and run back into obscure caves whence you catch flashes of red and green and gold as the broken sunbeams chance on piles of silk or carpets, fresh garden-stuff, hammered copper ware, or jars of spices. As you pass from the bazaar of one trade to that of another you gain ever some new effect: in the cloth-market the whole alley-way is festooned with gaudily-coloured stuffs; the jewellers' bazaar has its rows of glass boxes where gold and silver trinkets gleam with flashes caught from the live coals of the gold-smith's brazier; the vegetable market is one mass of green, with crates of oranges and heaps of white and purple grapes in their season, or fat yellow melons and early apricots; the Sûk el Nahasin where the copper-smiths are at work all day long is a blaze of burnished metal and a babel of hammering: there are the glowing ovens of the cook-shops, where the counter is spread with sesame-cakes steeped in honey, and cavernous restaurants where many-coloured sherbets are served to you in tumblers full of snow. You can wander literally for miles through these vaulted alleys, and jostled by the crowd and deafened with the noise of their chaffering you will find it hard to realize that the stone roof above your head is indeed that wide field which from the castle you saw green with grass and dotted with goats placidly at feed.

Notes

(Unless otherwise stated, books in English are published in London, books in French in Paris.)

Introduction

1 Abdullah Hadjar, *Historical Monuments of Aleppo* (Aleppo, 2000), p. 1.
2 Ibn Jubayr, *Travels*, ed. R. J. C. Broadhurst (1952), p. 261.
3 Georges Tschalenko, *Villages antiques de la Syrie du Nord*, 2 vols (1953), passim.
4 A. J. Arberry, *Poems of al-Mutanabbi: A Selection with Introduction, Translations and Notes* (Cambridge, 1967), pp. 46, 62, 76, 124.
5 Ibn Jubayr, *Travels*, pp. 261–3.
6 Paule Charles-Dominique, ed., *Voyageurs arabes* (1995), p. 430.
7 Caroline Finkel, *Osman's Dream: The Story of the Ottoman Empire 1300–1923* (2005), p. 109.
8 Eugene Rogan, *The Arabs: A History* (2011), pp. 25, 27.

1 The Ottoman City

1 George W. F. Stripling, *The Ottoman Turks and the Arabs 1511–1574* (Urbana, IL, 1942), pp. 49, 51.
2 Alexander Russell, *The Natural History of Aleppo, containing a description of the city and the principal natural productions in its neighbourhood, together with an account of the climate, inhabitants and diseases; particularly the plague*, 2nd edn, revised, enlarged and illustrated with notes, 2 vols (1794), vol. I, pp. 323, 327.

3 Abdul-Karim Rafeq, 'Relations between the Syrian Ulamā and the Ottoman State in the Eighteenth Century', *Oriente Moderno*, 79 (1999), p. 82.

4 Lewis V. Thomas, *A Study of Naima* (New York, 1972), pp. 6, 9.

5 Abraham Marcus, *The Middle East on the Eve of Modernity: Aleppo in the Eighteenth Century* (New York, 1989), p. 81.

6 Metin Kunt and Christine Woodhead, eds, *Suleyman the Magnificent and his Age* (1995), pp. 168–9. In 1638, during another Ottoman–Iranian war, another sultan, Murad IV, also stayed in Aleppo.

7 Jean Chesneau, *Le voyage de Monsieur d'Aramon, ambassadeur pour le roy en Levant* (Geneva, repr. 1970), pp. xxxviii, 101.

8 Heghnar Zeitlian Watenpaugh, *The Image of an Ottoman City: Imperial Architecture and Urban Experience in Aleppo in the 16th and 17th Centuries* (Leiden, 2004), pp. 38–9, 121, 177.

9 John Ray, *A Collection of Curious Travels and Voyages*, 2 vols (2nd edn, 1738), vol. I, p. 46.

10 Philip Mansel, *Constantinople: City of the World's Desire 1453–1924* (1995), pp. 7–8, 18.

11 Bruce Masters, *The Origins of Western Economic Dominance in the Middle East: Mercantilism and the Islamic Economy in Aleppo, 1600–1750* (New York, 1988), pp. 19–21; cf. T. J. Gorton, *Renaissance Emir: A Druze Warlord at the Court of the Medici* (2013), pp. 50–2; Karen Barkey, *Bandits and Bureaucrats: The Ottoman Route to State Centralization* (Ithaca, NY, 1994), pp. 189, 214–17.

12 Talk by Frederico Frederici, Durham, 26 September 2013.

2 Emporium of the Orient World

1 Jacques Gassot, *Le discours du voyage de Venise à Constantinople* (1550), p. 31.

2 Michael Strachan, *The Life and Times of Sir Thomas Coryate* (Oxford, 1962), p. 197.

3 John Ray, *A Collection of Curious Travels and Voyages*, 2 vols (2nd edn, 1738), vol. I, p. 62.

4 Watenpaugh, *Image of an Ottoman City*, pp. 94–8.

5 Masters, *Origins of Western Economic Dominance*, pp. 16–17.

6 Hadjar, *Historical Monuments*, p. 31.

7 Antoine Abdel Nour, *Introduction à l'histoire urbaine de la Syrie ottomane (XVIe–XVIIIe siècle)* (Beirut, 1982), pp. 284–5, 287–9.

8 Olivier Salmon, *Alep dans la littérature de voyage européenne pendant la période ottomane (1516–1918)*, 3 vols (Aleppo, 2011), vol. II, p. 1069.

9 Gerald Maclean, *The Rise of Oriental Travel: English Visitors to the Ottoman Empire 1580–1720* (2004), p. 84.

10 Fynes Morison, *An Itinerary*, 4 vols (Glasgow, repr. 1907), vol. II, pp. 59–61; for more information on English merchants in Aleppo at this

time, see John Sanderson, *Travels [...] in the Levant, 1584–1602* (repr. 1931), passim.

11 Cf. for an account of trade in 1638, Jean-Baptiste Tavernier, *Les six voyages*, 2 vols (1676), vol. I, p. 137.

12 Abdul Rahman Hamide, *La ville d'Alep. Étude de géographie urbaine* (Damascus, 1959), p. 151.

13 Sebouh David Aslanian, *From the Indian Ocean to the Mediterranean: The Global Trade Networks of the Armenian Merchants from New Julfa* (Berkeley, CA, 2011), pp. 27–8, 67; Rudoph P. Matthee, *The Politics of Trade in Safavid Iran: Silk for Silver 1600–1730* (Cambridge, 1999), pp. 91, 143–5.

14 Matthee, *The Politics of Trade*, p. 141.

15 Simeon of Poland, *The Travel Accounts*, ed. George A. Bournoutian (Costa Mesa, CA, 2007), pp. 265–9.

16 Quoted in Niels Steengaard, *The Asian Trade Revolution of the Seventeenth Century: The East India Companies and the Decline of the Caravan Trade* (Chicago, 1973), pp. 177, 181–2.

17 Information kindly communicated by B. T. Kudsi.

18 Chevalier d'Arvieux, *Mémoires*, 6 vols (1735), vol. II, p. 469.

19 Elizabeth Longford, *A Pilgrimage of Passion: The Life of Wilfred Scawen Blunt* (1982 edn), p. 127.

20 Donna Landry, *Noble Brutes: How Eastern Horses Transformed English Culture* (Baltimore, 2009), pp. 1, 62, 85, 89, 99, 100–7, 203.

21 Marcus, *Middle East on the Eve of Modernity*, p. 221.

22 Ibid., p. 50.

3   Consuls and Travellers

1 Cf. Philip Mansel, 'Cities of the Levant – the Past for the Future?', *Asian Affairs*, 45, 2 (2014), p. 221.

2 Ugo Tucci, ed., *Lettres d'un marchand vénitien: Andrea Berengo (1553–1556)* (1957), p. 7.

3 Hussein I. el-Mudarris and Olivier Salmon, *Les relations entre les Pays-Bas et la Syrie ottomane au XVIIe siècle* (Aleppo, 2007), passim.

4 Despina Vlami, *Trading with the Ottomans: The Levant Company in the Middle East* (2014), p. 33.

5 Gedoyen 'le Turc', *Journal et correspondance*, ed. A. Boppe (1909), p. 165–9; d'Arvieux, *Mémoires*, vol. V, pp. 510–17; Edward B. Barker, ed., *Syria and Egypt under the Last Five Sultans of Turkey: Being Experiences during Fifty Years of Consul General Barker*, 2 vols (1876), vol. I, pp. 63, 125.

6 Bernard Heyberger, *Les chrétiens du Proche-Orient au temps de la Réforme Catholique* (Rome, 1994); Robert Paris, *Histoire du commerce de Marseille*, vol. V, *Le Levant* (1957), pp. 268, 272, 559. Descriptions of the consul's residence earlier in the century can be found in Salmon, *Alep dans la littérature de voyage*, vol. II, pp. 846–8.

7 Georges Goyau, *François Picquet, consul de Louis XIV à Alep et évêque de Babylone* (1942), p. 59; d'Arvieux, *Mémoires*, vol. VI, pp. 1–2.

8 Douglas Carruthers, *The Desert Route to India* (1929), p. xxivn; François Charles-Roux, *Les échelles de Syrie et de Palestine au XVIIIe siècle* (1928), p. 202.

9 Pierre Clément, ed., *Lettres, instructions et mémoires de Colbert*, 7 vols (1863–70), vol. VII, pp. 355–6, letter of 23 June 1668.

10 Salmon, *Alep dans la littérature de voyage*, vol. I, p. 95.

11 d'Arvieux, *Mémoires*, vol. V, pp. 510, 524, 530–5, 537, 539, 550, 558; vol. VI, pp. 422, 460, 463.

12 Ibid., vol. VI, p. 63.

13 Ibid., vol. V, p. 560.

14 Ibid., vol. VI, pp. 5, 11–13, 59.

15 Maurits H. van den Boogert, *The Capitulations and the Ottoman Legal System: Qadis, Consuls and Beratlis in the 18th Century* (Leiden, 2005), pp. 98, 110–11.

16 d'Arvieux, *Mémoires*, vol. V, pp. 521, 549; vol. VI, p. 22.

17 Ibid., vol. VI, pp. 282, 315.

18 Cf. Maclean, *The Rise of Oriental Travel*, pp. 55, 63, 66–72, 86–99 on William Biddulph, English chaplain at Aleppo, in 1599–1608.

19 Simon Mills, 'The English Chaplains at Aleppo', *CBRL Bulletin*, 6 (2011), pp. 13–20.

20 Christine Laidlaw, *The British in the Levant* (2010), p. 86.

21 Paris, *Le Levant*, p. 269.

22 J. Griffiths, *Travels in Europe, Asia Minor and Arabia* (1805), p. 338; Masters, *Origins of Western Economic Dominance*, pp. 78–9.

23 Bruce Masters, 'Ottoman Policies towards Syria in the 17th and 18th Centuries', in Thomas Philipp, ed., *The Syrian Land in the 18th and 19th Centuries* (Stuttgart, 1992), pp. 19–21.

24 Adrian Tinniswood, *The Verneys: A True Story of Love, War and Madness in Seventeenth-Century England* (2007), pp. 393–7, 424. I am grateful for this reference to Sonia Anderson.

25 Laidlaw, *The British in the Levant*, p. 204; Ralph Davis, *Aleppo and Devonshire Square* (1967).

26 Sonia P. Anderson, 'Sources for the English factory at Aleppo 1650–1700', unpublished presentation at ASTENE conference, Durham, 10 July 2009; cf. for accounts of the English in Aleppo, Davis, *Aleppo and Devonshire Square*; James Mather, *Pashas: Traders and Travellers in the Islamic World* (2009), pp. 72–82.

27 Maurits H. van den Boogert, *Aleppo Observed: Ottoman Syria through the Eyes of Two Scottish Doctors, Alexander and Patrick Russell* (2010), pp. 96, 136, 146, 155, 164.

28 Russell, *Natural History of Aleppo*, vol. II, pp. 19–21.

29 d'Arvieux, *Mémoires*, vol. I, p. 184.

30 Dirk van der Cruysse, *Le noble désir de courir le monde. Voyager en Asie au XVIIe siècle* (2002), pp. 73, 134, 409.

31 Alexander Russell, *The Natural History of Aleppo*, 1st edn (1756), pp. 135–6.

32 John Bramsen, *Letters of a Prussian Traveller*, 2 vols (1818), vol. II, pp. 46, 397.

33 Carruthers, *The Desert Route to India*, p. xvii.

34 Salmon, *Alep dans la littérature de voyage*, vol. I, p. 113; Herbert Bodman, *Political Factions in Aleppo 1760–1826* (Chapel Hill, NC, 1963), p. 40, for his use of Russell as a source of information on municipal and legal administration.

35 André Raymond, 'Aux origines du plan d'Alep par Rousseau: le plan de Vincent Germain de 1811', in Peter Sluglett with Stefan Weber, eds, *Syria and Bilad al-Sham under Ottoman Rule: Essays in honour of Abdul Karim al-Rafeq* (Leiden, 2010), pp. 499–512.

36 d'Arvieux, *Mémoires*, vol. VI, p. 59.

37 James Capper, *Observations on the Passage to India, through Egypt. Also by Vienna through Constantinople to Aleppo, and from thence by Bagdad, and Directly across the Great Desert, to Bassora* (1783), passim; cf. Abraham Parsons, *Travels in Asia and Africa; including a Journey from Scanderoon to Aleppo and over the Desert to Bagdad and Bussora* (1808); Sarah Searight, *Steaming East: The Forging of Steamship and Rail Links between Europe and Asia* (1991), pp. 56–7; for information on van der Steen, see the forthcoming article on him by Brian Taylor.

38 Carruthers, *The Desert Route to India*, p. xxviii.

4 Entertainments

1 William F. Sinclair, ed., *Travels of Pedro Texeira* (1902), p. 122.

2 Roland Bowen, *Cricket: A History of its Growth and Development throughout the World* (1970), p. 45.

3 Cornelis le Bruyn, *Voyage au Levant*, 6 vols (1725), vol. II, pp. 361, 364–5; Henry Maundrell, *A Journey from Aleppo to Jerusalem at Easter AD 1697* (1703), p. 198, 10 March 1698; Carruthers, *The Desert Route to India*, pp. xxiv–xxv; cf. Yoram Shalit, 'European Foreigners in Damascus and Aleppo during the Late Ottoman Period', in Moshe Ma'oz, Joseph Ginat and Onn Winckler, eds, *Modern Syria: From Ottoman Rule to Pivotal Role in the Middle East* (Brighton, 1999), pp. 150–69. I am grateful for this reference to Peter Clark.

4 Francis Vernon, *Voyages and Travels of a Sea Officer* (Dublin, 1792), pp. 161, 165.

5 Sinclair, *Travels of Pedro Texeira*, p. 121.

6 Masters, *Origins of Western Economic Dominance*, pp. 132–3; Watenpaugh, *Image of an Ottoman City*, p. 162.

7 Russell, *Natural History of Aleppo*, vol. I, pp. 147, 179.

8 Griffiths, *Travels in Europe, Asia Minor and Arabia*, pp. 336–7.
9 Bodman, *Political Factions*, pp. x, 40.
10 Van den Boogert, *Aleppo Observed*, p. 156.
11 Paris, *Le Levant*, pp. 275, 413; d'Arvieux, *Mémoires*, vol. VI, p. 414, 'Description de la ville d'Alep, novembre 1683'.
12 Marcus, *Middle East on the Eve of Modernity*, pp. 33–5, 296.
13 Haim Sabato, *Aleppo Tales* (New Milford, CT, 2004), pp. 3, 11.

5 Muslims, Christians, Jews

1 Peter Sluglett with Edmund Burke III, 'Introduction', in Peter Sluglett, ed., *The Urban Social History of the Middle East 1750–1950* (Syracuse, NY, 2008), p. 38.
2 Salmon, *Alep dans la littérature de voyage*, vol. I, pp. 59–60.
3 Van den Boogert, *Capitulations and the Ottoman Legal System*, pp. 136, 143, 145.
4 Elyse Semerdjian, *Off the Straight Path: Illicit Sex, Law and Community in Ottoman Aleppo* (Syracuse, NY, 2008), p. xxxiv; Marcus, *Middle East on the Eve of Modernity*, pp. 41, 112–13.
5 Abdel Nour, *Introduction à l'histoire urbaine*, p. 107.
6 Watenpaugh, *Image of an Ottoman City*, p. 171n.
7 Masters, *Origins of Western Economic Dominance*, p. 178; Marcus, *Middle East on the Eve of Modernity*, p. 98; Semerdjian, *Off the Straight Path*, p. xviii.
8 Abdul-Karim Rafeq, 'The Economic Organisation of Cities in Ottoman Syria', in Sluglett, *Urban Social History*, p. 118.
9 Marcus, *Middle East on the Eve of Modernity*, pp. 54, 157; Masters, *Origins of Western Economic Dominance*, p. 177.
10 Vlami, *Trading with the Ottomans*, p. 250.
11 Rafeq, 'Economic Organisation', pp. 116–17; Marcus, *Middle East on the Eve of Modernity*, p. 159.
12 Sabato, *Aleppo Tales*, pp. 13, 157.
13 Julia Gonnella and Jens Kroger, eds, *Angels, Peonies and Fabulous Creatures: The Aleppo Room in Berlin* (Munster, 2008), passim, esp. Michael Rogers, 'Safavids versus Ottomans: The Origins of the Decorative Repertoire of the Aleppo-Zimmer', pp. 127–31.
14 I am grateful for these translations to Jean-Claude David.
15 Russell, *Natural History of Aleppo*, vol. II, p. 58.
16 Sinclair, *Travels of Pedro Texeira*, p. 116.
17 Walter P. Zenner, *A Global Community: The Jews from Aleppo* (Detroit, 2000), passim; Israel Museum, *Treasures of the Aleppo Community* (Jerusalem, 1994), pp. 21–2.
18 Elyse Senerdjian, 'Nude Anxiety', *International Journal of Middle East Studies*, 45 (2013), pp. 651–76.

19 Major John Taylor, *Travels from England to India in the Year 1789*, 2 vols (1799), vol. I, p. 217.
20 Russell, *Natural History of Aleppo*, vol. I, pp. 134, 138–9.
21 Agnès-Mariam de la Croix and François Zabbal, *Icones arabes. Art chrétien du Levant* (Méolans-Revel, 2003), p. 31.
22 Hanna Dyab, *D'Alep à Paris. Les pérégrinations d'un jeune Syrien au temps de Louis XIV* (2015), pp. 26–7.
23 Bruce Masters, *Christians and Jews in the Ottoman Arab World: The Roots of Sectarianism* (Cambridge, 2001), p. 113.
24 Barker, *Syria and Egypt under the Last Five Sultans*, vol. II, pp. 317; vol. I, pp. 33, 47.
25 Ulrich Seetzen, a German who studied Arabic in Aleppo from November 1803 to April 1805, however, had the opposite opinion to his friend John Barker. He observed feelings of 'hatred and disgust' and suspicion prevailing between Christians, Muslims and Jews. Muslims might dine with Christians, but never with Jews: Carsten Walbiner, 'Ulrich Jasper Seetzen in Aleppo (1803–1805)', presentation at ASTENE conference, Birmingham, 13 July 2013.
26 Marcus, *Middle East on the Eve of Modernity*, pp. 101, 331; Watenpaugh, *Image of an Ottoman City*, p. 56.
27 John Lewis Burckhardt, *Travels in Syria and the Holy Land*, 2 vols (1822), vol. II, p. 654.
28 See Philip Mansel, *Levant: Splendour and Catastrophe on the Mediterranean* (2010), pp. 3, 34, 36, 56, 121.

6   Catholics against Orthodox

1 Salmon, *Alep dans la littérature de voyage*, vol. I, pp. 62–7; vol. II, pp. 906–13; John Joseph, *Muslim–Christian Relations and Inter-Christian Rivalries in the Middle East: The Case of the Jacobites in an Age of Transition* (Albany, NY, 1983), pp. 38–44.
2 Salmon, *Alep dans la littérature de voyage*, vol. II, p. 1156, letter of 17 December 1674.
3 Albert Vandal, *Les voyages du marquis de Nointel* (1900), pp. 8–9, 156; d'Arvieux, *Mémoires*, vol. V, 544; vol. VI, pp. 35, 40.
4 Thomas Philipp, *The Syrians in Egypt 1725–1975* (Stuttgart, 1985), p. 15; Heyberger, *Les chrétiens du Proche-Orient*, pp. 396–403 and passim.
5 Masters, *Christians and Jews in the Ottoman Arab World*, pp. 83, 86, 89–90, 93.

7   Janissaries against Ashraf

1 Marcus, *Middle East on the Eve of Modernity*, pp. 149, 153, 338.
2 Ibid., p. 48.

3 Masters, *Origins of Western Economic Dominance*, p. 191.

4 Marcus, *Middle East on the Eve of Modernity*, pp. 257–9; Barker, *Syria and Egypt under the Last Five Sultans*, vol. I, p. 165, Barker to Isaac Morier, 27 May 1814.

5 Marcus, *Middle East on the Eve of Modernity*, p. 62; Burckhardt, *Travels in Syria and the Holy Land*, vol. II, pp. 649, 652.

6 Russell, *Natural History of Aleppo*, vol. I, p. 321.

7 Burckhardt, *Travels in Syria and the Holy Land*, vol. II, p. 649.

8 Barker, *Syria and Egypt under the Last Five Sultans*, vol. I, p. 302.

9 Russell, *Natural History of Aleppo*, vol. II, p. 375.

10 Marcus, *Middle East on the Eve of Modernity*, pp. 138, 140, 143.

11 Ibid., p. 73; Taylor, *Travels from England*, vol. I, p. 223; Bodman, *Political Factions*, p. 46.

12 Francis William Newman, *Personal Narrative in Letters, Principally from Turkey, in the Years 1830–33* (1856), letter XII, 10 February 1831, pp. 16–17.

13 Burckhardt, *Travels in Syria and the Holy Land*, vol. II, p. 654.

14 Nora Lafi, 'From a Challenge to the Empire to a Challenge to Urban Cosmopolitanism? The 1819 Aleppo Riots and the Limits of Imperial Urban Domestication of Factional Violence', in Ulrike Freitag and Nora Lafi, eds, *Urban Governance under the Ottomans: Between Cosmopolitanism and Conflict* (2014), pp. 58–75.

15 Ibid., p. 66; cf. Waclaw Rzewuski, *Impressions d'Orient et d'Arabie. Un cavalier polonais chez les Bédouins, 1817–1819* (2002), pp. 258–9.

16 Bodman, *Political Factions*, pp. 61–2, 133–5.

17 Albert Hourani, *The Emergence of the Modern Middle East* (1981), p. 65.

18 Sarah Shields, 'Interdependent Spaces: Relations between the City and the Countryside in the Nineteenth Century', in Sluglett, *Urban Social History*, p. 65; Philip S. Khoury, *Urban Notables and Arab Nationalism: The Politics of Damascus 1860–1920* (Cambridge, 1983), p. 271.

19 Eugen Wirth, 'Alep dans la première moitié du XIXe siècle', in Viviane Fuglestad-Aumeunier, ed., *Alep et la Syrie du nord* (1991), p. 139; Barker, *Syria and Egypt under the Last Five Sultans*, vol. I, pp. 25, 176.

20 See e.g. Louis Damoiseau, *Voyage en Syrie et dans le désert [...] pour l'achat d'étalons arabes* (1833), passim; Salmon, *Alep dans la littérature de voyage*, vol. I, pp. 126–7.

21 Salmon, *Alep dans la littérature de voyage*, vol. I, pp. 300, 357. See Rosalie Rzewuska, *Mémoires de la Comtesse Rzewuska*, ed. Giovannella Caetani Grenier, 3 vols (Rome, 1939–1950), vol. III, pp. 29–43.

22 Salmon, *Alep dans la littérature de voyage*, vol. II, p. 1692; David Morray, 'The Consul's Retreat', *Cornucopia*, 10 (1996), pp. 72–80.

23 Laidlaw, *The British in the Levant*, pp. 209–10.

24 Burckhardt, *Travels in Syria and the Holy Land*, vol. II, p. 652.
25 Bruce Masters, 'The 1850 Events in Aleppo: An Aftershock of Syria's Incorporation into the Capitalist World System', *International Journal of Middle East Studies*, 22 (1990), p. 9.
26 Bernard le Calloch, 'La dynastie consulaire des Picciotto (1784–1894)', *Revue d'Histoire Diplomatique*, 1 (1991), pp. 135, 139, 152, 154, 161; cf. Salmon, *Alep dans la littérature de voyage*, vol. II, pp. 1561, 1706, for accounts of the family in 1820 and 1842.
27 Salmon, *Alep dans la littérature de voyage*, vol. III, p. 1839.

8 Ottoman Renaissance

1 Newman, *Personal Narrative*, letters XVI–XXIV, April–June 1831, pp. 23–4, 30–1, 36–8.
2 Salmon, *Alep dans la littérature de voyage*, vol. III, p. 1836.
3 Masters, '1850 Events in Aleppo', pp. 9, 16.
4 Masters, *Christians and Jews in the Ottoman Arab World*, pp. 158–61; Paul Baurian, *Alep autrefois et aujourd'hui* (Aleppo, 1930), p. 109.
5 Salmon, *Alep dans la littérature de voyage*, vol. III, p. 1724; Moshe Ma'oz, *Ottoman Reform in Syria and Palestine* (Oxford, 1968), pp. 102–3.
6 Barker, *Syria and Egypt under the Last Five Sultans*, vol. II, p. 288.
7 Salmon, *Alep dans la littérature de voyage*, vol. III, p. 1711.
8 Ma'oz, *Ottoman Reform*, p. 106.
9 Masters, *Christians and Jews in the Ottoman Arab World*, p. 182.
10 Ibid., p. 179; Gertrude Bell, *The Desert and the Sown* (1907), p. 265.
11 Norman N. Lewis, *Nomads and Settlers in Syria and Palestine 1800–1980* (Cambridge, 1987), pp. 39–43, 47, 54–6.
12 Brian Masters, 'Aleppo, the Ottoman Empire's Caravan City', in Edehm Eldem, Daniel Goffman and Bruce Masters, eds, *The Ottoman City between East and West: Aleppo, Izmir, and Istanbul* (Cambridge, 1999), p. 56.
13 Zeynep Çelik, *Empire, Architecture and the City: French–Ottoman Encounters 1830–1914* (Seattle, 2008), pp. 84, 108, 197; Salmon, *Alep dans la littérature de voyage*, vol. III, p. 1861; Bernard Hourcade, 'The Demography of Cities and the Expansion of Urban Space', in Sluglett, *Urban Social History*, p. 171n.
14 Bruce Masters, 'Power and Society in Aleppo in the Eighteenth and Nineteenth Centuries', in Fuglestad-Aumeunier, *Alep et la Syrie du nord*, p. 157.
15 Charles Issawi, *The Fertile Crescent 1800–1914: A Documentary Economic History* (Oxford, 1988), pp. 74, 386.
16 Newman, *Personal Narrative*, letter XII, 10 February 1831, pp. 16–17.
17 Sabato, *Aleppo Tales*, pp. 114, 141.

18 Salmon, *Alep dans la littérature de voyage*, vol. III, p. 1869.
19 Salim Dermarker, 'La spoliation de Nigoghos Der Markarian drogman du consulat d'Angleterre à Alep 1886–1887', in Bernard Heyberger and Chantal Verdeil, eds, *Hommes de l'entre-deux. Parcours individuels et portraits de groupes sur la frontière de la Méditerranée XVIe–XXe siècle* (2009), pp. 256–74.
20 Julia Gonnella, 'As-Sayyid Abu'l-Huda al-Sayyadi in Aleppo', in Jens Hanssen, Thomas Phillip and Stefan Weber, eds, *The Empire in the City* (Beirut, 2002), pp. 297–310; François Georgeon, *Abdulhamid II: le sultan calife* (2003), p. 200.
21 Salmon, *Alep dans la littérature de voyage*, vol. III, p. 1993.
22 Information kindly communicated by Professor Nicola Corrado.
23 Jeremy Collingwood, *A Lakeland Saga: The Story of the Collingwood and Altounyan Family in Coniston and Aleppo* (Ammanford, 2012), pp. 83–4.
24 For a history and description, see Charles Glass, *Tribes with Flags* (1990), pp. 90–100.
25 See Shereen Khairallah, *Railways in the Middle East 1856–1948* (Beirut, 1991), p. 82.
26 Interview with M. Georges Antaki, Beirut, 1 May 2013.
27 Jean-Claude David and Thierry Boissière, *Alep et ses territoires. Fabrique et politique d'une ville 1868–2011* (Beirut, 2014), pp. 72–5.
28 Peter Sluglett, 'Will the Real Nationalists Stand Up? The Political Activities of the Notables of Aleppo 1918–1946', in Nadine Méouchy, ed., *France, Syrie et Liban 1918–1946* (Damascus, 2002), p. 279; Khaldun al-Husri, *Three Reformers* (Beirut) 1966, p. 92.
29 Cf. for an account of Aleppo at this time, Gertrude Bell, *Amurath to Amurath*, 2nd edn (1924), pp. 4–5.
30 Hasan Kayali, *Arabs and Young Turks: Ottomanism, Arabism and Islamism in the Ottoman Empire 1908–1918* (Berkeley, CA, 1997), pp. 136–7.
31 Anthony Sattin, *Young Lawrence: A Portrait of the Legend as a Young Man* (2014), pp. 173, 179–80; Jeremy Wilson, *Lawrence of Arabia: The Authorized Biography of T. E. Lawrence* (1989), pp. 946–8, report by US Consul F. Willoughby Smith, 9 December 1912, p. 997, Fontana to Sir G. Lowther, 15 June 1913.
32 T. E. Lawrence, *The Seven Pillars of Wisdom* (repr. 1962), pp. 342–3.

9   The French Mandate

1 Document kindly communicated by M. Georges Antaki. Mme Homsy was said to have been one of Cemal Pasha's mistresses.
2 Jean-Claude David and Thierry Grandin, 'L'habitat permanent des grands commercants dans les khans d'Alep à l'époque ottomane', in Daniel Panzac, ed., *Les villes dans l'empire ottoman. Activités et sociétés*, 2 vols

(1994), vol. II, pp. 92–4; cf. Glass, *Tribes with Flags*, pp. 116–19; Mafalda Ade, *Picknick mit den paschas. Aleppo und die levantinische Handelsfirma Fratelli Poche (1853–1880)* (Beirut, 2013), reproducing photographs and documents.

3 See Vartan Dérounian, *Mémoire arménienne. Photographies du camp de réfugiés d'Alep 1922–1936* (Beirut, 2010), passim and pp. 16–20.

4 Taner Akçam, *A Shameful Act: The Armenian Genocide and the Question of Turkish Responsibility* (New York, 2006), pp. 167, 182.

5 See Hilmar Kaiser, *At the Crossroads of Der Zor: Death, Survival and Humanitarian Resistance in Aleppo 1915–1917* (Princeton, NJ, 2002), pp. 15, 24–9 and passim.

6 Lord Kinross, *Atatürk: The Rebirth of a Nation* (Nicosia, repr. 1981), pp. 122–4; Baurian, *Alep autrefois*, pp. 114–15; Taqui Altounyan, *Chimes from a Wooden Bell* (1990), p. 25; Collingwood, *Lakeland Saga*, p. 91; A. J. Hill, *Chauvel of the Light Horse* (Melbourne, 1978), p. 189.

7 Ali A. Allawi, *Faisal I of Iraq* (2014), p. 160.

8 Ibid., pp. 167, 239.

9 Jafar Pasha al-Askari, *A Soldier's Story* (2003), pp. 162, 168, 171–2, 209.

10 Jane Priestland, ed., *Records of Syria 1918–1973*, 10 vols (Slough, 2005), vol. II, p. 301, despatch by J. B. Jackson, US Consul, 30 July 1920.

11 Khoury, *Urban Notables and Arab Nationalism*, pp. 128, 272–3, 440.

12 James L. Gelvin, *Divided Loyalties: Nationalism and Mass Politics in Syria at the Close of Empire* (Berkeley, CA, 1998), pp. 82–5, 129.

13 Peter Sluglett, 'Urban Dissidence in Mandatory Syria: Aleppo 1918–1936', in Kenneth Brown, Bernard Hourcade, Michèle Jolé, Claude Liauzu, Peter Sluglett and Sami Zubaida, eds, *État, ville et mouvements sociaux au Maghreb et au Moyen Orient* (1989), p. 314.

14 Priestland, *Records of Syria*, vol. III, p. 179, Smart to Curzon, 12 February 1923; cf. p. 214, Smart to Curzon, 30 May 1923.

15 Charlotte Trumpler, ed., *Agatha Christie and Archaeology* (2001), pp. 274, 281, 294.

16 Khoury, *Urban Notables and Arab Nationalism*, pp. 186, 344, 373.

17 Taqui Altounyan, *In Aleppo Once* (1969), p. 106.

18 William Dalrymple, *From the Holy Mountain: A Journey in the Shadow of Byzantium* (1997), p. 153.

19 Nachat Chehade, 'Aleppo', in Morroe Berger, ed., *The New Metropolis in the Arab World* (New Delhi, 1963), pp. 80–1.

20 *The Hilltop 1957–1958* (Aleppo, 1958), passim.

10   Independence

1 Major-General Sir Edward Spears, *Fulfilment of a Mission: Syria and Lebanon 1941–1944* (1977), pp. 70n, 116.

2 Richard Pearse, *Three Years in the Levant* (1949), pp. 77–81.

3 Ibid., pp. 103, 106.

4 Nigel Davidson, personal communication, 6 June 1991.

5 F. H. Hinsley, *British Intelligence in the Second World War* (1993), p. 165.

6 Khoury, *Urban Notables and Arab Nationalism*, p. 361.

7 Priestland, *Records of Syria*, vol. VIII, p. 674, despatch of 11 June 1946.

8 Joseph A. D. Sutton, *Aleppo Chronicles* (New York, 1988), pp. 110, 127.

9 Amnon Shamosh, *Michel Ezra Safra et fils* (1986), pp. 35, 73, 85.

10 Israel Museum, *Treasures of the Aleppo Community* (Jerusalem, 1994), p. 22.

11 *Financial Times*, 16 August 2014, p. 9.

12 Patrick Seale, *The Struggle for Syria: A Study of Post-War Arab Politics 1946–1958* (1965), p. 135.

13 Khoury, *Urban Notables and Arab Nationalism*, p. 623.

14 Baurian, *Alep autrefois*, pp. 219, 302.

15 Account by Bartholomew Plaisted, 1750, in Carruthers, *The Desert Route to India*, p. 107.

16 Newman, *Personal Narrative*, letter XXII, June 1831, pp. 33–4.

17 Sabato, *Aleppo Tales*, p. 3.

18 Marie Seurat, *Salons, coton, révolutions. Promenade à Alep* (1995), pp. 135, 137, 141.

19 Florence Ollivry, *Les secrets d'Alep. Une grande ville arabe révélée par sa cuisine* (Arles, 2006), pp. 20, 92, 176–80.

20 Nabih Moukayed, personal communication, 24 June 2015.

21 Altounyan, *Chimes from a Wooden Bell*, p. 152.

22 Cecil Hourani, *An Unfinished Odyssey: Lebanon and Beyond* (1984), pp. 40–1; Collingwood, *Lakeland Saga*, pp. 98, 117.

23 Hasham Sarkis, 'Civic Pride', in Joan Busquets, ed., *Aleppo: Rehabilitation of the Old City* (Cambridge, MA, 2005), p. 33.

24 Interview with Faisal Kudsi, London, 10 May 2015.

25 Claudia Roden, *The Book of Jewish Food* (1997), pp. 486–7.

11   Years of the Assads

1 Cf. Nikolaos van Dam, *The Struggle for Power in Syria: Sectarianism, Regionalism and Tribalism in Politics 1961–1978* (1979), pp. 99–102.

2 Patrick Seale, *Asad of Syria: The Struggle for the Middle East* (1988), pp. 325, 328.

3 David and Boissière, *Alep et ses territoires*, pp. 12, 25.

4 Glass, *Tribes with Flags*, pp. 87, 100. Others called it 'a slow-motion city'.

5 See the catalogue, *Les malles de la famille Antaki* (Sadberk Hanim Muzesi, Istanbul, 2000); and Glass, *Tribes with Flags*, p. 122.

6 Anette Gangler et al, eds., *My Aleppo*, (Stuttgart, 2011), passim and pp. 39, 77, 122.

7 David and Boissière, *Alep et ses territoires*, p. 325.

8 Hadjar, *Historical Monuments*, p. 33.

9 W. J. Childs, *Across Asia Minor on Foot* (1917), p. 421; Jonathan Beard and Erol Makzume, personal communications, 4 November 2014.

10 Anette Gangler *et al.*, eds, *My Aleppo* (Stuttgart, 2011), p. 233, quoting Suleyman Tewfiq.

11 Jonathan Holt Shannon, *Among the Jasmine Trees: Music and Modernity in Contemporary Syria* (Middletown, CT, 2006), pp. 27–34, 132–9, 146–7, 156–7.

12 AMAR, Foundation for Arab Music Archiving and Research, accessed 18 July 2013, www.amar-foundation.org.

12 Death of a City

1 Khaled Khalifa, interview with al-Mustafa Najjar, 1 April 2014, www. Arablit.org.

2 Malu Halasa, Zaher Omareen and Nawara Mahfoud, *Syria Speaks: Art and Culture from the Frontline* (2014), p. 213.

3 BBC News, 18 August 2013, 'From Our Own Correspondent'.

4 BBC News, 12 December 2012.

5 Charles Glass, 'How Syria Is Being Destroyed', *New York Review of Books*, 20 December 2012, pp. 36–9; cf. *International Herald Tribune*, 19 December 2012, p. 3, reporting that rebels from rural areas 'did not share Aleppo's cosmopolitan fabric'.

6 *The Times*, 2 July 2013, p. 9.

7 BBC News, 28 April 2014.

8 *International New York Times*, 12 March 2015, p. 6; BBC News, 28 April 2014.

9 'Aleppo: A Syrian Nightmare – in Pictures', *Guardian*, 12 March 2015; BBC News, 5 May 2015.

10 A popular bar.

11 Ahram Online, 2 February 2015.

12 *International New York Times*, 15 August 2014, pp. 1, 4.

13 *International New York Times*, 11 November 2014, p. 4.

Bibliography

(Unless otherwise stated, books in English are published in London, books in French in Paris.)

Abdel Nour, Antoine, *Introduction à l'histoire urbaine de la Syrie ottomane (XVIe–XVIIIe siècle)* (Beirut, 1982).

Ade, Mafalda, *Picknick mit den Paschas. Aleppo und die levantinische Handelsfirma Fratelli Poche (1853–1880)* (Beirut, 2013).

Adjemian, J., *Guide commercial illustré des pays du Levant sous mandat français* (Beirut, 1939).

Akçam, Taner, *A Shameful Act: The Armenian Genocide and the Question of Turkish Responsibility* (New York, 2006).

Allawi, Ali A., *Faisal I of Iraq* (2014).

Altounyan, Taqui, *In Aleppo Once* (1969).

———— *Chimes from a Wooden Bell* (1990).

Anderson, Sonia P., 'Sources for the English factory at Aleppo 1650–1700', unpublished presentation, *ASTENE*, 10 July 2009.

Arberry, A. J., *Poems of al-Mutanabbi: A Selection with Introduction, Translations and Notes* (Cambridge, 1967).

al-Askari, Jafar Pasha, *A Soldier's Story* (2003).

Aslanian, Sebouh David, *From the Indian Ocean to the Mediterranean: The Global Trade Networks of the Armenian Merchants from New Julfa* (Berkeley, CA, 2011).

Barker, Edward B., ed., *Syria and Egypt under the Last Five Sultans of Turkey: Being Experiences during Fifty Years of Consul General Barker*, 2 vols (1876).

Barkey, Karen, *Bandits and Bureaucrats: The Ottoman Route to State Centralization* (Ithaca, NY, 1994).

Baurian, Paul, *Alep autrefois et aujourd'hui* (Aleppo, 1930).

Bell, Gertrude, *Syria: The Desert and the Sown* (1907).

—— *Amurath to Amurath*, 2nd edn (1924).

Berger, Morroe, ed., *The New Metropolis in the Arab World* (New Delhi, 1963).

Bodman, Herbert, *Political Factions in Aleppo 1760–1826* (Chapel Hill, NC, 1963).

Bowen, Roland, *Cricket: A History of its Growth and Development throughout the World* (1970).

Bramsen, John, *Letters of a Prussian Traveller*, 2 vols (1818).

Brown, Kenneth, Bernard Hourcade, Michèle Jolé, Claude Liauzu, Peter Sluglett and Sami Zubaida, eds, *État, ville et mouvements sociaux au Maghreb et au Moyen Orient* (1989).

Browne, William George, *Travels in Africa, Egypt and Syria from the Year 1792 to 1798* (1806).

le Bruyn, Cornelis, *Voyage au Levant*, 6 vols (1725).

Buckingham, James Silk, *Travels among the Arab Tribes Inhabiting the Countries East of Syria and Palestine* (1825).

Burckhardt, John Lewis, *Travels in Syria and the Holy Land*, 2 vols (1822).

le Calloch, Bernard, 'La dynastie consulaire des Picciotto (1784–1894)', *Revue d'Histoire Diplomatique*, 1 (1991), pp. 135–75.

Capper, James, *Observations on the Passage to India, through Egypt. Also by Vienna through Constantinople to Aleppo, and from thence by Bagdad, and Directly across the Great Desert, to Bassora* (1783).

Carruthers, Douglas, *The Desert Route to India* (1929).

Çelik, Zeynep, *Empire, Architecture and the City: French–Ottoman Encounters 1830–1914* (Seattle, 2008).

Charles-Dominique, Paule, ed., *Voyageurs arabes* (1995).

Charles-Roux, François, *Les échelles de Syrie et de Palestine au XVIIIe siècle* (1928).

Chesneau, Jean, *Le voyage de Monsieur d'Aramon, ambassadeur pour le roy en Levant* (Geneva, 1970).

Childs, W. J., *Across Asia Minor on Foot* (1917).

Clément, Pierre, ed., *Lettres, instructions et mémoires de Colbert*, 7 vols (1863–70).

Collingwood, Jeremy, *A Lakeland Saga: The Story of the Collingwood and Altounyan Family in Coniston and Aleppo* (Ammanford, 2012).

Cowper, Henry Swainson, *Through Turkish Arabia: A Journey from the Mediterranean to Bombay* (1894).

Dalrymple, William, *From the Holy Mountain: A Journey in the Shadow of Byzantium* (1997).

Damoiseau, Louis, *Voyage en Syrie et dans le désert [...] pour l'achat d'étalons arabes* (1833).

d'Arvieux, Chevalier, *Mémoires*, 6 vols (1735).

David, Jean-Claude, 'L'espace des chrétiens à Alep. Ségrégation et mixité: stratégies communautaires 1750–1950', *Revue du Monde Musulman et de la Méditerranée*, 55, 1 (1990), numéro thématique: *Villes au Levant*, pp. 150–70.

David, Jean-Claude and Thierry Boissière, *Alep et ses territoires: fabrique et politique d'une ville 1868–2011* (Beirut, 2014).

David, Jean-Claude and Gerard Degeorge, *Alep* (2002).

David, Jean-Claude and Thierry Grandin, 'L'habitat permanent des grands commercants dans les khans d'Alep à l'époque ottomane', in Daniel Panzac, ed., *Les villes dans l'empire ottoman: activités et sociétés*, 2 vols (1994), vol. II, pp. 85–124.

Davis, Ralph, *Aleppo and Devonshire Square* (1967).

de la Croix, Agnès-Mariam and François Zabbal, *Icônes arabes. Art chrétien du Levant* (Méolans-Revel, 2003).

Dermarker, Salim, 'La spoliation de Nigoghos Der Markarian drogman du consulat d'Angleterre à Alep 1886–1887', in Bernard Heyberger and Chantal Verdeil, eds, *Hommes de l'entre-deux. Parcours individuels et portraits de groupes sur la frontière de la Méditerranée XVIe–XXe siècle* (2009), pp. 256–74.

Dérounian, Vartan, *Mémoire arménienne: photographies du camp de réfugiés d'Alep 1922–1936* (Beirut, 2010).

de Volney, Constantin-François, *Voyage en Syrie et en Egypte pendant les années 1783, 1784 et 1785*, 3 vols (1787).

Dweck, Poopa, *Aromas of Aleppo: The Legendary Cuisine of Syrian Jews* (New York, 2007).

Dyab, Hanna, *D'Alep à Paris. Les pérégrinations d'un jeune Syrien au temps de Louis XIV* (2015).

Finkel, Caroline, *Osman's Dream: The Story of the Ottoman Empire 1300–1923* (2005).

Freitag, Ulrike and Nora Lafi, eds, *Urban Governance under the Ottomans: Between Cosmopolitanism and Conflict* (2014).

Fuglestad-Aumeunier, Viviane, ed., *Alep et la Syrie du nord* (1991).

Fuller, John, *Narrative of a Tour through Some Parts of the Turkish Empire* (1829).

Gangler, Anette et al., eds., *My Aleppo* (Stuttgart, 2011).

Gassot, Jacques, *Le discours du voyage de Venise à Constantinople* (1550).

Gaube, Heinz and Eugen Wirth, *Aleppo. Historische und geographische Beiträge zur baulichen Gestaltung* (Wiesbaden, 1984).

Gedoyen 'le Turc', *Journal et correspondance*, ed. A. Boppe (1909).

Gelvin, James L., *Divided Loyalties: Nationalism and Mass Politics in Syria at the Close of Empire* (Berkeley, CA, 1998).

Georgeon, François, *Abdulhamid II. Le sultan calife* (2003).

Glass, Charles, *Tribes with Flags* (1990).

——— 'How Syria Is Being Destroyed', *New York Review of Books*, 20 December 2012, pp. 36–9.

Gonnella, Julia, 'As-Sayyid Abu'l-Huda al-Sayyadi in Aleppo', in Jens Hanssen, Thomas Phillip and Stefan Weber, eds, *The Empire in the City* (Beirut, 2002), pp. 297–310.

Gonnella, Julia and Jens Kroger, eds, *Angels, Peonies and Fabulous Creatures: The Aleppo Room in Berlin* (Munster, 2008).

Gorton, T. J., *Renaissance Emir: A Druze Warlord at the Court of the Medici* (2013).

Goyau, Georges, *François Picquet, consul de Louis XIV à Alep et évêque de Babylone* (1942).

Griffiths, J., *Travels in Europe, Asia Minor and Arabia* (1805).

Hadjar, Abdullah, *Historical Monuments of Aleppo* (Aleppo, 2000).

Halasa, Malu, Zaher Omareen and Nawara Mahfoud, *Syria Speaks: Art and Culture from the Frontline* (2014).

Hamide, Abdul Rahman, *La ville d'Alep. Étude de géographie urbaine* (Damascus, 1959).

Hamilton, Alistair, Alexander Hendrik de Groot and Maurits H. Van Den Boogert, eds, *Friends and Rivals in the East: Studies in Anglo-Dutch Relations in the Levant from the Seventeenth to the Early Nineteenth Centuries* (Leiden, 2007).

Heyberger, Bernard, *Les chrétiens du Proche-Orient au temps de la Réforme Catholique* (Rome, 1994).

Hill, A. J., *Chauvel of the Light Horse* (Melbourne, 1978).

Hinsley, F. H., *British Intelligence in the Second World War* (1993).

Hourcade, Bernard, 'The Demography of Cities and the Expansion of Urban Space', in Peter Sluglett, ed., *The Urban Social History of the Middle East 1750–1950* (Syracuse, NY, 2008), pp. 154–81.

Hourani, Albert, *The Emergence of the Modern Middle East* (1981).

Hourani, Cecil, *An Unfinished Odyssey: Lebanon and Beyond* (1984).

al-Husri, Khaldun, *Three Reformers* (Beirut, 1966).

Ibn Jubayr, *Travels*, ed. R. J. C. Broadhurst (1952).

Israel Museum, *Treasures of the Aleppo Community* (Jerusalem, 1994).

Issawi, Charles, *The Fertile Crescent 1800–1914: A Documentary Economic History* (Oxford, 1988).

Joseph, John, *Muslim–Christian Relations and Inter-Christian Rivalries in the Middle East: The Case of the Jacobites in an Age of Transition* (Albany, NY, 1983).

Kaiser, Hilmar, *At the Crossroads of Der Zor: Death, Survival and Humanitarian Resistance in Aleppo 1915–1917* (Princeton, NJ, 2002).

Kayali, Hasan, *Arabs and Young Turks: Ottomanism, Arabism and Islamism in the Ottoman Empire 1908–1918* (Berkeley, CA, 1997).

Khairallah, Shereen, *Railways in the Middle East 1856–1948* (Beirut, 1991).

Khalifa, Khaled, *In Praise of Hatred* (2012).

Khoury, Philip S., *Urban Notables and Arab Nationalism: The Politics of Damascus 1860–1920* (Cambridge, 1983).

Kinross, Lord, *Atatürk: The Rebirth of a Nation* (Nicosia, repr. 1981).

Kociejowski, Marius, ed., *Syria: Through Writers' Eyes* (2006).

Kunt, Metin and Christine Woodhead, eds, *Suleyman the Magnificent and his Age* (1995).

Lafi, Nora, 'From a Challenge to the Empire to a Challenge to Urban Cosmopolitanism? The 1819 Aleppo Riots and the Limits of Imperial Urban Domestication of Factional Violence', in Ulrike Freitag and Nora Lafi, eds, *Urban Governance under the Ottomans: Between Cosmopolitanism and Conflict* (2014), pp. 58–75.

Laidlaw, Christine, *The British in the Levant* (2010).

Landry, Donna, *Noble Brutes: How Eastern Horses Transformed English Culture* (Baltimore, 2009).

Lawrence, T. E., *The Seven Pillars of Wisdom* (repr. 1962).

Lewis, Norman N., *Nomads and Settlers in Syria and Palestine 1800–1980* (Cambridge, 1987).

Longford, Elizabeth, *A Pilgrimage of Passion: The Life of Wilfred Scawen Blunt* (1982).

Maclean, Gerald, *The Rise of Oriental Travel: English Visitors to the Ottoman Empire 1580–1720* (2004).

Mansel, Philip, *Constantinople: City of the World's Desire 1453–1924* (1995).

—— *Levant: Splendour and Catastrophe on the Mediterranean* (2010).

—— 'Cities of the Levant – the Past for the Future?', *Asian Affairs*, 45, 2 (2014), pp. 220–42.

Ma'oz, Moshe, *Ottoman Reform in Syria and Palestine* (Oxford, 1968).

Ma'oz, Moshe, Joseph Ginat and Onn Winckler, eds, *Modern Syria: From Ottoman Rule to Pivotal Role in the Middle East* (Brighton, 1999).

Marcus, Abraham, *The Middle East on the Eve of Modernity: Aleppo in the Eighteenth Century* (New York, 1989).

Masson, Paul, *Histoire du commerce français dans le Levant au XVIIIe siècle* (1911).

Masters, Bruce, *The Origins of Western Economic Dominance in the Middle East: Mercantilism and the Islamic Economy in Aleppo, 1600–1750* (New York, 1988).

—— 'The 1850 Events in Aleppo: An Aftershock of Syria's Incorporation into the Capitalist World System', *International Journal of Middle East Studies*, 22 (1990), pp. 3–20.

—— 'Power and Society in Aleppo in the Eighteenth and Nineteenth Centuries', in Viviane Fuglestad-Aumeunier, ed., *Alep et la Syrie du nord* (1991), pp. 151–8.

—— 'Ottoman Policies towards Syria in the 17th and 18th Centuries', in Thomas Philipp, ed., *The Syrian Land in the 18th and 19th Centuries* (Stuttgart, 1992), pp. 11–26.

—— 'Aleppo, the Ottoman Empire's Caravan City', in Edhem Eldem, Daniel Goffman and Bruce Masters, eds, *The Ottoman City between East and West: Aleppo, Izmir, and Istanbul* (Cambridge, 1999), pp. 17–78.

—— *Christians and Jews in the Ottoman Arab World: The Roots of Sectarianism* (Cambridge, 2001).

Mather, James, *Pashas: Traders and Travellers in the Islamic World* (2009).

Matthee, Rudolph P., *The Politics of Trade in Safavid Iran: Silk for Silver 1600–1730* (Cambridge, 1999).

Maundrell, Henry, *A Journey from Aleppo to Jerusalem at Easter AD 1697* (1703).

Mills, Simon, 'The English Chaplains at Aleppo', *CBRL Bulletin*, 6 (2011), pp. 13–20.

Morison, Fynes, *An Itinerary*, 4 vols (Glasgow, repr. 1907).

Morray, David, 'The Consul's Retreat', *Cornucopia*, 10 (1996), pp. 72–80.

el-Mudrarris, Hussein I. and Olivier Salmon, *Les relations entre les Pays-Bas et la Syrie ottomane au XVIIe siècle* (Aleppo, 2007).

—— *Le Consulat de France à Alep au XVIIe siècle* (Aleppo, 2009).

Newman, Francis William, *Personal Narrative in Letters; Principally from Turkey, in the Years 1830–33* (1856).

Ollivry, Florence, *Les secrets d'Alep. Une grande ville arabe révélée par sa cuisine* (Arles, 2006).

Paris, Robert, *Histoire du commerce de Marseille*, vol. V, *Le Levant* (1957).

Parsons, Abraham, *Travels in Asia and Africa; including a Journey from Scanderoon to Aleppo and over the Desert to Bagdad and Bussora* (1808).

Paton, Andrew, *The Modern Syrians* (1844).

Pearse, Richard, *Three Years in the Levant* (1949).

Philipp, Thomas, *The Syrians in Egypt 1725–1975* (Stuttgart, 1985).

Plaisted, Bartholomew, *A Journal from Calcutta in Bengal, by Sea, to Busserah: from thence across the Great Desart to Aleppo: and from thence to Marseilles, and through France to England. In the Year 1750* (1757).

Priestland, Jane, ed., *Records of Syria 1918–1973*, 10 vols (Slough, 2005).

Rabbath, Antoine, *Documents inédits pour servir à l'histoire du Christianisme en Orient* (1905).

Racy, A. J., *Making Music in the Arab World: The Culture and Artistry of Tarab* (Cambridge, 2003).

Rafeq, Abdul-Karim, 'Relations between the Syrian Ulamā and the Ottoman State in the Eighteenth Century', *Oriente Moderno*, 79 (1999), pp. 67–95.

——— 'The Economic Organisation of Cities in Ottoman Syria', in Peter Sluglett, ed., *The Urban Social History of the Middle East 1750–1950* (Syracuse, NY, 2008), pp. 104–40.

Ray, John, *A Collection of Curious Travels and Voyages*, 2 vols, 1st edn (1693).

——— *A Collection of Curious Travels and Voyages*, 2 vols, 2nd edn (1738).

Raymond, André, 'Aux origines du plan d'Alep par Rousseau: le plan de Vincent Germain de 1811', in Peter Sluglett with Stefan Weber, eds, *Syria and Bilad al-Sham under Ottoman Rule: Essays in Honour of Abdul Karim al-Rafeq* (Leiden, 2010), pp 499–512.

Robson, Charles, *Newes from Aleppo* (1628).

Roden, Claudia, *The Book of Jewish Food* (1997).

Rogan, Eugene, *The Arabs: A History* (2011).

Russell, Alexander, *The Natural History of Aleppo*, 1st edn (1756).

——— *The Natural History of Aleppo*, 2 vols, 2nd edn (1794).

Russell, Francis, *Places in Syria: A Pocket Grand Tour* (2011).

Rzewuska, Rosalie, *Mémoires de la Comtesse Rzewuska*, ed. Giovannella Caetani Grenier, 3 vols (Rome, 1939–50).

Rzewuski, Waclaw, *Impressions d'Orient et d'Arabie. Un cavalier polonais chez les Bédouins, 1817–1819* (2002).

Sabato, Haim, *Aleppo Tales* (New Milford, CT, 2004).

Sadberk Hanim Müzesi, *Les malles de la famille Antaki* (Istanbul, 2000).

Salmon, Olivier, *Alep dans la littérature de voyage européenne pendant la période ottomane (1516–1918)*, 3 vols (Aleppo, 2011).

Sanderson, John, *Travels [...] in the Levant, 1584–1602* (repr. 1931).

Sarkis, Hasham, 'Civic Pride', in Joan Busquets, ed., *Aleppo: Rehabilitation of the Old City* (Cambridge, MA, 2005), pp. 33–6.

Sattin, Anthony, *Young Lawrence: A Portrait of the Legend as a Young Man* (2014).

Sauvaget, Jean, *Alep. Essai sur le développement d'une grand ville syrienne, des origines au milieu du XIXe siècle* (1941).

Seale, Patrick, *The Struggle for Syria: A Study of Post-War Arab Politics 1946–1958* (1965).

———— *Asad of Syria: The Struggle for the Middle East* (1988).

Seaman, John, *Edmond J. Safra: A Life* (work in progress).

Searight, Sarah, *Steaming East: The Forging of Steamship and Rail Links between Europe and Asia* (1991).

Semerdjian, Elyse, *Off the Straight Path: Illicit Sex, Law and Community in Ottoman Aleppo* (Syracuse, NY, 2008).

———— 'Nude Anxiety', *International Journal of Middle East Studies*, 45 (2013), pp. 651–76.

Seurat, Marie, *Salons, coton, révolutions. Promenade à Alep* (1995).

Shalit, Yoram, 'European Foreigners in Damascus and Aleppo during the Late Ottoman Period', in Moshe Ma'oz, Joseph Ginat and Onn Winckler, eds, *Modern Syria: From Ottoman Rule to Pivotal Role in the Middle East* (Brighton, 1999), pp. 150–69.

Shamosh, Amnon, *Michel Ezra Safra et fils* (1986).

Shannon, Jonathan Holt, *Among the Jasmine Trees: Music and Modernity in Contemporary Syria* (Middletown, CT, 2006).

Shields, Sarah, 'Interdependent Spaces: Relations between the City and the Countryside in the Nineteenth Century', in Peter Sluglett, ed., *The Urban Social History of the Middle East 1750–1950* (Syracuse, NY, 2008), pp. 43–66.

Simeon of Poland, *Travel Accounts*, ed. George A. Bournoutian (Costa Mesa, CA, 2007).

Sinclair, William F., ed., *The Travels of Pedro Texeira* (1902).

Sluglett, Peter, 'Urban Dissidence in Mandatory Syria: Aleppo 1918–1936', in Kenneth Brown, Bernard Hourcade, Michèle Jolé, Claude Liauzu, Peter Sluglett and Sami Zubaida, eds, *État, ville et mouvements sociaux au Maghreb et au Moyen Orient* (1989), pp. 301–16.

———— 'Will the Real Nationalists Stand Up? The Political Activities of the Notables of Aleppo 1918–1946', in Nadine Méouchy, ed., *France, Syrie et Liban 1918–1946*, (Damascus, 2002), pp. 273–90.

———— ed., *The Urban Social History of the Middle East 1750–1950* (Syracuse, NY, 2008).

Sluglett, Peter with Edmund Burke III, 'Introduction', in Peter Sluglett, ed., *The Urban Social History of the Middle East 1750–1950* (Syracuse, NY, 2008), pp. 1–42.

Sluglett, Peter with Stefan Weber, eds, *Syria and Bilad al-Sham under Ottoman Rule: Essays in Honour of Abdul Karim al-Rafeq* (Leiden 2010).

Spears, Major-General Sir Edward, *Fulfilment of a Mission: Syria and Lebanon 1941–1944* (1977).

Steengaard, Niels, *The Asian Trade Revolution of the Seventeenth Century: The East India Companies and the Decline of the Caravan Trade* (Chicago, 1973).

Strachan, Michael, *The Life and Times of Sir Thomas Coryate* (Oxford, 1962).

Stripling, George W. F., *The Ottoman Turks and the Arabs 1511–1574* (Urbana, IL, 1942).

Sutton, Joseph A. D., *Aleppo Chronicles* (New York, 1988).

Tavernier, Jean-Baptiste, *Les six voyages*, 2 vols (1676–7).

Taylor, Bayard, *The Lands of the Saracen; or, Pictures of Palestine, Asia Minor, Sicily and Spain* (1857).

Taylor, Major John, *Travels from England to India in the Year 1789*, 2 vols (1799).

Thomas, Lewis V., *A Study of Naima* (New York, 1972).

Thubron, Colin, *Mirror to Damascus* (1967).

Tinniswood, Adrian, *The Verneys: A True Story of Love, War and Madness in Seventeenth-Century England* (2007).

Trumpler, Charlotte, ed., *Agatha Christie and Archaeology* (2001).

Tschalenko, Georges, *Villages antiques de la Syrie du Nord*, 2 vols (1953).

Tucci, Ugo, ed., *Lettres d'un marchand vénitien: Andrea Berengo (1553–1556)* (1957).

Vandal, Albert, *Les voyages du marquis de Nointel* (1900).

van Dam, Nikolaos, *The Struggle for Power in Syria: Sectarianism, Regionalism and Tribalism in Politics 1961–1978* (1979).

van den Boogert, Maurits H., *The Capitulations and the Ottoman Legal System: Qadis, Consuls and Beratlis in the 18th Century* (Leiden, 2005).

——— *Aleppo Observed: Ottoman Syria through the Eyes of Two Scottish Doctors, Alexander and Patrick Russell* (2010).

Van der Cruysse, Dirk, *Le noble désir de courir le monde. Voyager en Asie au XVIIe siècle* (2002).

Vernon, Francis, *Voyages and Travels of a Sea Officer* (Dublin, 1792).

Vlami, Despina, *Trading with the Ottomans: The Levant Company in the Middle East* (2014).

Walpole, Frederick, *The Ansayrii and the Assassins; with Travels in the Further East in 1850–51* (1851).

Watenpaugh, Heghnar Zeitlian, *The Image of an Ottoman City: Imperial Architecture and Urban Experience in Aleppo in the 16th and 17th Centuries* (Leiden, 2004).

Wilkins, Charles L., *Forging Urban Solidarities: Ottoman Aleppo 1640–1700* (Leiden, 2010).

Wilson, Jeremy, *Lawrence of Arabia: The Authorized Biography of T. E. Lawrence* (1989).

Wirth, Eugen, 'Alep dans la première moitié du XIXe siècle', in Viviane Fuglestad-Aumeunier, ed., *Alep et la Syrie du nord* (1991), pp. 133–49.

Woolley, Leonard, *Dead Towns and Living Men* (1932).

Zenner, Walter P., *A Global Community: The Jews from Aleppo* (Detroit, 2000).

Index

Numbers in italics with *pl* are plates.

Abbas, Shah 10
Abbasid caliphs 2
Abdulaziz, Sultan 42
Abdulhamid II/'Abdu'l Hamid,
     Sultan 42, 43–5, 199, 207
Abdullah Bey Babilsi 40–1
Abdulmecid, Sultan 41
'Abdurrahman' 63
Abraham 1–2, 25, 190, 195, 205
agriculture 71–4, 96, 99–101
Akkad, Mustafa 56
Alawi community 58
alcohol 82
   arak 189
   wine 80–1, 101, 113, 119, 189
Alep dans la littérature de voyage
     européenne pendant la période
     ottomane (Salmon) 21
Aleppo *xiv, xv, 1pl*
  name of 1–2, 25, 190, 195, 205
  origins of 1–2, 190

'Aleppo button' ('mal d'Alep') 19, 44,
     162–3, 174
Aleppo Codex 29, 54
Aleppo College 51
Aleppo Dispersion 33, 56–7, 64
Aleppo Tales (Sabato) 25, 55
Ali (son-in-law of the Prophet) 9
Ali Pasha 10
Altounyan, Assadour 44
Altounyan, Ernest 56
Altounyan, Taqui 56
Altounyan Hospital 48, 56
Amnesty International 64
Amurath IV, Sultan 196
Amurath to Amurath (Bell) 206–14
animals 59
Ansayrii (or Assassins), The
     (Walpole) 158–68
Antaki, Georges 59
Antioch, Browne on 131
Arab conquest 2

Arab Spring 61–2
arak 189
Armenians 13, 48, 51
   dress 109
   Mazloumian family 44
ashraf, sherifs
   against janissaries 34–8
   al-Sayyadi, Abul Huda 43–4
   Browne on 128
   Burckhardt on 135–6,138–9
al-Askari, Jafar 49
Asmahan 53
al-Assad, Bashar 59, 64, 65
al-Assad, Hafez 58
Assad Pasha 41
asses/mules 182–3
Azizia Hotel 187–9

Bab Antaki 12
Bab el-Farraj (Bab el Faradge) (Gate
   of Fair Prospect) 12, 44, 160
Bab el-Nasr 12
Baghdad, railway 201
al-Baghdadi, Abu Bakr 64
Bakhash, Na'um 42
Balta Liman (treaty) 40
barber's shops 191–2
Barker, John 30, 36, 37–8
   Buckingham on 143–53
   Fuller on 155
Baron Hotel 44, 50, 53, 55
barrel bombs 63–4
bashaws *see* pashas
baths 29, 87–8, 102
   Russell on 104–5, 114, 115
bazaars *see* souks
Beit Ghazaleh *6pl*, 28–9
Beit Sada 161
Beit Wakil 28, 59, 62
Bell, Gertrude 45, 199–214
Bem, Josef (Murad Pasha) 40, 160,
   173, 175
Britain/British *11pl*, 118–20
   consuls 15–16, 18, 19, 30, 178
   trade 19–20

Browne, William George
   37, 127–32
Buckingham, James Silk, *Travels
   among the Arab Tribes* 143–53
Burckhardt, John Lewis, *Travels in
   Syria and the Holy Land* 30, 35,
   36, 133–42
Byzantine Empire 2

cafes/coffee houses 24, 107, 148
Canbulatoglu family 10
canes 77
caravanserai *see* khans
Cassas, Louis-François 21
castle (Citadel of Aleppo)
   Bell on the 200, 212–13
   Browne on the 131
   Burckhardt on the 138
   Cowper on the 192–6
   Rauwolff on the 70
   Russell on the 93
   Tavernier on the 86
   Walpole on the 159
   Woolley on the 216
Catholics
   Greek *10pl*, 40, 203
   Newman on 180
   and Orthodox 32–3, 36
cats, hospital for 174–5
Cavafy, Constantine, 'City, The'
   (poem) 57
Celal Bey 48
Celebi, Evliya 24, 30
Çelebi effendi 35
Cemal Pasha 47
champs *see* khans
character of Aleppines 142, 162
   Newman on 174
cholera 48, 190
Christians 18, 26–31, 42
   after the Young Turk Revolution
      207, 209–10, 211
   Catholics
      and Orthodox 32–3, 36
   rivalries 18

churches 41
and the French mandate 51
and Jews 54
Maronites 32, 42, 88
marriage/weddings 172–3
and Muslims 31, 49, 184–5
Newman on 184–5
Orthodox 27, 32–3, 36, 41, 51
population 51
Tavernier on 88
tax 8, 34
Taylor on 172–3
and trade 42
use of canes 77
violence against 41–2, 79
Walpole on 160
Christie, Agatha 50
churches 41, 87
Church of the Forty Martyrs 13
Ciary, Jack 54
citadel *see* castle
'City, The' (poem) (Cavafy) 57
civil war 61–5, 137–9
climate 97–9
clock towers 43
Club d'Alep/Nadi Halab *13pl*, 55
coffee 24, 80, 103, 113, 129
see also cafes/coffee houses
Colbert (French minister) 17
*Collection of Curious Travels and
Voyages, A* (Rauwolff) 69–84
colleges 87
commodities 88, 130
coffee 24, 80, 103, 113, 129
cotton 37, 42, 100, 128–9, 191
gemstones 76, 76–7
olives 100
silk 10, 13, 37, 59, 88, 128–9, 191
soap 13, 37, 63, 71, 88, 100
spices 76
tobacco 17, 20, 100, 103–4,
129, 188
wheat 42, 71, 99
wine 17, 80–1, 101, 113, 189
conscience, freedom of 12

consuls/consulates *xv*, 15–20,
37, 38, 42
Austrian 48
Dutch 155–6
English 15–16, 18, 19, 50
see also Barker, John
French 14, 118
German 48
in the Netherlands 59
Newman on 180–1
and travellers 171
Venetian 48
corbeaux d'Alep, Les (Mamarbashi) 55
Corrado, Michele 44
Coryate, Thomas 11
cotton 37, 42, 100, 128–9, 191
coups 55, 58
courts of law 27–8
Cowper, Henry Swainson, *Through
Turkish Arabia* 186–98
crime 142
Newman on 177

Dalrymple, William 51
Damascus 54–5
dancing 108, 171–2
Dar Zamaria 59, 62
d'Aramon, Monsieur 9
d'Arvieux, Chevalier 14, 17–18, 20, 25
'Darley Arabian' 14
Darley, Thomas 14
Da'ud (cobbler) 27
David Pasha 179
de Bruyn, Cornelis 23
Dead Towns and Living Men
(Wooley) 215–17
desertification 35, 61
diseases 19, 111
'Aleppo button' ('mal d'Alep') 19,
44, 162–3, 174
cholera 48, 190
influenza 190
lock-jaw 163
malaria 34
plague 34–5, 36, 129

diseases (*cont.*)
　typhus 48
　venereal disease 24
divan 8
Djezzar Pasha 134, 136–7
dress 19, 59, 111, 129–30
　of entertainers and musicians 109
　Greek Catholic archbishop 203
　janissaries 109, 135
　Jewish women 156–7, 172, 182
　Newman on 182
　for non-Muslims/Europeans 27, 119
　Russell on 102
　Walpole on 165
　Western 40, 43
drugs 74, 77, 104
　hashîsh 131, 179
　kief 159, 166
Drummond, Alexander 19, 92

earthquakes 36, 155, 170, 174, 187
education 109–11
　colleges 87, 109–10
　Newman on 181
Egypt
　and the Battle of Nezib 40
　union with Syria 55–6
Eldred, John 12
England/English *see* Britain/British
entertainment 23–5
　after Second World War 55
　baths 29
　cafes 24, 107
　dancing 108
　games 107
　music 61, 82, 108–9
　　Taylor on 171
　　Walpole on 167–8
　Russell on 103
Euphrates (river) 88–9
Europeans (Franks)
　Fuller on 155–6
　Russell on 118–20
　see also individual countries
exercise for health 106, 120

Faisal, Emir 48, 49
Fakhri, Sabah 60
Farhat, Germanos 30
Ferhat Pasha (General Stein) 175
First World War 47
food and drink 55, 59
　Browne on 130
　Cowper on 188, 189, 196
　Rauwolff on 71–4, 76, 81,
　　82, 83–4
　Russell on 100–1, 102–3, 112–13
　Walpole on 166, 167
Fouad, Mohammad Fouad 64
France/French 42–3
　consuls 15, 16, 17
　mandate 47–51
　railway 200
　and Suleyman 'the Magnificent' 9
Franks *see* Europeans
Free Syrian Army 63, 64
freedom of conscience 12
Fuller, John, *Narrative of a Tour*
　　through Some Parts of the
　　Turkish Empire 154–7
funerary practices 116–17, 129
　Browne on 132
　Cowper on 197–8
　Walpole on 163–4
Furat (newspaper) 45

Galland, Antoine 30
games 107
Gangler, Anette 59
Gassot, Jacques 11
Gate of Fair Prospect *see* Bab
　　el-Farraj
Ghazeleh, Rizkallah 44
Gedoyen, Monsieur (French
　　consul) 16
gemstones 76–7
　Le Bleu de France 85
Germain, Vincent 21
Germany 200
Ghadban, Zoe 51
Ghazaleh house *6pl*, 28–9

Girardi family 43
glass 95
Glass, Charles 58–9, 63
government of Aleppo 8
    Tavernier on 89
    Vernon on 125–6
    see also pashas
granaries 100
Great Mosque 9, 24, 63, 147–8, 192
'Greenheads' 35
Griffiths, John 19
Guys, Henri 36

al-Halabi, Yusuf 35, 42
Haleb *see* Aleppo
Halifax, William 18
Hamdanid dynasty 2
Hamidiye cavalry 44
Harley, Nathaniel 14, 19
hashîsh 131, 169
health
    and the civil war 62
    and exercise 106, 120
    see also diseases; medicine
'hell cannons' 64
Hindiyya 30
Homsi family 44, 47, 203
horses 14, 27, 37, 106, 119
hospitality 170–1
hospitals 44, 48, 56
hotels 59, 87
    Azizia 187–9
    Baron Hotel 44, 50, 53, 55
houses 93–4, 122–3, 128
    Cowper on 190–1
    merchant mansions 28–9, 119
Huda, Abul 44, 45
Hunter, Henry Lannoy *2pl*, 23
hunting 23, 119
Husrev Pasha 9
Hussein (son of the Prophet) 9

Ibn Battuta 2
Ibn Hassan Aga Khalas 137
Ibn Jubayr 2

Ibrahim Beg 135–6
Ibrahim Pasha 136–7, 167
Ibrahim Pasha Katiraghasi 9
Ibrahim Pasha Milli 44–5
In Praise of Hatred (Khalifa) 61
independence from the French 52–7
industry 37
    cloth 40
    printing 42
influenza 190
Iran 9, 10
    silk trade 13
    and the Syrian government 62
    war with Aleppo 9, 34
ISIL *see* 'Islamic State in Iraq and the
        Levant'
Iskenderun 12
Islam
    Browne on 130–1
    Russell on 102, 114
    Walpole on 160–1
'Islamic State in Iraq and the Levant'
        (ISIL) 64–5

Jabiri family 36–7
Jackson, J. B. 49
Jaleel (servant) 188–9
Jamiliye quarter 42
janissaries 8
    against *ashraf* 34–8
    Burckhardt on 135–6, 138–42
    civil war 135–6, 138–9
    Cowper on 196
    dress 109, 135
    Tavernier on 89
Jemil Pasha 43
Jesuits 18
jewellers 78
    see also gemstones
Jews 10, 26–31, 49
    Fuller on 156–7
    Italian 119
    Newman on 178, 180–1
    and the Ottoman Empire 70–1
    population 51

Jews (*cont.*)
  riots against 54
  Russell on 117–18
  Taylor on 171–2
  and trade 42
  Vernon on 125
  weddings 172
Journal from Calcutta in Bengal, by
    Sea, to Buserah, A
    (Plaisted) 121–3
Journey from Aleppo to Jerusalem
    at Easter AD 1697, A
    (Maundrell) 18
Judayda district 24, 28, 63, 161
judicial system 90
Jumblatt family *5pl*, 10

kadi 8, 16, 17, 20, 140
Kara Bekir Pasha 18
al-Kawakibi, Abdul Rahman 45
Kemal, Mustafa 48, 50
Kettle, Tilly 22
Khalifa, Khaled 61
  In Praise of Hatred 61
Khan al-Gumruk 12, 16, 18, 38, 44
Khan al-Nahasin 48
Khan al-Wazir *4pl*, 19, 197
khans (*champs*) xv, 9, 12, 75, 94, 155
  Cowper on 196–7
  Fuller on 155
  Newman on 179–80
  Russell on 119
Khoury, Philip 50–1
Kiāzim Pasha 201–2
kief 159, 166
  see also hashîsh
Kohl, Martha 28
Kudsi, Adly 59
Kurds
  Browne on 132
  Canbulatoglu family 10
  cure for lock-jaw 163
  Ibrahim Pasha Milli 44–5
  Russell on 120
  in the Second World War 53

Landry, Donna 14
Lands of the Saracen (Taylor) 169–75
language
  Arabic 30, 43, 54, 125, 128
    Cowper on 188
    Newman on 180–1
  French 43
  Hebrew 177–8
  Italian 19, 43, 124, 171
Lawrence, T. E. 45–6, 56
Layard, Henry 37
Levant Company 16, 34
libraries 24
livestock 82
lock-jaw 163
'londra' 13
'Lord Harley's Dun' 14

Makzume, Elena (*née* Girardi) 43
'mal d'Alep' *see* 'Aleppo button'
El Malik eẓ Ẓāhir 212
Mamarbashi, Marie, *corbeaux*
    d'Alep, Les 55
Mamluk sultans 3, 26, 65
Manna 75
manners 25
Mansouriya Palace 59
manufacturing
  Browne on 128–9
  and the civil war 62, 63
  cloth 13, 128
  glass 95
Marie, Houssam 64
markets *see* souks
Maronites 32, 42, 88
marriage/weddings 37, 90, 101–2
  Russell on 114–15, 118
  Taylor on 172, 173–4
  Walpole on 164
Masters, Bruce 42
Maundrell, Henry, *Journey from*
    Aleppo to Jerusalem at Easter
    AD 1697, A 18
Mazloum, Mgr 40
Mazloumian family 44

medicine 110–11
Mehmed II, Sultan 10
Mehmed Kibrisli Pasha 41
merchants 118
Modern Syrians, The (Paton) 40
Mohammed Ali Pasha 37, 39, 204
Mohammed Beg 136–7
Mohammed Pasha 137, 138, 139
mohassil 20
Morison, Fynes 13
mosques 9, 70
   Bell on 211
   cat hospital 174–5
   Great Mosque 9, 24, 63,
      147–8, 192
   Rauwolff on 87
   Russell on 94
   Taylor on 183, 174–5
el-Mudarris, Hussein 59
Muhammad (Prophet) 9
Murad Pasha (Josef Bem) 40, 160,
      173, 175
music 61, 82, 108–9, 167–8
   Taylor on 171
Muslims 26–31
   and Christians 49
   and Jews 54
al-Mutanabbi 2, 60
mutsellim 17, 135, 140
My Aleppo (Gangler) 59

Naima, Mustafa 9
Narrative of a Tour through Some
      Parts of the Turkish Empire
      (Fuller) 154–7
Nasser, Gamal Abdul 55
nationalisation 55
Natural History of Aleppo, The
      (Russell) 19–20, 92–120
Nāzim Pasha 204–5
Neale, Frederick Arthur 41
Netherlands, consuls 15, 155–6
Newman, Francis William 39,
      43, 176–85
Nezib (Nizip) (Turkey), Battle of 40

Nicephorus Phocas 2
Nointel, Marquis de 32–3
Nuri Bey 48

olives 100
opium 104
Order of Saint Stephen 10
Orontes (river) 97
Orthodox Christians 27, 32–3,
      36, 41, 51
Ottoman rule 3, 7, 39–46
   after the Young Turk
      Revolution 205–14
   Burckhardt on 134–5
   defeat of 48–9
   and religious tolerance 7–8, 26–31

pashas (bashaws, bashas) 20, 36
   Ali Pasha 10
   Assad Pasha 41
   Cemal Pasha 47
   David Pasha 179
   Djezzar Pasha 134, 136–7
   Ferhat Pasha (General Stein) 175
   Husrev Pasha 9
   Ibrahim Pasha 136–7, 167
   Ibrahim Pasha Katiraghasi 9
   Ibrahim Pasha Milli 44–5
   Jemil Pasha 43
   Kara Bekir Pasha 18
   Kiāzim 201
   Mehmed Kibrisli Pasha 41
   Mohammed Ali Pasha 37, 39, 204
   Mohammed Pasha 137, 138, 139
   Murad Pasha (Josef Bem) 40, 160,
      175
   Nāzim Pasha 204
   Sokollu Mehmed Pasha 12
   Tavernier on 89
Paton, Andrew, *Modern*
      Syrians, The 40
pattens 182
Pearse, Richard 53
Picciotto family 36, 38, 40, 44, 54, 156
   Taylor on 170, 173–4

plague 19, 34–5, 36, 129
Plaisted, Bartholomew 55
  Journal from Calcutta in Bengal, by
      Sea, to Busserah, A 121–3
Poché, Guillaume 47–8
Pococke, Edward 18, 193
poetry 111
population 51, 59, 64, 125
Project for Restoration 59
prostitution 24
protectors, and janissaries 141
proverbs 14, 24, 28, 164

quarries 71, 129

railways 44, 50, 200–1, 216
  Rayak-Hamah 200
  Taurus Express 53
Ransome, Arthur 56
Rauwolff, Leonhard 9–10, 11–12, 24
  Collection of Curious Travels and
      Voyages, A 69–84
Rayak-Hamah railway 200
religious fanaticism 39
religious tolerance 12
  and the Ottoman Empire
      7–8, 70–1
Rezko, Tony 56
riots/violence 37, 42
  against the French 51–2
  anti-Jewish 54
  Catholics and Orthodox 33, 36
  Muslims and Christians 40
  over dress 40
  tax 35
rivers
  Coic/Coik/Koeyk/Kuwaik 95,
      128, 131, 158
  Euphrates 88–9
  Orontes 97
  Tigris 88–9
Roden, Claudia 57
Roman Empire 2
Rössler, Walter 48
Runciman, Steven 50

Russell, Alexander 8, 19–21, 24, 29,
      35, 153
  on Kurdish tribes 35
  Natural History of Aleppo, The
      19–20, 92–120
Russell, Patrick 19, 29, 92
Rzewuski (Tag el-Fakir), Count
      Waclav 37

Sabato, Haim, *Aleppo Tales* 25, 55
Sacquatz 79
Sada family 161
Safra brothers 54
Saif al-Daula 2
Salmon, Olivier, *Alep dans la*
      littérature de voyage européenne
      pendant la période ottomane 21
al-Sayyadi, Abul Huda 43–4
Second World War 52
Selim, Yavuz 3, 8, 49, 65
Selucia 131–2
Seven Pillars of Wisdom, The
      (Lawrence) 45–6
Sharia law 33
Shawa, Sami 60
Shi'a/Sunni conflict 30, 58, 62
  Ottoman rule 9
silk 10, 13, 37, 59, 88, 128–9, 191
Simeon of Poland 13
Six Voyages of Jean-Baptiste
      Tavernier, The
      (Tavernier) 85–91
slavery 115, 163
sleeping habits 106–7
smoking 99, 103–4, 107, 113, 117,
      157, 188
Smyrna 13–14
soap 13, 37, 63, 71, 88, 100
Sokollu Mehmed Pasha 12
Soldi, Andrea, *Portrait of Henry*
      Lannoy Hunter 2pl, 23
souks *3pl*, 12, 59–60, 78–80,
      82–3, 101
  Cowper on 191, 197
  Russell on 94–5

Walpole on 159
Woolley on 216–17
Spears, Sir Edward 52–3
spices 12, 13, 76, 77, 106, 216
Stanhope, Lady Hester 37, 143, 145,
    146, 148
Steen, Jan van der 22
Suez Canal 42
Sufi Muslims 43, 60
Suleyman 'the Magnificent'
    9–10, 70–1
'Sultan al-Rum' 8
Summerhayes, Christopher 52–3
Sunni/Shi'a conflict 30, 58, 62
    Ottoman rule 9
Sykes, Mark 44
Syria *xiv*
    Burckhardt on 134
    Russell on 97
Syria: The Desert and the Sown (Bell)
    200–5

Tag el-Fakir (Count Waclav
    Rzewuski) 37
Tavernier, Jean-Baptiste, *Six Voyages
    of Jean-Baptiste Tavernier,
    The* 85–91
taxes 3, 7, 8, 26, 36, 141, 183–4
    rioting 35
Taylor, Bayard, *Lands of the
    Saracen* 169–75
Taylor, John 29, 35
Ter-Petrosyan, Levon 56
Texeira, Pedro 23, 24, 29
theatres/music halls 24
Thévenot, Jean 24
Through Turkish Arabia
    (Cowper) 186–98
Tigris (river) 88–9
tobacco 17, 20, 100, 103–4, 129, 188
trade 2, 11–14, 56
    Bell on 201
    Browne on 129
    decline 34
    Fuller on 155

Rauwolff on 74–7
and the Suez Canal 42
Tavernier on 88–9
Vernon on 125
see also souks
transport
    asses 182–3
    horses 14, 27, 37, 106
travellers 20–2, 42, 82
    Bell 45, 199–214
    Browne 37, 127–32
    Buckingham 143–53
    and consuls 171
    Cowper 186–98
    on cuisine 55
    Fuller 154–7
    Ibn Jubayr 2
    Newman 39, 43, 176–85
    Plaisted 55, 121–3
    Rauwolff 9–10, 11–12, 24, 69–84
    Russell 8, 19–21, 24, 29, 153
        on Kurdish tribes 35
        *Natural History of Aleppo,
        A* 92–120
    Tavernier 85–91
    Taylor 169–75
    Vernon 24, 124–6
    Walpole 158–68
    Woolley 215–17
Travels among the Arab Tribes
    (Buckingham) 143–53
Travels in Syria and the Holy Land
    (Burckhardt) 133–42
Tshelebi Effendi 135
Tuscany, Grand Duke 10

Umayyad caliphs 2
UNESCO World Heritage Site 59
United Nations 41

Venice, consuls 48
Verney, John 19
Vernon, Francis, *Voyages and
    Travels of a Sea Officer*
    24, 124–6

Vernon, Luisa 27
Verschuer, Richard 27
Voyages and Travels of a Sea Officer
        (Vernon) 124–6

Wahhabis/Wahabees 36, 130, 151
Walpole, Frederick, *Ansayrii and the
        Assassins, The* 158–68
war, with Iran 9, 34
water sources 95
weddings *see* marriage/weddings
wells 95, 166, 187, 189, 191, 195,
        205, 212, 213, 216
wheat 42, 100
wine 80–1, 101, 113, 119, 189
women
    apartments (*haram*) 94, 116
    and baths 88, 105–6

Christian 27
dress and appearance 102, 111–12,
        116, 129–30, 171, 172
and health 111
Jews 156, 171, 172
and marriage 101–2, 114–15
milk drinking 160
social life 55, 181–2
transport 106
Vernon on 124–5
Walpole on 162, 165
Woolley, Leonard, *Dead Towns and
        Living Men* 215–17

Young Turks 45, 47

Zacharias, St 192
Zammar, Mohammed Hayder 56

Also by Philip Mansel

Louis XVIII

Pillars of Monarchy: An Outline of the Political and Social History of Royal Guards 1400–1984

Sultans in Splendour: Monarchs of the Middle East 1869–1945

The Court of France 1789–1830

Constantinople: City of the World's Desire, 1453–1924

The French Émigrés in Europe and the Struggle against Revolution, 1789–1814 (co-edited with Kirsty Carpenter)

Paris between Empires 1814–1852

Prince of Europe: The Life of Charles-Joseph de Ligne (1735–1814)

Dressed to Rule: Royal and Court Costume from Louis XIV to Elizabeth II

Levant: Splendour and Catastrophe on the Mediterranean

Monarchy and Exile: The Politics of Legitimacy from Marie de Médicis to Wilhelm II (co-edited with Torsten Riotte)

The Eagle in Splendour: Inside the Court of Napoleon